Starting and Managing
A Nonprofit Organization

Starting and Managing A Nonprofit Organization

A Legal Guide

BRUCE R. HOPKINS

WILEY

John Wiley & Sons

New York • Chichester • Brisbane • Toronto • Singapore

Material in Chapter 20 includes reference to J. Naisbitt, *Megatrends: Ten Directions Transforming Our Lives.* (New York: Warner, 1982); and to A. Toffler, *Future Shock.* (New York: Random House, 1970).

Library of Congress Cataloging in Publication Data:

Hopkins, Bruce R.
   Starting and managing a nonprofit organization.

   Bibliography: p.
   Includes index.
   1. Corporations, Nonprofit—United States.
2. Corporations, Nonprofit—Taxation—United States.
I. Title.
KF1388.H66   1989   346.73′064   88-20878
ISBN 0-471-61711-3   347.30664

Printed in the United States of America

10 9 8 7 6 5 4 3 2 1

To my parents, Frederick and Jane,
who, as teachers, professional and otherwise,
encouraged me, in their own way and
in ways they may not realize, to write this book,
with love.

Contents

Preface

This book was conceived on a memorable occasion about three years ago, approximately five minutes into a speech before managers of relatively small nonprofit organizations. I was assigned some esoteric topic on the law of tax-exempt organizations and had launched into my presentation when I suddenly realized, from the glazed-over looks, that far too many in the audience had not the faintest idea what it was I was talking about. Preservation instincts took over as I realized the assignment to be a hopeless one, and I abandoned my intended remarks. Instead, we talked about what they wanted to hear: some of the basics of the laws affecting nonprofit organizations.

I recount this, not to insult the level of knowledge of that particular audience, but rather to illustrate the massive gap that exists between the goals desired by those responsible for nonprofit organizations and their knowledge of the law that can either help them achieve those goals or prevent them from succeeding in their aspirations.

Five minutes into that speech, I was struck by the thought that those in that room and their many counterparts need a summary of the laws that affect them in their operation of nonprofit organizations. This summary, as I envisioned it, would be something inherently contrary to a lawyer's normal inclinations: a summary without citations and without footnotes—just text, and, thanks to the editing of Nancy M. Land, relatively readable text.

In my practice and as the result of speeches over the last 20 years, and as part of my teaching a law school course on the subject of tax-exempt organizations for 15 years, I have been privileged to be the beneficiary of a lot of questions. Following that fateful speech, I began recalling these questions and noting subsequent ones, and was surprised to realize how many of the same questions are asked again and again. The purpose of this book is to provide answers to these basic questions.

The questions are good ones—they are fundamental, important—yet are bred of confusion. The confusion is understandable because the law in this field is confusing—for all too many, overwhelming. The ultimate purpose of this book is to decipher, to translate the intricacies of the law in these areas and to try to make them understandable to those who engage in the valuable function of managing and otherwise helping nonprofit organizations.

For several reasons, much is left out of this book. It is, after all, a summary of the basics. Those who want more detail will find it in my book, *The Law of Tax-Exempt Organizations,* published by John Wiley (with ample citations and footnotes) and annually updated.

The law affecting nonprofit organizations is volatile. Ongoing change is the order of the day and many changes lie ahead. This book is intended to be sufficiently general to withstand most of this change. Yet, once the basics in this field are grasped, the reader may want more—more detail and more current information. This is the purpose of my monthly newsletter, *The Nonprofit Counsel,* also published by John Wiley. It is hoped that readers will find the newsletter to be a useful resource in keeping up with the developments in the law as it affects nonprofit organizations.

The purpose of this book is to present the basics of the law of nonprofit organizations in a way as to make the rules, which can be tedious and confusing, generally understandable. For some, there may be more in the book than they need at this time . ... or at least some will perceive that to be the case.

This may be particularly true for those individuals who are just beginning to establish a nonprofit organization or are in the process of thinking about doing so. It is appropriate to pause at this point and offer a perspective for the newcomer to the world, including the law, of nonprofit organizations.

There are many types of nonprofit organizations. Nearly always, those who start a nonprofit organization want it to be tax-exempt. Quite frequently, they want it to be eligible to receive tax-deductible contributions. Thus, many equate "nonprofit" organizations with "tax-exempt" organizations and perhaps with "charitable" organizations.

For those who already know that what they want is a "charitable" entity, Chapter 4 may be extraneous. For others, Chapter 4 is the place to begin, for therein is an inventory of the various types of tax-exempt organizations.

Thus, the fictional Campaign to Clean Up America is used throughout as an illustration of how to organize and qualify a tax-exempt charitable organization. Most individuals, as noted, when contemplating the establishment of a nonprofit organization, are thinking in terms of a charity, even if that thinking is only subconscious. Rarely have they already made the selection between a "public" versus a "private" charity. Usually, they are thinking about the establishment of a "foundation."

But there is more to the universe of nonprofits than charity. An individual interested in establishing a nonprofit organization should first clearly understand what it is that the nonprofit organization is going to do. Just like starting a business, the first step is to determine the organization's functions—then match the category of tax-exempt status (if any) to the organization's purposes and functions. Too often, individuals start with a type of nonprofit organization (usually, a charitable one) and try to force the round peg of what they want to do with it into the square hole of the requirements of law imposed upon that type of organization.

Chapter 4 is designed to assist in this sorting-out process. A *charity* will not fit the requirements of all. Here are some of the other choices:

- *Advocacy organizations.* These are groups that are to be used to attempt to influence the legislative process and/or the political process, or otherwise advocate positions. Useful in this context is the "social welfare organization" or perhaps the "political action committee." Not all advocacy is lobbying and not all political activity is political campaign activity. While some of this type of program can be accomplished through a charitable organization, it is rare for that to be the case where the advocacy is the organization's primary undertaking. In some instances, two nonprofit organizations are used to have it both ways—a blend of charitable and advocacy activities.

- *Membership groups.* Some nonprofit organizations are structured as membership organizations. Predominant among these are associations, veterans' groups, and fraternal organizations. This is not to say that a charitable organization may not be structured as a membership entity—it can—but there are other categories of membership groups. Frequently, these are "business leagues."

- *Social or recreational organizations.* Nonprofit organizations may be organized as formal "social clubs" (like country clubs, and tennis and golf clubs), or hobby, garden, or sports tournament organizations. Again, this is a matter of primary purpose, since some social activity can be tolerated in charitable groups. Here again there is some overlap with other categories, such as the fact that a social organization can be structured as a membership entity.

- *Satellite organizations.* Some nonprofit organizations are deliberately organized as auxiliaries or subsidiaries of other organizations. Examples of this type of organization include title-holding companies, the various types of cooperatives, and retirement and other employee benefit funds. Sometimes, the "parent" organization is a for-profit entity, such as a business corporation with a related foundation.

- *Employee benefit funds.* The world of compensation is an intricate one, regardless of whether the employer is a for-profit or nonprofit organization. Various benefits for the employees, both current and deferred, are provided, including retirement and profit-sharing programs. When properly organized and operated, these funds are tax-exempt entities.

Once the category of tax-exempt organization is decided upon, the reader can, if desired, skip Chapter 5, which discusses the concept of "private inurement." However, it may be useful to briefly review that chapter because, among other things, it offers an explanation of the basic distinctions between nonprofit and for-profit organizations. An understanding of these distinctions may well avoid some difficulties later on. Sooner or later, an understanding of the private inurement doctrine will be necessary.

In selecting the type of nonprofit organization that is to come into existence, consider the activities in which the organization will engage. If attempts to influence legislation are to be in the picture, a jump ahead and a reading of Chapter 13 is essential. Likewise, if the organization is to engage in efforts to intervene or participate in political campaign activities, a perusing of Chapter 14 is necessary.

For charitable organizations, another jump ahead in the book may be in order. Since all charitable organizations are presumed to be "private foundations" and since there is little advantage in being so classified, most charitable entities strive to avoid private foundation status if they can. Therefore, a review of the basic differences between "public" and "private" charities is important at the outset. A discussion of these differences is included in Chapter 11.

In addition to being tax-exempt, an organization may have charitable donee status. While not every tax-exempt organization can receive tax-deductible gifts, many can. Chapter 4 identifies those that are charitable donees; Chapter 8 provides the basic charitable giving rules. Hopefully, the new charitable giving program will include at least the rudiments of a planned giving program; this type of giving is described in Chapter 17. If a charitable gift solicitation program is to be undertaken, it is essential that the organization keep in mind the state and federal laws pertaining to fund-raising. These laws are summarized in Chapter 11.

Charitable organizations must obtain a ruling from the IRS that they are tax-exempt and eligible to receive deductible gifts. Most other categories of tax-exempt organizations may wish to obtain IRS rulings but are not required to do so. The process of obtaining such a ruling is the subject of Chapter 6. Thus, this is a necessary chapter for the newcomer.

Another important chapter for the newcomer is Chapter 7 in which the various returns and reports a tax-exempt organization must file, both under federal and state law, are outlined.

The balance of the book can be read as needed. Chapter 10 focuses on compensation programs other than basic salaries. Chapter 15 deals with the use of subsidiaries and Chapter 16 details involvements in partnerships.

The final chapters (19 and 20), which look at the future of nonprofit organizations, are not critical immediate reading for the newcomer. However, they provide some insight as to the direction of the federal tax law in this area and can be reviewed from that perspective as time allows.

Having said all this, the inherent danger is obvious: How is an organization to progress if it does not absorb and act on new information? Yet an organization may stagnate in frustration and not progress at all if it is overwhelmed with unnecessary detail, particularly in the beginning stages. The trick, of course, is balance.

Let us assume that the newcomer will read the initial four chapters of the book, then only Chapters 6 through 9. The balance of the book may be put aside to pick up as need dictates.

The balance is in understanding the basics, at least for now. Take the matter of Chapter 18, concerning planned giving. Assume that, despite all we've said, the management of a charitable organization refuses to entertain even a preliminary thought about launching a planned giving program at this time. Hopefully, there will be an employee or perhaps a trustee who will have the foresight to at least try to understand what "planned giving" is, and perhaps become aware of at least the basic terms. Even if the management of a charitable organization elects to turn down a planned giving program for now, at least they will have some idea of what it is they are turning down.

For those who are tempted to spurn Chapter 18, perhaps a few minutes devoted to contemplating the following will be a few minutes well spent:

- The basic concept of planned giving
- The likelihood of securing a planned gift immediately
- The reasons for postponing the advent of a planned giving program
- The "charitable remainder trust"
- The "charitable gift annuity"
- The "pooled income fund"
- The "charitable lead trust"
- The use of insurance as the basis for a charitable gift
- Integrating estate planning and charitable giving
- The need for an endowment for the organization
- Existing fund-raising resources that might more productively be devoted to a planned giving program

Someday, someone may ask a trustee, officer, or employee of a charitable organization: "Do you have a pooled income fund?" It would be nice for the potentially hapless respondent to have some idea as to what a "pooled income fund" is.

The same may be said for the chapter on subsidiaries and/or the one on partnerships (15 and 16). Those starting a nonprofit organization may believe (and rightfully so) that the use of a taxable subsidiary or an involvement in a joint venture is the farthest thing from their minds. Yet, it would be nice to know at least the basics regarding the use of a subsidiary. For example:

- Would the tax-exempt status of the organization be disturbed, enhanced, or preserved if one or more activities were housed in a separate organization?

- Aside from tax considerations, do management or other factors dictate the use of a subsidiary?
- How is the subsidiary to be funded, either as to initial capitalization or ongoing operations?
- How does the "parent" organization maintain control over the subsidiary?
- What are the circumstances that might cause the activities of the subsidiary to be attributed back to the tax-exempt parent?

As to partnerships, it would be appropriate if the newcomer knew such fundamentals as:

- The purpose of using a partnership (frequently simply a financing device)
- The difference between a "general partnership" and a "limited partnership"
- When property is best acquired by a partnership rather than by a participating nonprofit organization
- When to use (and when not to use) a for-profit partner
- How and why it may be beneficial for a nonprofit organization to lease property from a partnership in which it is a partner
- When to become involved in a joint venture . . . and when not to
- The circumstances where involvement by the exempt organization in a partnership might cause the organization to forfeit its tax-exempt status

Finally, there are the concluding two chapters, offering both a short-run look and a long-run look ahead (Chapters 19 and 20). These two chapters are not intended to be a discussion of basic legal principles as are the other chapters; they are designed to offer a look at the evolving context in which the new exempt organization will be functioning. The chapters are not crucial essential reading but a review of them along the way may enhance the value derived from the "mandatory" chapters.

Thus, each chapter is designed to have some practical import. Yet for the newcomer, some chapters are of greater necessity than others. Therefore, this portion of the book will serve as a guide to the rudimentary chapters and a plea to not wholly abandon the rest. At all times, when in doubt as to the meaning of a word or phrase, the glossary is available.

The book is no substitute for good legal or other professional advice. But, sometimes, the manager of a nonprofit organization is afraid to seek advice—out of embarrassment for asking "dumb questions" or fear of the costs involved. Or, the operator of a nonprofit organization may not even realize the presence of a legal problem. The book is intended to ease those fears and close those gaps.

Acknowledgments

This book is possible because of the contributions of many people: clients, participants at conferences and seminars, students, and colleagues.

There are five individuals who warrant particular mention. Three of them reviewed drafts of the manuscript and offered many very helpful suggestions. They are Robert Smucker, Vice-President for Government Relations at Independent Sector; Carolyn Fazio, Chairman of Fazio International, and Charles Fazio, President of Fazio International. I very much appreciate their assistance; the book is better because of their efforts. Any mistakes of fact, law, or judgment are mine.

The fourth individual is Jeffrey W. Brown, Executive Editor at John Wiley & Sons, Inc. Jeff was the editor on this project and also serves as editor on my other efforts with Wiley, including the newsletter, *Nonprofit Counsel*. Jeff has offered more encouragement, help, and overall support for this book and the other endeavors than I can possibly describe, and I acknowledge his contributions here with thanks.

Finally, Carol J. Barbitta deserves acknowledgment for her extraordinary support including review of and comments on the the final text.

Starting and Managing
A Nonprofit Organization

Part I

Starting a Nonprofit
Organization

1

Why Start a Nonprofit Organization? A Perspective

One unique aspect of life in the United States is that when an individual perceives a problem, either personal or involving society, he or she does not always have to turn to a government for the resolution of the matter. Rather, the individual has the opportunity to attempt to remedy the problem himself or herself, by acting individually or collectively by turning to a nongovernmental body. There are exceptions to this sweeping statement, of course, and governments obviously provide a wide range of services that individuals acting together otherwise are not likely to create. Nonetheless, in U.S. culture, more so than in any other, an individual is often likely to use nongovernmental means to remedy, or at least attack, a problem.

A BIT OF PHILOSOPHY

This mindset stems from the very essence of our political history: distrust of government. We really do not like government controls and prefer to act freely, as individuals, to the extent it is realistic and practical to do so. As the great political philosopher Alexis de Tocqueville wrote in 1835, "Americans of all ages, all conditions, and all dispositions constantly form associations" and "[w]henever at the head of some new undertaking you see the government in France, or a man of rank in England, in the United States you will be sure to find an association." Over 100 years later, John W. Gardner, founder of Common Cause, observed: "In the realm of good

3

works this nation boasts a unique blending of private and governmental effort. There is almost no area of educational, scientific, charitable, or religious activity in which we have not built an effective network of private institutions."

This "effective network of private institutions" comprising the nation's nonprofit organizations constitutes what is called the *independent sector* or the *voluntary sector* of U.S. society. For-profit organizations are the business sector, while the third of these sectors, the governmental sector, is made up of the branches, departments, agencies, and bureaus of the federal, state, and local governments.

Nonprofit organizations, particularly charitable ones, are regarded as fostering pluralism of institutions and voluntarism in the U.S. social order. That is, society is regarded as benefiting not only from the application of private wealth to specific purposes in the public interest but also from the variety of choices made by individual philanthropists (making gifts of all sizes) as to which activities to support. This decentralized choice making is perceived as more efficient and responsive to public needs than the cumbersome and less flexible allocation process of government. As John Stuart Mill once observed, "Government operations tend to be everywhere alike. With individuals and voluntary associations, on the contrary, there are varied experiments, and endless diversity of experience."

Contemporary writing is replete with examples of these fundamental principles. Those who have addressed the subject include:

> . . . the associative impulse is strong in American life; no other civilization can show as many secret fraternal orders, businessmen's "service clubs," trade and occupational associations, social clubs, garden clubs, women's clubs, church clubs, theater groups, political and reform associations, veterans' groups, ethnic societies, and other clusterings of trivial or substantial importance.—Max Lerner

> . . . in America, even in modern times, communities existed before governments were here to care for public needs.—Daniel J. Boorstein

> . . . voluntary association with others in common causes has been thought to be strikingly characteristic of American life.—Merle Curti

> We have been unique because another sector, clearly distinct from the other two [business and government], has, in the past, borne a heavy load of public responsibility.—Richard C. Cornuelle

> The third sector is . . . the seedbed for organized efforts to deal with social problems.—John D. Rockefeller

> . . . the ultimate contribution of the Third Sector to our national life—namely, what it does to ensure the continuing responsiveness, creativity and self-renewal of our democratic society . . . .—Waldemar A. Neilsen

> . . . an array of its [the independent sector's] virtues that is by now fairly familiar: its contributions to pluralism and diversity, its tendency to enable individuals to participate in civic life in ways that make sense to them and help to combat that corrosive feeling of powerlessness that is among the dread social

diseases of our era, its encouragement of innovation and its capacity to act as a check on the inadequacies of government.—Richard W. Lyman

The problems of contemporary society are more complex, the solutions more involved and the satisfactions more obscure, but the basic ingredients are still the caring and the resolve to make things better.—Brian O'Connell

AN ILLUSTRATION: A NEW ORGANIZATION

Suppose you decide that something must be done about the trash that is strewn about your community and, for that matter, seemingly wherever you go in this country. You intensely dislike the condition of the environment caused by this assortment of bottles, cans, and other trash, and you resent those who do the littering. You realize that this is not a problem that you can conquer singlehandedly, and you suspect (correctly) that there is not much money in the coffers of your town, county, state, or federal treasuries to be used for more trash control. Yet you suspect (also correctly) that others in your community and around the nation feel the same about accumulating litter as you do.

In the best tradition of problem solving in the United States, you decide to form an organization to "do something." In your opinion, the trash problem can be solved in two basic ways: pickup and disposal, and public education. You envision scores of volunteers, combing the streets, parks, and other areas of their communities, picking up trash and distributing anti-litter literature. Your hope is that greater sensitivity to the trash problem will inhibit littering and encourage citizens to be more willing to clean up their communities and keep them clean. (More details of these program activities are in Chapter 6.)

Being not a major philanthropist but a person of modest means, you begin thinking about the funding of this organization and the specific nature of its programs. As your plans take shape, you mention your ideas to a neighbor, who is a labor relations lawyer. She has only a vague idea of what to do, but suggests that you contact one of her law partners who practices in the field of corporate and tax law.

This you do and, while driving to the first appointment, you hear, on the radio, a fund-raising message on behalf of a charitable organization, replete with a catchy name and some memorable slogans. Suddenly, you realize that your organization-to-be must likewise be a charitable one (so as to be exempt from taxes and to receive deductible gifts) and that it needs a suitable name. By the time you reach the lawyer's office, you know what the name will be: "Campaign to Clean Up America."

In an attempt to impress the lawyer—a specialist in the field of nonprofit, tax-exempt organizations—with your basic understanding of nonprofit organizations, you recite some quotations you have read, such as those on pages 4 and 5. The lawyer is duly impressed and, in an effort to deepen your knowledge of the subject, he brings down from his bookshelf the 1977 report of the Commission on Private Philanthropy and Public Needs. He reads:

> The practice of attending to community needs outside of government has profoundly shaped American society and its institutional framework. . . . This vast and varied array is, and has long been widely recognized as part of the very fabric of American life. It reflects a national belief in the philosophy of pluralism and in the profound importance to society of individual initiative.

Replacing that volume, he produces a copy of congressional testimony in 1973, when George P. Shultz, then Secretary of the Treasury, said that charitable organizations "are an important influence for diversity and a bulwark against overreliance on big government."

Then, as befitting a lawyer, he reaches into the casebooks. He turns to an opinion of a federal court of appeals which, in the context of explaining the rationale for tax-exempt status for nonprofit organizations, wrote:

> [o]ne stated reason for a deduction or exemption of this kind is that the favored entity performs a public service and benefits the public or relieves it of a burden which otherwise belongs to it.

Then, the lawyer turns to a U.S. Supreme Court decision and shares this with you:

> The State has an affirmative policy that considers these groups as beneficial and stabilizing influences in community life and finds this classification [tax exemption] useful, desirable, and in the public interest.

He then reads from a federal district court opinion, one concerning the charitable contribution deduction, with the court writing that the reason for the deduction has "historically been that by doing so, the Government relieves itself of the burden of meeting public needs which in the absence of charitable activity would fall on the shoulders of the Government."

By this time, your enthusiasm and vision is nearly boundless. Here you are, thinking and acting in the finest American traditions: approaching and solving a problem, invoking the principles of pluralism and voluntarism, demonstrating your care and "resolve to make things better"—all without governmental assistance and yet relieving government of a responsibility that society must assume. You feel that, almost singlehandedly, you are ensuring the "continuing responsiveness, creativity and self-renewal of our democratic society."

Twenty minutes later, however, your soaring enthusiasm for ridding the United States of its litter has plummeted into deep confusion. What seemed like such a wonderful concept has been quickly and repeatedly punctured with swirls of advice about state corporate law intricacies, warnings of personal liability, gobbledegook as to the law of deductible charitable giving, babble about related and unrelated activities, something about state regulation of fund-raising, talk of a Form 1023 and Form 990, and—here the lawyer totally lost you—a discourse on the distinctions between private foundations and public charities.

Discouraged and rapidly abandoning any more thoughts about saving your country from the onslaught of more rubbish, you dejectedly mumble something about paying his fee for the consultation and prepare to leave. Sensing your dejection and despair, the lawyer assures you that, while the matter may be more complex than you thought, you have a good idea and he can help you (for a reasonable fee) through the maze of laws to your goal. Implicitly trusting him, you agree to proceed—and in a few short months have a successful, nationwide, multimillion-dollar charitable organization to combat the blight of trash in the American environment. In fact, you have since quit your job and are now the full-time, paid president of the Campaign to Clean Up America.

AN INITIAL CHECKLIST

Looking back, you review the lawyer's questions that you and he resolved:

- What should be the form of the organization? Why? In what jurisdiction should it be formed?
- Who should be its directors and officers? Why? What about their personal liability? Should there be employees? Consultants? Compensation arrangements?
- What will be the organization's programs? Will they be related or unrelated?
- How will the organization achieve its goals at the community level? Will it have chapters? Members? In either case, what will be the criteria?
- How can the organization be exempt from federal and state taxation?
- How will the organization be funded? Gifts? Grants? Income from the performance of exempt functions? Endowment income? Unrelated income?
- Will the organization be "public" or "private"?
- To what extent will gifts to the organization be deductible?
- What reports must be filed with federal and state governmental agencies?
- What are the state law fund-raising requirements?
- Can or should the organization engage in lobbying or political campaign activities?

You cannot help but reflect upon the subquestions within each of these categories, as well as the tens of other questions that came up along the way, are before you now, and that you presume (correctly) lie ahead.

2

Getting Started

Being enthusiastic, imaginative, and creative about establishing a nonprofit organization is one thing. Actually forming the entity and making it operational is another.

For better or worse, the exercise is much like establishing one's own business. It is a big move and an important one, and thus it should be done carefully and properly. The label "nonprofit" does not mean "no planning." Forming a nonprofit organization is a serious undertaking.

Many nonprofit organizations are started on a shoestring, with the individuals involved doing jobs they would never do if starting a commercial enterprise. One of the reasons for this is the "nonprofit mentality"—the thought that since the undertaking is nonprofit, it need not pay for services rendered. Encumbered with this view, the sponsors of the organization will, in abundant good faith and with the best of intentions seek—indeed, expect—free assistance. Sometimes, this attitude carries over to the acquisition of equipment and supplies.

In some instances, this nonprofit mentality is wonderful. It enables the skilled manager to parlay a horde of earnest volunteers into a magnificent service-providing organization. However, the truly skilled are rare, and anyone considering organizing and operating a nonprofit organization is well-advised not to skimp with respect to three consultants: lawyer, accountant, and fund-raiser. The professional services of these individuals are crucial. The old adage that "you get what you pay for" is amply applicable in this context.

With that as background, the basic components of forming and operating a nonprofit organization will be considered. These are not, by any means, all of the considerations but, in keeping with the scope of this book, these are the ones that must be confronted.

LOCATION AND LEGAL FORM

What form should a prospective nonprofit organization take? A lawyer may say, "It must be a separate legal entity." But what does that mean?

Any nonprofit organization legally must be one of three types: a corporation, a trust, or an "other" (usually an unincorporated association). (Occasionally, a nonprofit organization is created by statute.) A common element in each is that there should be a creating document—articles of organization—and a document containing operational rules—bylaws.

Keep in mind that before an organization can be tax-exempt, it must be a nonprofit organization. Nonprofit organizations are basically creatures of state law; tax-exempt organizations are basically subjects of federal tax law.

Location

The place to begin in organizing a nonprofit organization is state law. But which state? An organization can be created in only one jurisdiction. Although it can operate in more than one jurisdiction, it can be formed under the law of only one jurisdiction (at a time).

In most instances, selecting the jurisdiction where the organization is to be created is easy: It will be the same jurisdiction in which the organization will operate (be headquartered). For example, if you (the founder of the Campaign to Clean Up America) live and work in the state of Michigan, chances are that you will form the Campaign under Michigan law. Some people feel that a national organization should be formed under the law of a jurisdiction such as New York, the District of Columbia, or Delaware (the for-profit corporate mecca). However, no matter what state the organization is created in, it will have to qualify to function in the jurisdiction where there is an operational relationship with that jurisdiction. Thus, if you plan to operate the Campaign in Michigan, you can incorporate it in, for example, the District of Columbia but you will also have to qualify the organization to "do business" in Michigan.

Since the process of qualifying an organization to do business in a state is about the same as incorporating it, there usually is no point in working with two different states. There are exceptions to this rule, such as where a stock-based nonprofit organization is appropriate or where only one director is desired. If an organization is formed in one state, but has offices in one or more other states, this duplication of effort is unavoidable. Thus, if the Campaign to Clean Up America is formed in Michigan and has offices in other states, it must registered to function in each of the other states.

A caution: If a nonprofit organization is formed in one jurisdiction and the plan is to qualify it in another, be certain that the organization will meet the requirements of the law of the state of qualification. For example, not all states allow a nonprofit organization to be formed as a corporation with stock.

Legal Form

Once the headquarters jurisdiction of the nonprofit organization is selected, or the place of formation is otherwise determined, consideration must be given to the legal form of the organization. Since this is basically a matter of state law, the laws of the state in which the headquarters is based will govern this decision.

Assuming that the nonprofit organization is expected to qualify as a tax-exempt organization under federal law, as well, it is essential to see if a particular form of organization is dictated by federal tax law. In most cases, federal law is neutral on the point. However, in a few instances, a specific form of organization is a prerequisite to qualification as a tax-exempt organization. For example, a federal government instrumentality and a title-holding organization must, under federal tax law, be formed as corporations, while entities such as supplemental unemployment benefit organizations, Black Lung benefit organizations, and multiemployer plan funds must be formed as trusts. A multibeneficiary title-holding organization can be formed as either a corporation or a trust. On occasion, a federal law other than the tax law will have a direct bearing on the form of a tax-exempt organization. For example, the federal political campaign regulation laws prevent the making of political campaign contributions by corporations, therefore, a political committee must avoid the corporate form.

In the absence of the federal law requiring a particular form for the organization, the choice is basically that of those who are establishing the entity.

There are several factors to take into account in selecting the form of a nonprofit organization. Given the reality of our litigious society, personal liability looms as a major element in the decision. Personal liability means that one or more managers of a nonprofit organization (its trustees, directors, officers, and/or key employees) may be found *personally* liable for something done or not done while acting on behalf of the organization.

The Four "I"s. Some of this exposure can be limited by one or all of four ways: indemnification, insurance, immunity, and incorporation.

Indemnification occurs (assuming indemnification is legal under state law) when the organization agrees (usually by provision in its bylaws) to pay the judgments and related expenses (including legal fees) incurred by those who are covered by the indemnity as the result of a misdeed (commission or omission) while acting in the service of the organization. The indemnification cannot extend to criminal acts and perhaps not to certain willful acts in contravention of civil law. Since an indemnification involves the resources of the organization, the economic viability of an indemnification is dependent upon the economic viability of the organization—in times of financial difficulties for a nonprofit organization, an indemnification of its directors and officers can be a classic "hollow promise."

Insurance is similar to indemnification. However, instead of shifting the risk of liability from the individuals involved to the nonprofit organization, the risk of liability is shifted to an independent third party—an insurance company. Certain risks cannot be shifted via insurance, such as criminal law liability. The insurance contract will likely exclude from coverage certain forms of civil law liability, such as libel and slander, employee discrimination, and antitrust matters. Insurance, even where adequate coverage is available, can be costly; premiums can easily be thousands of dollars annually, even with a sizable deductible.

Immunity is available when the law provides that a class of individuals, under certain circumstances, is not liable for a particular act or set of acts, or failure to undertake a particular act or set of acts. Several states are enacting immunity laws for officers and directors of nonprofit organizations, protecting them in the case of asserted civil law violations, particularly where these individuals are functioning as volunteers.

Notwithstanding indemnification, insurance, and immunity, an additional form of protection against personal liability may be desired. This extra protection is afforded by means of *incorporation*. A corporation is regarded as a separate legal entity, whose liability is confined to the organization, and does not normally extend to those who manage it. For this reason alone, a nonprofit organization should probably be incorporated.

Another advantage to incorporation is that the law may provide answers to many of the questions that will inevitably arise when forming and operating a nonprofit organization. Some examples:

- How many directors must the organization have? What are their voting rights? How is a quorum ascertained? How is notice properly given? What is the length and number of their terms of office?
- What officers must the organization have? What are their duties? What is the length and number of their terms of office? Can more than one office be held by the same individual?
- How frequently must the governing board meet? Must they always meet in person, or can the meetings be by telephone conference call or video teleconferencing? Can the board members vote by mail or unanimous consent? Can they use proxies?
- If there are members, what are their rights? When must they meet? What notice of the meetings must be given? How can they vote?
- What issues must be decided by members (if any)? Directors?
- May there be an executive committee of the governing board? If so, what are its duties? What limitations are there on its functions?

- What about other committees, including an advisory committee? Which are standing committees?
- How are the organization's governing instruments amended?
- How must a merger of the organization with another occur?
- What is the process for dissolving the organization? For distributing its assets and net income upon dissolution?

Nearly every state has a nonprofit corporation act. The answers to these and many other questions may be found in that law. If the organization is not a corporation, these and other questions are usually unanswered under state law. If that is the case, the organization must add to its rules the answers to all the pertinent questions (assuming they can be anticipated) or live with the uncertainties.

There is a third reason for the corporate form: You and others know what the entity is. People are familiar with corporations. The IRS knows corporations. Private foundations understand corporations as potential grantees. In general, the world in which the nonprofit organization will be functioning is comfortable with the concept of a corporation.

In contrast to the three advantages of incorporation—limitation against personal liability, availability of information concerning operations, and the comfort factor—what are the disadvantages of incorporation? Generally, the advantages far outweigh the disadvantages. The disadvantages stem from the fact that incorporation entails an affirmative act of the state government: It "charters" the entity. In exchange for the grant of corporate status, the state usually expects certain forms of compliance by the organization, such as adherence to rules of operation, an initial filing fee, annual reports, and annual fees. However, these costs are frequently nominal and the reporting requirements are usually not that extensive.

A nonprofit organization that is a corporation is formed by preparing and filing articles of incorporation, with its operating rules embodied in bylaws. The contents of the articles of incorporation are established by state law and will usually include:

- The name of the organization
- A general statement of its purposes
- The name(s) and address(es) of its initial director(s)
- The name and address of its registered agent
- The name(s) and address(es) of its incorporator(s)
- Language referencing the applicable federal tax law requirements

The bylaws of an incorporated nonprofit organization will usually include provisions with respect to:

- Its purposes (it is a good idea to restate them in the bylaws)
- The election and duties of its directors
- The election and duties of its officers
- The role of its members (if any)
- Meetings of members and directors, including dates, notice, quorum, and voting
- Role of executive and other committees

Trusts. A nonprofit organization may be formed as a trust. This is rarely an appropriate form for a nonprofit organization other than a charitable entity or some of the funds associated with employee plans. Many private foundations, for example, are trusts (sometimes created as testamentary trusts).

Most nonprofit organizations, however, are ill-suited to be structured as trusts, particularly those organizations that will have a membership.

The principal problem with structuring a nonprofit organization as a trust is that most state laws concerning trusts are written for the regulation of charitable trusts. These rules are rarely as flexible as contemporary nonprofit corporation acts, and frequently impose fiduciary standards and practices that are more stringent than those for nonprofit corporations.

A nonprofit corporation that is to be a trust is formed by the execution of a trust agreement or a declaration of trust. Frequently, only one trustee is necessary—in reflection of the usual narrow use of trusts.

The trustees of a trust *do not* have the protection against personal liability that is afforded by the corporate form.

While a fee to the state is rarely imposed upon the creation of a trust, most states impose an annual filing requirement on trusts for the trust agreement or declaration of trust.

It is unusual—although certainly permissible—for the trustee(s) of a trust to also adopt a set of bylaws.

The Unincorporated Association. The final type of nonprofit organization, labeled "other," is the *unincorporated association.*

To the uninitiated, a nonprofit corporation and a nonprofit unincorporated organization might look alike. For example, a membership association has the same characteristics, whether or not incorporated. However, the shield against individual liability provided by the corporate form is unavailable in the case of the unincorporated association.

An unincorporated association is formed by the preparation and adoption of a constitution. The contents of a constitution are much the same as the contents of articles of incorporation (see previous discussion). Likewise, the contents of bylaws of an unincorporated association are usually the same as the contents of the bylaws of a nonprofit corporation.

It is relatively uncommon for an unincorporated association to have to register with and annually report to a state (other than for fund-raising regulation purposes, see Chapter 9).

Occasionally, there are nonprofit organizations that have articles of incorporation, a constitution, and bylaws. This is technically improper, so that, in the case of an incorporated nonprofit organization, the constitution is a redundancy.

Consequently, trusts and unincorporated associations are likely to have less contact with the state than nonprofit corporations. However, as noted, this advantage is usually overshadowed by more substantive disadvantages.

In some states (such as California and New York), the nonprofit corporation and trust law is far more refined than in others. Careful examination of these and like laws is essential when an organization is to be formed in, or operate in, one or more of these places. In addition, some states have far more stringent laws concerning mergers and dissolutions.

In summary, as a general rule, a nonprofit organization has clear advantages being organized as a corporation. Nonetheless, the facts and circumstances of each situation must be carefully examined to be certain that the most appropriate form is selected.

Focus on the Campaign to Clean Up America

After consideration of all of the relevant factors, the decision is made (in conformance with the lawyer's advice) to form the Campaign to Clean Up America as a nonprofit corporation. The aspect of limited personal liability is of particular interest and you can see few disadvantages to incorporation of the entity. (As to the matter of personal liability, the lawyer advises the use of an indemnification provision and points out that in some instances, under Michigan law, directors and officers of nonprofit organizations are immunized from personal liability.) Therefore, you instruct the lawyer to prepare the articles of incorporation for the Campaign and to incorporate it in your home state of Michigan.

BOARD OF DIRECTORS

Every nonprofit organization—irrespective of form—must have at least one director (or trustee). However, few nonprofit organizations have just one "manager." (In tax law language, directors, officers, and key employees are managers.)

The directors are those who generally administer the organization. The word "generally" is used here because day-to-day management is supposed to be the province of the employees and sometimes the officers. Thus, the directors are the policymakers of the organization—those who develop plans for the organization and oversee its affairs. In reality, it is very difficult to set precise lines of demarcation as to the scope of authority of directors and officers—where the authority of the board of directors stops and the officers begins. The same is true with respect to the authority of directors and officers in relation to that of employees. All too frequently, the matter is resolved on an occasion-by-occasion basis—and often in the political arena, not the legal one, by the sheer force of personalities.

Many state nonprofit corporation laws require at least three directors; however, many nonprofit organizations have governing boards far larger than three. State laws never set a maximum number of nonprofit organization directors. The optimum size of a governing board of a nonprofit organization depends upon many factors.

One factor that affects the size of a nonprofit organization's governing board is the manner in which its membership is elected. Because there are so many possibilities, we will not enumerate them all here.

If there are bona fide members of the nonprofit organization, it is likely that these members will elect some or all of the members of the governing board. This may be done by mail ballot or by voting at an annual meeting. In some instances, the board may include some ex officio positions (such as one or more of the officers, one or more past-presidents, or individuals holding positions in another but related organization). It is quite possible, however, for a nonprofit organization with a membership to have a governing board that is not elected by that membership.

In the absence of a membership (or a membership with no vote on the matter), the governing board of a nonprofit organization may be a so-called "self-perpetuating board." In this case, the initial board may continue with those who are elected by that and subsequent boards. Again, there may also be one or more ex officio positions.

In many instances, the source of the membership of the governing board of a nonprofit organization is foreordained. Some examples include the typical membership organization that elects the board (for example, a trade association, a country club, or a veterans' organization); a hospital, college, or museum that has a governing board generally reflective of the community; and a private foundation that has one or more trustees representative of a particular family or a corporation.

Much of this must be left to the realm of the political. Some membership organizations, for example, may appear to have an "open" election system, yet the process is controlled by a small group comprising the nominating committee. Some advocacy groups may feature a membership that is not a true membership at all and have a governing board that is tightly controlled by a small group of insiders.

The combinations of ways to generate members of a governing board are numerous. One fundamental principle to keep in mind, however, is that no one "owns" a nonprofit organization. "Control" of a nonprofit organization is another matter. A membership may control a nonprofit organization without owning it; in most instances, nonetheless, the board of directors of a nonprofit organization controls the organization, notwithstanding the presence of a membership.

This matter of selection of directors and control of a nonprofit organization is of particular consequence in the case of a single-purpose organization that is started by one individual or a close-knit group of individuals. Here, there is a dilemma: The individuals who launched a nonprofit organization do not want to put their blood, sweat, and tears and perhaps dollars into the organization, only to watch others assume control over it. Yet these founders are usually desirous of having a "representative" governing board which, if created, would clearly put them in a minority, without control.

One solution to this problem may be an advisory committee. This is a group of individuals who do not substitute for the board of directors but who provide technical input as to the programs of the organization. Since the members of an advisory committee lack voting rights, their number is governed only by what is practical. Such a committee allows individuals to serve without the potential of incurring the type of personal liability that may accrue to directors and officers and without incurring the larger set of responsibilities held by the directors. An advisory committee further enables an organization to surround itself with prominent names in the field; it can lead to some impressive stationery!

FOCUS ON THE CAMPAIGN TO CLEAN UP AMERICA

How should the Campaign to Clean Up America organize its governing board? Let us assume that you wish to retain control and also assume that the state law under which the Campaign is formed requires at least three directors (recall that the decision was to form the Campaign as a nonprofit corporation). You, presumably, are one of the three. The other two may be a combination of your spouse, best friend, lawyer, accountant, or someone else that you trust. Thus, as a matter of fact (but not necessarily law), you presumably are in control of the Campaign.

There are some deficiencies with this approach. One is that, because loyalties can shift, you can never be certain that you are in fact always in control. Another is that your ability to advance the cause may be hindered in the absence of a "public" board. Still another is the possibility that the IRS may allege the presence of private benefit or private inurement if the governing board is too small and incestuous.

Here are some options:

- The Campaign may be formed in a state that requires only one director, then become qualified to function in the state from which it will operate.

- The Campaign may be formed in a state that allows nonprofit corporations to issue stock, you become the sole stockholder, the bylaws are written so that the directors of the Campaign are selected by the shareholder, and the Campaign then becomes qualified to function in the state from which it will operate.
- An intimate, small (for example, three-person) board is created, to be accompanied by a separate advisory committee composed of "outsiders"; the advisory committee has no binding vote as to corporate policy.
- The governing board of the Campaign is elected by a membership or some other means so that it is representative of those interested in the cause, and you trust your political skills to enable you to retain operational control.

After due consideration, you doubt your political skills and, when incorporating the Campaign, you do so in the state where you live (Michigan) and name as the three initial board members yourself, your spouse, and a close personal friend. (You invited your lawyer to be on the board but he declined, on the grounds of potential personal liability and a conflict of interest.) The bylaws of the Campaign are written to provide for a self-perpetuating board and to create an advisory committee that is generally representative of the anti-trash cause. You resolve, however, to—later in life—make the governing board of the Campaign more representative of its constituency.

In the meantime, while you are not interested in a membership with full voting rights, you begin thinking about a nonvoting membership so as to be able to build a network of individuals who can serve the Campaign as volunteers at the local level. Moreover, this group of individuals can become the heart of a very important set of persons: Those who become regular donors to the Campaign.

OFFICERS

Nearly every nonprofit organization has officers. The basic exception is the trust, which usually has only one or more trustees.

Here again, as with the board of directors, levels of authority are difficult to articulate. In the case of a nonprofit organization with members, directors, officers, and employees, setting a "clear" distinction as to who has the authority to do what is nearly impossible. General principles can be stated but are generally nearly useless in practice. For example, it can be said that the members set basic policy, the board of directors also sets policy but within the policy parameters established by the membership, the officers implement policy, and the employees also implement policy albeit more on a day-to-day basis. Yet the reality is that, at all four levels, policy is established. Worse, at all four levels, policy is implemented.

In a nonprofit organization, for example, who decides what new programs will be undertaken, who is hired and fired as employees, the nature of the retirement plan arrangements, who the lawyers and accountants will be, the type of fund-raising program, the format of the journal, or the organization's physical location? Depending upon the circumstances, the answer may be: the members, the board, the chairman of the board, the president, the vice-president, the executive director, or any number of others.

For the most part, the answers to these questions relate to politics and personalities. A nonprofit corporation statute may spell out the duties of directors and officers, but these are broad ranges of responsibilities. Who is to stop a board majority that wants a green tint to an organization's newsletter rather than a blue one? Or the board majority that wants the organization to use the services of a particular bank, lawyer, or pension plan administrator? Yet there is many a nonprofit organization where the directors and officers are mere putty in the hands of its executive director. There are all too many nonprofit organizations that have volunteer members of the board of directors, each of whom believe it is their duty to delve deeply into the day-to-day management of the organization.

One cannot generalize as to the origins of officers, except to say that they are usually elected. They may be elected by the membership and/or by the board of directors. Some may be appointed by other officers who are elected.

Here are the common patterns:

- A membership elects the directors and the officers.
- A membership elects the directors and the directors elect the officers.
- A self-perpetuating board elects the officers.
- In relation to one of the foregoing combinations, some of the officers are appointed.

The governing instruments of the organization, usually the bylaws, should identify the offices of the organization, state the duties and responsibilities of the officers, provide for the manner of their selection, state the terms of office, address the matter of reelections to office, and so forth. As to the terms of office, some organizations find it useful to stagger the terms, so that only a portion of the board is up for election at any one time, thereby providing some continuity of service and expertise. In some states, the nonprofit corporations law will impose some requirements as to officers, terms of office, and the like.

For example, a typical pattern is as follows. A membership elects a board of directors. The directors elect a president, secretary, and treasurer. The president appoints an assistant treasurer, an assistant secretary, and an executive director. A variation is to have the members directly elect the officers.

Another common pattern is for an organization to have a self-perpetuating board of directors that elects the officers. For the most part, the law allows a nonprofit organization to use whatever governing structure it wants.

Normally, a chairman of the board is not a corporate officer. He or she is selected by the board of directors as its leader. But in many nonprofit organizations, the chairman of the board and president are the same individual. In others, the chairman of the board assumes the responsibilities normally expected of a president. Sometimes, what is normally termed an executive director is labeled the president. Here, too, the possibilities are numerous. How can the roles of a chairman of the board and a president be differentiated? What is the difference between an executive director and an executive vice president?

Can a strong, aggressive chairman of the board dominate the board of directors, the officers, and the staff? Can a strong, aggressive executive director dominate the other staff members, the officers, and the board of directors? The answer to both questions is yes.

─────────── FOCUS ON THE CAMPAIGN TO ───────────
CLEAN UP AMERICA

The Campaign to Clean Up America decided to have the board of directors of the Campaign elect the officers. The officers must be members of the board. You are elected the president and your spouse is elected the secretary-treasurer. Given the size of the organization at this time, there is no need to have a chairman of the board or a vice-president.

ORGANIZATIONAL MINUTES

Another document—in addition to the articles of organization and the bylaws—that is important when forming a nonprofit organization are the organizational minutes. If there is a membership, there must be organizational minutes of that body. The same is true with respect to the board of directors. If there is no membership, the only organizational document will be that of the board of directors.

In this document (or documents), the following actions, at a minimum, will be reflected: ratification of the adoption of the articles of organization; adoption of the bylaws; election of the officers; passage of the requisite resolution(s) for the establishment of a bank account (or accounts); and passage of resolutions selecting legal counsel, an accountant, and perhaps a fundraising consultant; and authorizing reimbursement of expenses incurred in establishing the entity. (As to the bank account resolution(s), the bank that is selected will provide the form of the resolution(s) that it wishes passed.) Of course, these minutes may reflect other actions, such as a discussion of program activities and/or development of the fund-raising program.

All minutes of meetings concerning a nonprofit organization are important, but the organizational minutes are particularly important. Minutes need not be filed with the IRS when pursuing recognition of tax-exempt status (see Chapter 6) but are important documents in other settings, such as an audit.

Minutes should be kept in a minute book, along with other important documents (including the articles of organization and bylaws). These books may be purchased commercially. While a formal minute book is not required—a simple ring binder will suffice—there is something about the formality of a true minute book that seems to get the organization off to a good start, organizationally. Obviously, to be useful, a minute book needs to be maintained, although there is nothing inherent in a good minute book that will cause the organization to be successful, operationally.

IDENTIFICATION NUMBER

Every nonprofit organization must have an "identification number." This is assigned by the IRS and is acquired by filing a properly completed Form SS-4. This form may be filed as soon as the entity is formed or with the application for recognition of tax-exempt status. (Some banks want the number as part of the process of opening a bank account.)

There is much confusion about this requirement. Part of the confusion comes from its name. In some contexts, it is known as an "employer identification number," but it is required even though the organization does not have any employees. It is also known as a "taxpayer identification number." Again, it is required even though the organization is not a "taxpayer."

As discussed in Chapter 3, there is no such thing as a "tax-exempt number." A tax-exempt organization must have an IRS-assigned identification number but the number has nothing to do with tax-exempt status. An identification number is required of every entity as a matter of course, be it a corporation, trust, partnership, estate, or whatever.

CHECKLIST

The legal status of a nonprofit organization—new or old—may be tested by use of the Checklist that follows the Glossary.

3

Debunking Some
Myths and Misperceptions

Those who manage and consult with nonprofit organizations all too frequently labor with misunderstandings as to the nature of the entities they are working with and the law that applies to them. What follows is offered with the hope that it will, at least for the readers, put an end to these myths and misunderstandings.

MYTH 1

An Organization Must Be Incorporated
to Be Tax-Exempt

In general, this is not the law. As discussed in Chapter 2, a tax-exempt organization may be one of three forms. While incorporation may be desirable (and usually it is), generally it is not mandatory. However, the federal tax law mandates that certain tax-exempt organizations be incorporated, such as an instrumentality of the United States and a single-parent title-holding organization.

MYTH 2

Every Nonprofit Organization Qualifies as a Tax-Exempt Organization

This is not the case. While nearly every tax-exempt organization is a non-profit organization, not all nonprofit organizations are eligible to be tax-exempt. Thus, the concept of a nonprofit organization (see Chapter 5) is broader than that of a tax-exempt organization. This is indicative of the fact that there are some types of nonprofit organizations (such as mutual, self-help type entities) that do not, as a matter of federal law, qualify for tax-exempt status.

MYTH 3

Being Tax-Exempt Means That the Organization Does Not Have to Pay Any Taxes

As Chapters 11 to 14 indicate, this is certainly not the case, and those chapters relate only to federal income and excise taxes. Even with complete exemption from federal taxation, there may still be exposure to state and/or local income, sales, use, and/or property taxation. Moreover, there are several civil law penalties (that are not really taxes but are payments to a government nonetheless) that are applicable to nonprofit organizations.

MYTH 4

All Tax-Exempt Organizations Are Eligible to Receive Contributions That Are Deductible for Federal Income Tax Purposes

Not true. Just as nonprofit organizations are a larger universe than tax-exempt organizations, tax-exempt organizations are a larger universe than charitable organizations.

MYTH 5

A Tax-Exempt Organization Must Have a Ruling from the IRS Stating That It Is Tax-Exempt

For the most part, this *is not* the law. First, the IRS does not grant tax-exempt status—Congress does that; the IRS grants recognition of tax-exempt status (see Chapter 6). Second, this grant of recognition from the IRS is generally made by means of a *determination letter,* which technically is not a ruling. Third, only four types of tax-exempt organizations are required to have a determination letter, namely, charitable organizations, voluntary employees' beneficiary associations, supplemental unemployment benefit trusts, and prepaid legal service organizations. For other tax-exempt organizations, the pursuit of recognition of tax-exempt status is optional. This is not to say that a tax-exempt organization should not seek a determination letter if it does not have to (since in many cases that is advisable); the point simply is that generally a determination letter is not mandatory.

MYTH 6

There Is Something Called a "Tax-Exempt Number"

This is not true. As discussed in Chapter 2, every nonprofit organization (tax-exempt or not) must have an IRS-assigned identification number, but that number has nothing to do with tax-exempt status.

MYTH 7

Only Charitable Organizations Are Eligible to Receive Contributions That Are Deductible for Federal Income Tax Purposes

Not true. The fact is that Congress has provided charitable donee status for organizations in addition to those that are normally regarded as charitable organizations. Thus, in addition to organizations that are charitable, educational, religious, scientific, and the like, deductible charitable gifts may be made to governmental bodies, veterans' organizations, fraternal organizations, and cemetery companies (see Chapter 8).

MYTH 8

A Charitable Organization Cannot Engage in Legislative Activities

False. A charity is permitted to engage in far more lobbying efforts than most people realize. Indeed, under some circumstances, a charitable organization can spend more than one-fifth of its funds for legislative ends (see Chapter 13).

MYTH 9

A Charitable Organization Cannot Engage in Political Activities

Again, not true. While a charity cannot engage in political campaign activities without loss of its tax-exempt status (and eligibility to receive deductible contributions), it can engage in certain types of political activities. This practice may, however, trigger a tax—but not loss of exemption. Also, a charity can use a political action committee to engage in political activities that are not political campaign activities (see Chapter 14).

MYTH 10

Only the States Regulate the Process of Fund-Raising by Charitable Organizations

This is not true. While there is no federal charitable solicitations act (at least not yet), the federal authorities have figured out a variety of ways to regulate charitable fund-raising (see Chapter 9), mostly through the federal tax system.

MYTH 11

State Regulation of Fund-Raising for Charitable Purposes Has Declined

Wrong. This is a boom area of the law, with states that previously lacked fund-raising regulation statutes now enacting them and states with them finding ways to make them tougher (see Chapter 9).

MYTH 12

A Nonprofit Organization Must Be Represented by a Professional (Lawyer or Accountant) to Secure Recognition of Tax-Exempt Status from the IRS

Although the professionals may wish it otherwise, there is no requirement that a professional be involved in this process. That is, a nonprofit organization may secure recognition of tax-exempt status on its own. However, in complex circumstances (and circumstances may be more complex than most people may realize), a nonprofit organization usually will be far better off using the services of a competent professional who charges a reasonable fee to see the task done correctly. (By the way, the lawyer or other individual involved should be asked, in advance, for an estimate of total fees and expenses.) The problem is that if one or more mistakes are made, it is more costly to undo them and otherwise rectify the situation than it is to pay a fair fee to do it properly from the beginning.

MYTH 13

All Lawyers and Accountants Are Competent to Represent a Nonprofit Organization

As society becomes more complex and as fields of practice become correspondingly more specialized, this statement is becoming more and more a myth. A lawyer, for example, may be an excellent practitioner in the field of labor law, securities law, patent law, admiralty law, or domestic relations law, but that does not mean that he or she is competent to represent a nonprofit organization. Even a corporate or tax lawyer may not have the requisite expertise. Just as you would not go to a brain surgeon for a coronary bypass operation, you should not go to a divorce lawyer when assistance is needed in matters concerning nonprofit and tax-exempt organizations (and vice versa).

MYTH 14

It Is Easy to Find a Lawyer or Accountant Who Is Competent to Represent Nonprofit, Tax-Exempt Organizations

Related to Myth 13, this one is all too frequently untrue. There is no convenient master list of these individuals. Some lawyers and accountants who do not practice in this field are not shy about referring nonprofit organizations to practitioners who specialize in this area of the law. Most of these professionals, however, are not that self-confident (that is, willing to lose a client or prospective client to someone else, even if it is in the best interest of the organization). So, the pathway to a lawyer or accountant serving nonprofit organizations on a regular basis is the network—you must talk to those involved with other nonprofit organizations and learn who they rely on for legal and accounting services. Most lawyers and accountants who are good at what they do will tell you that referrals are their best source of new business.

MYTH 15

All Fund-Raisers Are Equal in Competence

This untruth rivals Myths 13 and 14. In a sense, the dilemma is magnified in this context because, not only are there good and bad, ethical and unethical, fund-raisers, there are good ones with important sub-specialties. Fund-raising consultants can be excellent when it comes to direct mail, special events, capital campaigns, fee-for-service projects, or planned giving, but it is rare that one has any true expertise in more than one or two of these areas. Be careful here—your direct mail consultant probably knows nothing about planned giving, and vice versa. Look for a fund-raiser with expertise in working with comparable types of organizations, such as colleges, hospitals, symphonies, or professional societies. Further, a "fund-raiser" may in reality be a "solicitor," thus presenting other types of problems.

MYTH 16

The IRS Is Always Right

Usually, the IRS is right. At least in the tax-exempt organizations context, the IRS usually is right. Once in a while, nonetheless, the IRS will err. As an example, the IRS has been known to take an erroneous position on an issue at the district office level, only to be overruled by its National Office in Washington, DC. Generally, the quality of IRS personnel is good; it is exceptionally high at the National Office. The point is that, although the IRS is usually correct, the answer received from the IRS in response to a particular inquiry may be less than fully accurate. While there are exceptions, IRS personnel do not provide tax planning services.

MYTH 17

There Is No Humor in the Federal Tax Law
Bearing on Tax-Exempt Organizations

Actually, this myth comes closer to the truth than any of them. However, there are exceptions.

The federal tax law definition of the term *agricultural* includes the art or science of "harvesting . . . aquatic resources." The comparable definition under the postal laws is the art or science of "harvesting . . . marine resources." It is not clear as to why this distinction was made but, since the word "aquatic" means "pertaining to water" and the word "marine" means "pertaining to the sea," an organization engaged in or associated with the harvesting of fresh waters can acquire classification as an "agricultural" organization for federal tax purposes but fail to so qualify for postal law purposes, with its emphasis on salt waters.

Maybe this one will spark more mirth. There are a variety of types of organizations that are exempt from the unrelated income rules. One of them is a category of radio station operated by a nonprofit organization that satisfies certain criteria. There are three basic tests to meet under these rules, although they are written in such a way that only one radio station qualifies. So as to make the point a little more obvious, the writers of the provision phrased the criteria in such a way that the first letter of each of the three tests is the same as the call letters of the beneficiary radio station (WWL, operated by Loyola University in New Orleans, Louisiana).

MYTH 18

Only the Technical Types (Like Lawyers and Accountants) Need to Know the Information in This Book

This may be the greatest misperception of all. There are too many professionals serving nonprofit organizations who are functioning without this necessary information. This book is designed to provide the basics of the law of the various subjects covered in the belief that everyone seriously serving one or more nonprofit organizations—be it as lawyer, accountant, fundraiser, other type of consultant, employee, or trustee—must understand the points of law surveyed in this book.

Part II

Being Nonprofit . . . Legally

4

Nonprofit Organizations . . . There's Much More Than Charity

For most, the concept of the nonprofit organization and the tax-exempt organization is the same. In addition, for most, nonprofit/tax-exempt organizations mean charitable organizations . . . but, neither is true. As explained in Chapter 5, the idea of a nonprofit organization is much broader than that of a tax-exempt organization. In this chapter, the different types of tax-exempt organizations are summarized. As will be seen, the charitable entity is merely one of many types of exempt organizations, albeit the most well-known.

Because they are so popular, the charitable organization will be discussed first. Note first that the federal tax law uses the term *charitable* in two ways. First, a charitable organization means all organizations that are eligible to receive deductible contributions. Used this way, the term includes entities that are religious, educational, scientific, and the like, as well as certain fraternal, cemetery, and veterans' organizations. In the first of the rare instances of a citation to a section of the Internal Revenue Code in this book (except for those in the Glossary), these organizations (other than the fraternal, cemetery, and veterans' groups) are 501(c)(3) organizations—probably the most widely recognized provision of the Code.

Second, the term charitable organization is used to describe organizations that are defined as that type of entity under the law, as opposed to religious, educational, scientific, and like entities. It is this narrower definition that applies to the organizations discussed next.

Charitable Organizations

To generalize, for many the charitable organization means an entity that works to aid the poor and the otherwise distressed. While some organizations certainly do that, it is by no means not the only way to be "charitable," at least as that term is defined for federal tax law purposes.

The federal tax law definition of a charitable organization contains at least 15 different ways for a nonprofit entity to be charitable. These definitions are found in the income tax regulations, IRS rulings, and federal and state court opinions and include: relieving the poor and distressed or the underprivileged; advancing religion, education, or science; lessening the burdens of government; beautifying and maintaining a community; preserving natural beauty; promoting health, social welfare, environmental conservancy, arts, or patriotism; caring for orphans or animals; promoting, advancing, and sponsoring amateur sports; and maintaining public confidence in the legal system.

The relief of poverty is perhaps the most basic and historically founded form of charitable activity. Originally, it meant largely the distribution of money or goods to the poor. In contemporary times, particularly as government has assumed some of this function, it means more the provision of services. Therefore, this type of charitable entity might operate a counseling center, provide vocational training, supply employment assistance, provide low-income housing, or offer transportation services.

Advancement of religion, as a charitable activity, frequently pertains to a collateral activity of a church. For example, such organizations may maintain church buildings, monuments, or cemeteries; distribute religious literature; or augment salaries. The organization may conduct programs unique to a particular religion, operate a retreat center, or maintain a religious radio or television station.

Advancement of education, as a charitable activity, includes providing student assistance, advancing knowledge through research, or disseminating knowledge by means of publications, seminars, lectures, and the like. This type of charitable function may be a satellite activity of a particular educational institution, such as a university, library, or museum.

Advancement of science, as a charitable activity, includes comparable activities devoted to the furtherance or promotion of science and the dissemination of scientific knowledge. Frequently, this type of charitable function involves conducting and/or disseminating the results of research.

One way for an organization to be "charitable" under the federal tax law is for it to lessen the burdens of government. This includes the erection or maintenance of public buildings, monuments, or works. The organization's activities must be those that a governmental unit considers to be its burdens and that actually lessen that burden. Charitable organizations of this type, for example, help finance assistance to police and firefighters, public transportation, recreational centers, and internship programs. They may provide public parks, preserve a lake, or beautify a city.

Somewhat overlapping with the concept of lessening burdens of government is the charitable activity of community beautification and maintenance, and the preservation of natural beauty. Again, an organization that is charitable under this definition is one that may maintain community recreational facilities, assist in community beautification activities, or work to preserve and beautify public parks.

The promotion of health is a separately recognized charitable purpose. In this context, this type of charity includes public and mental health. This function includes the establishment and maintenance of institutions and organizations such as hospitals, clinics, homes for the aged, and the like. Other illustrations of health providing (or promoting) organizations are health maintenance organizations, drug abuse treatment centers, blood banks, hospices, and home health agencies. It also includes the advancement of medical and similar knowledge through research, and, generally, the maintenance of conditions conducive to health. As discussed in Chapter 11, classification of an organization as a "hospital" or a "medical research organization" is an automatic pathway to avoidance of private foundation status.

The promotion of social welfare is one of the most indefinite categories of charitable endeavors. In the law of trusts, the concept of promotion of social welfare can include such purposes as the promotion of temperance or national security, and the erection or maintenance of tombs and monuments. In the federal tax context, the term embraces such ends as activities designed to accomplish charitable (as otherwise defined) purposes, lessen neighborhood tensions, eliminate prejudice and discrimination, defend human and civil rights secured by law, and combat community deterioration and juvenile delinquency.

An organization can be charitable because it endeavors to promote environmental conservation: a range of activities to preserve and protect the natural environment for the benefit of the public. The IRS has recognized an express national policy of conserving the nation's unique natural resources; this type of organization serves to implement that policy.

The promotion of patriotism is a charitable objective; organizations that, in the words of one IRS ruling, "inculcate patriotic emotions" are charitable. This type of organization may assist in the celebration of a patriotic holiday, provide a color guard, or underwrite flag-raising ceremonies.

Promotion of the arts is still another way for a nonprofit organization to be charitable. These organizations may operate a theater (for plays, musicals, concerts, and the like), work to encourage the talent and ability of young artists, promote filmmaking, sponsor festivals or exhibits, or otherwise promote public appreciation of one of the arts.

More than one of these various ways to be charitable can be present in relation to the purposes and activities of a nonprofit organization. For example, the hypothetical Campaign to Clean Up America (the programs of which are described in Chapter 6) endeavors to beautify communities, preserve natural beauty, lessen the burdens of government, and advance education. In addition, it promotes social welfare, protects the natural environment, and, in some instances, promotes health.

When the IRS classifies an organization as a tax-exempt entity because it is charitable (using that term in its broadest sense), it does not specifically determine the type(s) of charity it may be. However, the categories just discussed are useful in enabling an organization to describe its charitable activities to the IRS (and others) in terms that conform to the federal tax law requirements.

Educational Organizations

Educational organizations include schools, colleges, universities, libraries, museums, and similar institutions. To be a "formal" educational institution, an organization must have a regularly scheduled curriculum, a regular faculty, and a regularly enrolled body of students in attendance at the place where the educational activities are carried on.

The formal educational entities are, by reason of their very programming, exempted from classification as private foundations (see Chapter 11). Beyond these formal educational institutions, however, are a wide variety of organizations that are educational in nature.

One way to be educational, for federal tax law purposes, is to instruct or train individuals for the purpose of improving their capabilities. Within this category are organizations that provide instruction or training on a particular subject (although they may not have a regular curriculum, faculty, or student body). For example, organizations that operate apprentice training programs, correctional and rehabilitation centers, internship programs, and seminars, conferences, and lectures are educational. In addition, educational entities can include those that engage in study and research.

Another way to be educational is to instruct the public on subjects useful to the individual and beneficial to the community. Within this classification are organizations that provide counseling services, instruction on various subjects, endeavor to instruct the public in the field of civic betterment, publish material, and (again) engage in study and research. As to publishing activities, to be an educational function, the content of the publication must follow methods generally accepted as educational in character, the distribution of the material is necessary or valuable in achieving the organization's tax-exempt purposes, and the manner in which the distribution is accomplished must be distinguishable from ordinary commercial

There can be a fine line of distinction between an educational activity and a taxable business (see Chapter 12). Sometimes it is difficult to distinguish between an educational undertaking and one that amounts to propagandizing—the zealous propagation of a particular idea or doctrine without presentation of the material in a reasonably objective or balanced manner (see Chapter 13). Further, it is often impossible (indeed, unnecessary) to differentiate between organizations that are charitable because they advance education and those that are educational. As to the latter, for example, the Campaign to Clean Up America would be both charitable (as advancing education) and educational (as instructing the public on subjects that are beneficial to the community).

Religious Organizations

Religious organizations are the oldest form of tax-exempt organization. Unlike other areas of the law of tax-exempt organizations, religious organizations defy definition. This is due in large part to constitutional law considerations, in that the First Amendment to the U.S. Constitution bars Congress from making any law with respect to the establishment of religious organizations or prohibiting the free exercise thereof.

Thus, neither the U.S. Congress, the Department of the Treasury, nor the IRS has attempted to define the word "religion" (or "religious"). The courts are supposed to steer clear of definitions of the term as well. The U.S. Supreme Court has written that freedom of thought and religious belief "embraces the right to maintain theories of life and of death and of the hereafter which are rank heresy to followers of the orthodox faiths," and that, if judges undertake to examine the truth or falsity of religious beliefs, "they enter a forbidden domain."

With this in mind, one federal district court said that it will not consider the "merits or fallacies of a religion," nor will it "praise or condemn a religion, however excellent or fanatical or preposterous it may seem." The U.S. Tax Court has observed that, it is "loathe to evaluate and judge ecclesiastical authority and duties in the various religious disciplines." One aspect of the matter that is clear is that, for tax and other law purposes, religious belief is not confined to "theistic" belief. Another district court has noted that "an activity may be religious even though it is neither part of nor derives from a societally recognized religious sect."

Nonetheless, some courts have ventured into the "forbidden domain." One wrote that religious belief is "a belief finding expression in a conscience which categorically requires the believer to disregard elementary self-interest and to accept martyrdom in preference to transgressing its tenets." Another court found an activity to be religious because it was centered around belief in a higher being "which in its various forms is given the name 'god' in common usage." Even the U.S. Supreme Court has placed emphasis on belief in a "supreme being," and has looked to see whether "a given belief that is sincere and meaningful occupies a place in the life of its possessor parallel to that filled by the orthodox belief in God" and whether the belief occupies in the life of the individual involved "'a place parallel to that filled by . . . God' in traditional religious persons."

There are many kinds of religious organizations; the most common form is a church. But, here again, the federal tax law lacks a crisp definition of the word "church." The IRS has an informal definition of a church, which is an organization that satisfies at least some of the following criteria: It has a distinct legal existence, a recognized creed and form of worship, a definite and distinct ecclesiastical government, a formal code of doctrine and discipline, a distinct religious history, a membership not associated with any other church or denomination, a complete organization of ordained ministers ministering to their congregations and selected after completing prescribed courses of study, a literature of its own, established places of worship, regular congregations, regular religious services, Sunday schools for the religious instruction of the young, and schools for the preparation of its ministers.

Some courts are building upon these informal criteria. For example, the U.S. Tax Court has concluded that, to be a church, an organization must have, at a minimum, "the existence of an established congregation served by an organized ministry, the provision of regular religious services and religious education for the young, and the dissemination of a doctrinal code." On another occasion, the Tax Court concluded that a "church is a coherent group of individuals and families that join together to accomplish the religious purposes of mutually held beliefs" and that a "church's principal means of accomplishing its religious purposes must be to assemble regularly a group of individuals related by common worship and faith."

Other types of religious organizations, for tax purposes, include conventions of churches, associations of churches, integrated auxiliaries of churches, religious orders, apostolic groups, missionary organizations, bible and tract societies, and church-run organizations, such as schools, hospitals, orphanages, nursing homes, publishing entities, broadcasting entities, and cemeteries.

The law has become clouded in this area, because of the tax abuses involved in the establishment of alleged "churches." There have been many instances where an entity has been found to be a nonexempt entity on the finding that it is a "personal church."

Scientific Organizations

A scientific organization is one that is engaged in scientific research or otherwise operated for the dissemination of scientific knowledge. The tax-exempt scientific organization must be organized and operated to serve the public interest.

Once again, neither Congress, the Department of the Treasury, nor the IRS has endeavored to define the term "scientific." One dictionary states that "science" is a "branch of study in which facts are observed, classified, and, usually, quantitative laws are formulated and verified; [or which] involves the application of mathematical reasoning and data analysis to natural phenomena." One federal court has stated that the term "science" means "the process by which knowledge is systematized or classified through the use of observation, experimentation, or reasoning."

In this area, the focus is largely on the concept of "research." This term lacks precise definition in this setting as well. Generally, the concept differentiates between "fundamental" and "basic" research, as opposed to "applied" or "practical" research. While all may be scientific research for purposes of the law of tax-exempt organizations, the latter is suspect. Thus, scientific research does not include activities ordinarily carried on incident to commercial operations, as, for example, the testing or inspection of materials or products or the designing or construction of equipment or buildings.

Other Charitable Organizations

A nonprofit organization may be charitable, for federal tax purposes, because it is a literary organization. Or, it may be charitable by reason of the fact that it operates to prevent cruelty to children or animals. Further, it may be charitable because it qualifies as an amateur sports organization.

There are some organizations operated as cooperatives that can qualify as charitable entities. These are the cooperative hospital service organizations and cooperative educational service organizations. These types of organizations are subject to strict rules as to eligibility for tax-exempt status.

Organizations that test for public safety are eligible for tax-exempt status as charitable organizations. However, this type of charitable organization is ineligible to receive contributions that are deductible as charitable gifts.

Social Welfare Organizations

Traditionally, a social welfare organization is one that functions to, in the language of the tax regulations, advance the "common good and general welfare," and seeks "civic betterments and social improvements." This type of organization is expected to engage in activities that benefit the community in its entirety, rather than merely benefit its membership or other select group of individuals or organizations.

A contemporary use of the social welfare organization is as an advocacy entity. This is because the term *social welfare* can be broader than the term *charitable* (even though, as discussed above, the concept of *charitable* includes the promotion of social welfare), social welfare organizations can engage in an unlimited amount of legislative activity without endangering their tax-exempt status, and they can permissibly engage in some political campaign activity. Consequently, some charitable organizations utilize related social welfare organizations as means to engage in more lobbying activities than they are allowed to undertake directly.

Like many other tax-exempt organizations, social welfare entities may not engage in transactions that constitute private inurement (see Chapter 5) and may not operate unrelated businesses as a primary activity. The only type of social welfare organization to which contributions are deductible is a veterans' organization (see later section).

Business Leagues

The federal tax law uses the anachronistic term *business league* to describe what are known in the modern world as trade, business, and professional associations. The private inurement doctrine expressly applies to them.

A business league is a group of persons (an "association") having some common business interest, the purpose of which is to promote that common interest. Its activities are, if it is to be tax-exempt, directed to the improvement of business conditions of one or more lines of business, as distinguished from the performance of particular services for individual persons.

A unique association is accorded specific mention as a tax-exempt entity in the Internal Revenue Code: professional football leagues.

Chambers of Commerce

A tax-exempt chamber of commerce is an organization having a common business interest—the general economic welfare of a community. That is, it is an organization whose efforts are directed at promotion of the common economic interests of all of the commercial enterprises in a given trade community. Similar to the exempt chamber of commerce is the "board of trade" and the "real estate board."

Social Clubs

Social clubs are basically tax-exempt, although unlike most forms of exempt organizations, their investment income is taxable. A social club is a nonprofit organization, operated for pleasure, recreation, and social purposes, that is usually principally supported by membership dues, fees, and assessments. The exempt club must have an established membership, personal contacts, and fellowship.

The private inurement doctrine is expressly applicable to tax-exempt social clubs. Also, the law limits the extent to which an exempt social club can make its facilities available to the general public.

Labor Organizations

Federal tax law provides tax-exempt status for labor organizations. The purpose of these organizations is to better the conditions of workers, the improvement of the grade of their products, and the development of a higher degree of efficiency in the particular occupation. The most common example of this type of organization is a labor union whose purpose is to bargain collectively with employers, to secure better working conditions, wages, and similar benefits.

The private inurement doctrine is expressly applicable to labor organizations.

Agricultural Organizations

Like labor organizations, tax-exempt agricultural organizations must have as their purpose the betterment of the conditions of those engaged in the exempt pursuit, the improvement of the grade of their products, and the development of a higher degree of efficiency in the particular occupation.

For this purpose, the term *agricultural* includes (but is not limited to) the art or science of cultivating land, harvesting crops or aquatic resources, or raising livestock. However, the IRS will not grant agricultural status to an organization whose principal purpose is to provide a direct business service for its members' economic benefit. Again, the private inurement doctrine is applicable in this context.

Horticultural Organizations

The definition of a horticultural organization is much like that of the labor and agricultural organizations. For tax purposes, the term *horticultural* means the art or science of cultivating fruits, flowers, and vegetables. The private inurement doctrine is applicable in this setting as well.

United States Instrumentalities

A corporation that is organized pursuant to an act of Congress and is an "instrumentality" of the United States, is, if specifically so classified under federal tax law, an exempt organization. Certain federal credit unions are exempt under this rule.

Title-Holding Corporations

A corporation that is organized for the exclusive purpose of holding title to property, collecting income from the property, and turning the net income over to a tax-exempt organization is itself tax-exempt. An organization is ineligible for tax exemption under this rule if it has two or more unrelated parents. (Another rule, discussed below, provides for exempt status for multi-parent title-holding corporations.)

Title-holding corporations generally may not engage in any business other than that of holding title to property. These organizations can be particularly useful in holding title to property that may attract liability.

Local Employees' Associations

A form of tax-exempt organization is the local association of employees, the membership of which is limited to the employees of a designated employer or employers in a particular municipality. The private inurement doctrine is expressly applicable.

Fraternal Beneficiary Societies

Federal tax law provides tax-exempt status for fraternal beneficiary societies, orders, or associations operating under the lodge system or for the exclusive benefit of the members of a fraternal organization itself operating under the lodge system. The purpose of such groups is to provide for the payment of life, sick, accident, or other benefits to the members of the society, order, or association or their dependents.

Contributions to a fraternal beneficiary society are deductible where the gift is to be used exclusively for charitable purposes.

Voluntary Employees' Beneficiary Associations

Federal tax exemption is available for voluntary employees' beneficiary associations (VEBAs) that provide for the payment of life, sick, accident, or other benefits to its members or their dependents or designated beneficiaries. The private inurement doctrine is expressly applicable to VEBAs.

A VEBA is an increasingly popular vehicle for the provision of benefits to employees, usually of a common employer. Eligibility for membership may be restricted by geographic proximity or by objective conditions or limitations reasonably related to employment. Eligibility for benefits may be restricted by objective conditions relating to the type or amount of benefits offered.

Most VEBAs are subject to certain nondiscrimination requirements.

Domestic Fraternal Societies

Tax exemption is available for domestic fraternal societies, orders, or associations, operating under the lodge system, the net earnings of which are devoted exclusively to charitable purposes, and which do not provide for the payment of life, sick, accident, or other benefits to its members. An organization not providing these benefits but otherwise qualifying as a fraternal beneficiary society (see previous section) qualifies as a domestic fraternal society.

Teachers' Retirement Fund Associations

Federal tax law supplies tax-exempt status to teachers' retirement fund associations of a purely local character, if there is no private inurement (other than through the payment of retirement benefits) and the income consists wholly of amounts received from public taxation, amounts received from assessments on the teaching salaries of members, and income in respect of investments.

Benevolent or Mutual Organizations

Exemption is available for benevolent life insurance associations of a purely local character, mutual ditch or irrigation companies, mutual or cooperative telephone companies, or like organizations, if 85 percent or more of the income is collected from members for the sole purpose of meeting losses and expenses.

Cemetery Companies

A cemetery company is exempt from federal income taxation if it is owned and operated exclusively for the benefit of its members and if it is not operated for profit. The private inurement doctrine is expressly applicable. A tax-exempt cemetery generally is an entity that owns a cemetery, sells lots in it for burial purposes, and maintains these and the unsold lots in a state of repair and upkeep appropriate to, in the words of the IRS, a "final resting place."

An organization receiving and administering funds for the perpetual care of a nonprofit cemetery itself qualifies as a tax-exempt cemetery company. A nonprofit organization that provides for the perpetual care of a burial area in a community may also become so classified, even though it is not associated with a nonprofit cemetery.

Contributions to tax-exempt cemetery companies are deductible for federal income tax purposes.

Credit Unions

Credit unions without capital stock organized and operated for the mutual benefit of members and without profit are tax-exempt under federal law. Usually these organizations are chartered under state law. Those formed under federal law are likely to be tax-exempt as instrumentalities of the United States (see previous section).

Mutual Insurance Companies

Tax exemption is available for mutual insurance companies or associations other than life or marine (including interinsurers and reciprocal underwriters) if the gross amount received during the tax year from certain items (principally investment income) and premiums (including deposits and assessments) does not exceed $150,000. All of the policyholders must be members having common equitable ownership and control of the company.

Crop Operations Finance Corporations

Federal tax law provides exemption for corporations organized by a tax-exempt farmers' cooperative (see later section) or its members, for the purpose of financing the ordinary crop operations of the members or other producers, and operated in conjunction with this type of a cooperative. Under certain circumstances, this entity may issue capital stock.

Supplemental Unemployment Benefit Trusts

Tax exemption is available for certain trusts forming part of a plan providing for the payment of supplemental unemployment compensation benefits (SUB). Among other requirements, a SUB must be part of a plan that does not discriminate in favor of supervisory or highly compensated employees and that requires that benefits be determined according to objective standards. SUBs are intended to provide benefits to laid-off (and perhaps ill) employees, frequently in conjunction with other payments such as state unemployment benefits.

Veterans' Organizations

Federal tax law provides exemption for a post or organization of veterans, or an auxiliary unit or society thereof, or a trust or foundation for the entity. It must be organized in the United States or any of its possessions. At least 75 percent of its members must be past or present members of the armed forces of the United States and substantially all of the other members must be individuals who are cadets or spouses, widows, or widowers of such past or present members or of cadets. The private inurement doctrine is expressly applicable.

A special provision in the unrelated income tax rules (see Chapter 12) exempts from taxation income derived from members of these organizations attributable to payments for life, accident, or health insurance with respect to its members or their dependents, where the profits are set aside for charitable purposes.

Contributions to veterans' organizations are generally deductible. Some veterans' groups are tax-exempt as social welfare or charitable entities.

Farmers' Cooperatives

Exempt from federal income tax are farmers' cooperatives, which are farmer's, fruit grower's, or like associations organized and operated on a cooperative basis for the purpose of (1) marketing the products of members or other producers and returning to them the proceeds of sales, less the necessary marketing expenses, on the basis of either the quantity or the value of the products furnished by them, or (2) purchasing supplies and equipment for the use of members or other persons and turning over the supplies and equipment to them at actual cost plus necessary expenses.

One of the many other requirements for achievement of tax-exempt status as a farmers' cooperative is that any excess of gross receipts over expenses and payments to patrons must be returned to them in proportion to the amount of business done for them. With respect to a farmers' cooperative that issues stock, for the cooperative to be tax-exempt, substantially all of the capital stock must be owned by producers who market their products or purchase their supplies and equipment through the cooperative.

Shipowners' Protection and Indemnity Associations

Federal tax law provides that gross income does not include the gross receipts of nonprofit shipowners' mutual protection and indemnity associations. The private inurement doctrine is expressly applicable. These organizations are, however, taxable on income from interest, dividends, and rents.

Political Organizations

Tax exemption is basically available for the political organization. This entity is a political party, committee, association, fund, or other organization organized and operated primarily for the purpose of directly or indirectly accepting contributions and/or making expenditures for an *exempt function.* An exempt function includes influencing or attempting to influence the selection, nomination, election, or appointment of any individual to any federal, state, or local public office in a political organization, or the election of presidential or vice-presidential electors. The political organization thus includes political action committees or, more technically, separate segregated funds.

Income of a political organization, other than income from an exempt function, is taxable. This type of taxable revenue includes investment income.

Homeowners' Associations

A homeowners' association is tax-exempt if it satisfies five basic requirements. First, it must be organized and operated to provide for the acquisition, construction, management, maintenance, and care of association property. Second, at least 60 percent of the association's gross income for the year consists of exempt function income. Third, at least 90 percent of the annual expenditures of the association are to acquire, construct, manage, maintain, and care for or improve its property. Fourth, substantially all of the dwelling units in a condominium project or lots and buildings in a subdivision, development, or similar area must be used by individuals for residences. Fifth, the private inurement doctrine is expressly applicable.

Only the exempt function income of a homeowners' association escapes taxation; the remainder (including investment income) is fully taxed. This exemption must be elected.

Group Legal Service Organizations

Another type of tax-exempt organization is an entity formed as part of a qualified group legal services plan or plans. This type of plan provides benefits in the form of prepaid legal services for employees of an employer and their spouses and dependents. The group legal services plan must meet requirements with respect to nondiscrimination in contributions or benefits and in eligibility for enrollment.

Black Lung Benefits Trusts

Income tax exemption is available for a qualifying trust used by a coal mine operator to self-insure for liabilities under federal and state black lung benefits laws. Under federal law, a coal mine operator in a state deemed to not provide adequate workmen's compensation coverage for pneumoconiosis must secure the payment of benefits for which the operator may be found liable under the statute, either by means of commercial insurance or through self-insuring.

Multi-Employer Pension Plan Trusts

Also tax-exempt under federal law is a trust established by the sponsors of a multi-employer pension plan as a vehicle to accumulate funds in order to provide withdrawal liability payments to the plan.

Multi-Parent Title-Holding Organizations

Tax exemption is available for the multi-parent title-holding organization. This is an entity organized and operated for the exclusive purposes of acquiring and holding title to real property, collecting income from the property, and remitting the entire amount of income from the property (less expenses) to one or more qualified tax-exempt organizations that are shareholders of the title-holding corporation or beneficiaries of the title-holding trust. This category of tax-exempt organization was created in response to the position of the IRS that a title-holding company otherwise eligible for tax exemption under preexisting law (see above) cannot be exempt if two or more of its parent organizations are unrelated.

Other Tax-Exempt Organizations

While the foregoing represents a fast sweep through the various type of organizations that are conventionally known as tax-exempt organizations, there are many other entities that, under federal law, are also exempt from taxes.

These include governmental entities, such as states, political subdivisions of states, and other governmental bodies, whether termed "agencies," "bodies," or "instrumentalities." This type of tax-exempt status flows from the doctrine of intergovernmental immunity.

Tax-exempt status is accorded the funds underlying employee benefit plans, such as retirement and profit-sharing plans.

Other organizations that, in effect, are tax-exempt are partnerships (see Chapter 16), S corporations, some cooperatives (other than those referenced above), and planned giving vehicles (see Chapter 17) such as charitable remainder trusts and pooled income funds.

—————————— FOCUS ON THE CAMPAIGN TO ——————————
CLEAN UP AMERICA

The above survey of tax-exempt organizations illustrates the vast array of nonprofit entities that Congress has decided merit tax-exempt status. Certainly these organizations range far beyond the charitable entities and similar groups that are commonly thought of as nonprofit organizations.

The facts surrounding the hypothetical Campaign to Clean Up America illustrate the application of, and the interrelationship of, at least some of these rules. The Campaign is a charitable organization, in the broadest sense of that term. As discussed, it is in actuality a charitable and educational entity. The various reasons as to why it qualifies as a charitable organization, using that term in its more technical sense, are summarized above.

If, however, the Campaign were to want to engage in a greater degree of legislative activities than are allowed of charitable organizations, it could establish a related social welfare organization to conduct those activities. That social welfare organization may establish a political action committee. Alternately, the Campaign may establish a political action committee to engage in political activities other than political campaign activities.

Still other tax-exempt organizations may be involved. Certainly, in launching its planned giving program, the Campaign will be establishing at least one pooled income fund and (hopefully) many charitable remainder trusts (see Chapter 17). As it grows, it will have retirement and other benefits programs for its employees (see Chapter 10), the underlying funds of which will be tax-exempt. The time may come when a title-holding organization is appropriate.

As discussed throughout, today's tax-exempt organization is often part of a group of related organizations, some nonprofit (and tax-exempt) and some for-profit.

5

Nonprofits and Private Benefit

One fundamental requirement for qualification as a nonprofit organization is also one of the most misunderstood. This is because of the enormous misperception of the term *nonprofit*. Since an entity must be nonprofit before it can be tax-exempt, it is important to understand what the ramifications of this term *nonprofit* are. The meaning of the term is found in another confusing term; *private inurement*. Most nonprofit organizations are subject to the private inurement doctrine.

The concept of a nonprofit organization is best understood through a comparison with a for-profit organization. Indeed, the private inurement doctrine embodies the unique difference between nonprofit and for-profit organizations.

In many respects, the characteristics of the two categories of organizations are identical: both require a legal form, have a board of directors and officers, pay compensation, face essentially the same expenses, are able to receive a profit, make investments, and produce goods and/or services. However, a for-profit entity has owners—those who hold the equity in the enterprise, such as stockholders of a corporation. The for-profit organization is operated for the benefit of its owners; the profits of the enterprise are passed through to them, such as the payments of dividends on shares of stock. This is what is meant by a for-profit organization; it is one that is intended to generate a profit for its owners. In the jargon of the tax law, the transfer of the profits from the organization to its owners is *private inurement* of net earnings.

But, unlike the for-profit entity, the nonprofit organization is not permitted to distribute its profits (net earnings) to those who control and/or financially support it; a nonprofit organization usually does not have any owners (equity holders). (A few states allow nonprofit organizations to issue stock; this is done for control purposes only, in that the stock does not carry with it any dividend rights.) Thus, the private inurement doctrine is the substantive dividing line between the nonprofits and the for-profits.

The private inurement doctrine is, as noted, applicable to nearly all types of tax-exempt organizations. However, it is most pronounced with respect to charitable organizations. By contrast, in a few types of nonprofit organizations, private benefit is the exempt function; this is the case, for example, with employee benefit trusts, social clubs, and cemetery companies.

CHARITABLE ORGANIZATIONS

The federal law of tax exemption for charitable organizations requires that each such entity be organized and operated so that "no part of . . . [its] net earnings . . . inures to the benefit of any private shareholder or individual." Read literally, this means that the profits of a charitable organization may not be passed along to individuals in their private capacity, in the manner of, for example, dividend payments to shareholders. But, in fact, the private inurement rule, expanded and amplified by the IRS and the courts, today means much more.

The contemporary concept of private inurement is broad and wide-ranging. Recently, the IRS' lawyers advised that "[i]nurement is likely to arise where the beneficial benefit represents a transfer of the organization's financial resources to an individual solely by virtue of the individual's relationship with the organization, and without regard to accomplishing exempt purposes." That is a very apt description of the modern private inurement doctrine, yet it is a substantial embellishment of the statutory rendition of the rule.

The essence of the private inurement concept is to ensure that a charitable organization is serving public interests, *not* private interests. That is, to be tax-exempt, it is imperative for an organization to establish that it is not organized and operated for the benefit of private interests, such as designated individuals, the creator of the entity or his or her family, shareholders of the organization, persons controlled (directly or indirectly) by such private interests, or any persons having a personal and private interest in the activities of the organization.

One of the ways the law determines the presence of any proscribed private inurement is to look to the ultimate purpose of the organization. If the basic purpose of the organization is to benefit individuals in their private capacity, then it cannot be tax-exempt as a charitable organization (and probably not as any other type of exempt organization), even though exempt activities may also be performed. Conversely, it may well be (although the IRS officially believes the private inurement proscription to be an absolute one) that incidental benefits to private individuals will not defeat tax-exemption, as long as the organization otherwise qualifies for the exempt status.

Private inurement is not necessarily the same thing as commercial activities. A charitable organization may usually engage in commercial activities where done so for a larger exempt purpose. However, the existence of a single commercial or otherwise nonexempt substantial purpose will destroy or prevent the exemption.

The federal securities laws embody the notion of an *insider* with respect to a business corporation. An insider is one who has a special and close relationship with the corporation, frequently because he or she is a director, officer, and/or significant shareholder. The private inurement rules, using the phraseology of "private shareholder or individual," likewise contemplate a type of transaction between a charitable organization and a person in the nature of an insider, the latter able to cause the application of the organization's net earnings for private purposes as the result of his or her exercise of control or influence. The IRS basically adopts this view, once observing that, as a general rule, "[a]n organization's trustees, officers, members, founders, or contributors may not, by reason of their position, acquire any of its funds." Stating the matter another way, the IRS has rather starkly said that "[t]he prohibition of inurement, in its simplest terms, means that [with exceptions] a private shareholder or individual cannot pocket the organization's funds."

Therefore, impermissible private inurement involves two necessary components. One is that the private individual (insider) to whom the benefit inures has the ability to control or otherwise influence the actions of the charitable organization and does so to cause the private benefit to come into existence. The other is that the benefit conferred be intentionally conferred by the influenced organization and not be a permissible form of private inurement or not result coincidentally from happenstance.

The self-dealing rules that are applicable to private foundations represent, in essence, a codification of the private inurement doctrine (see Chapter 11). In that setting, the law is clear that an impermissible transaction must involve, in addition to the charitable entity (the foundation), a person in the nature of an insider—they are called *disqualified persons* (again, essentially, directors, trustees, officers, key employees, substantial contributors, and family members of and those who control or are controlled by the foregoing persons).

Persons can be privately benefited in many ways; however, thus private inurement has many manifestations. Still, it must be said at this point that a charitable organization may incur ordinary and necessary expenditures in its operations without losing its tax-exempt status. It may permissibly pay compensation, rent, interest, and the like—these are, of course, forms of payment to persons in their private capacity but they are done in furtherance of exempt purposes and (to be permissible) are reasonable and not excessive.

Compensation

Private inurement transactions take many forms. The most common of them is excessive and unreasonable compensation. Here, the contrast between allowable and nonallowable private inurement is the most obvious. When a charitable organization pays an employee a salary, it is—literally—paying a portion of what would otherwise be net earnings to an individual in his or her private capacity. However, that is not the meaning of private inurement. Instead, private inurement in the compensatory context means the payment of compensation that is excessive and unreasonable—and the payment of such compensation to one who is an insider. Most of the court cases on this point involve the payment of high compensation to the founder of the organization and/or the family members.

Whether compensation paid is or is not reasonable is a question of fact, to be decided in the context of each case. Generally, the law contemplates that the excessiveness (if any) of compensation is ascertained by comparing the compensation in question to that paid to individuals with similar responsibilities and expertise in the same or comparable communities. That is easier said than done. The key, nonetheless, is the reasonableness of the compensation. As the U.S. Tax Court once observed, "[t]he law places no duty on individuals operating charitable organizations to donate their services; they are entitled to reasonable compensation for their services."

There are two aspects of compensation that can make it unreasonable and excessive. One is the sheer size of the compensation, in absolute terms. One federal court, in finding private inurement because of excessive compensation, characterized the salaries as being a "substantial amount." Other courts will tolerate "substantial" amounts of compensation, where the employee's services and skills warrant that level of payment. Some courts evidence a distinct bias when it comes to compensation paid by nonprofit organizations, believing that it should be lower than that paid by for-profit organizations, even though all other material elements underlying the reasonableness of the compensation are the same. In many cases, the insider is not only receiving high cash compensation but also other financial benefits from the charity (such as fees, commissions, and royalties); often, family members are also participating in the largess. Most of the cases denying tax exemption to religious organizations do so, not on the ground that the entity is not religious in nature, but on the ground that the founder's are engaging in private inurement transactions, including unwarranted levels of compensation.

The other aspect of compensation that can lead to private inurement is the manner in which it is calculated. Basically, the courts and the IRS may struggle with compensation arrangements that are predicated upon a percentage of gross receipts. Although the caselaw on this point is inconsistent and unclear, the emerging rule, developed so far only by the U.S. Tax Court, seems to be that private inurement will not be found simply because a commission system is used, but rather the important fact is the reasonableness of the compensation actually paid. However, the Tax Court has found private inurement in this type of situation because the compensation arrangement, based on a percentage of gross receipts, did not include an upper limit on total compensation. Yet, in another instance, the Tax Court focused on the reasonableness of the percentage, not the reasonableness of the amount paid.

The special rules applying to self-dealing in the private foundation context, which exclude from the self-dealing constraints compensation arrangements where the payments are reasonable and not excessive, may be used as a guide in ascertaining the presence of private inurement in a situation involving a public charity.

As a general proposition, however, a charitable organization may, without causing undue private inurement, pay reasonable compensation to its employees, suppliers, and consultants—even those who are its insiders. This compensation may be in the form of salaries, wages, and/or fees. It can also include forms of fringe benefits, such as insurance, deferred compensation, and pension and retirement benefits (see Chapter 10).

Rents and Loans

As in the case of payment of compensation to employees and independent contractors, a charitable organization generally may lease property and pay rent. However, the private inurement doctrine requires, in addition to the fact that the rental arrangement be beneficial and desirable to the organization, that the rental payments be reasonable. That is, inflated rental prices may well amount to a private benefit inuring to the lessor. Again, loan arrangements between a private foundation and its disqualified persons are generally acts of self-dealing and those rules may be used as a guide to potential private inurement in other settings.

Like rental arrangements, the terms of a loan involving a charitable organization should be financially advantageous to the organization and commensurate with its exempt purposes. The interest charges, amount of security, repayment period, terms of repayment, and other aspects of the loan must be reasonable. This is true where the charity is the borrower; the scrutiny will heighten where an insider is borrowing from a charity. If a loan from a charity is not repaid timely, questions of private inurement will likely be raised. One federal court once observed that the "very existence of a private source of loan credit from an [charitable] organization's earnings may itself amount to inurement of benefit." Once again, the self-dealing rules may be looked to for general guidance.

Some charitable organizations are called upon to guarantee the debt of another entity, such as a related nonprofit or even for-profit organization. The terms of such an arrangement must be carefully reviewed; if the loan guarantee is not in advancement of exempt purposes or cannot be characterized as a reasonable investment, private inurement may be occurring.

Services

For charitable organizations, the interaction of the private inurement rules and the provision of services can be quite confusing. Of course, many charitable organizations provide services in advancement of their exempt functions. The point is, however, that an organization cannot qualify as a charitable entity where its primary purpose is the provision of services to individuals in their private capacity. By contrast, individuals can be benefited by a charity where they constitute members of a charitable class (such as the poor or students), the individual beneficiaries are considered merely instruments or means to a charitable objective, or the private benefit is merely incidental. (In this type of situation, where insiders are not involved, there may be "private benefit" rather than the more stringently prohibited "private inurement.")

Some illustrations will indicate these distinctions. Generally, organizations operated to advance the arts are charitable but a cooperative art gallery that exhibits and sells its members' works was held not to be a charitable entity because it is serving the private interests of its members. Quite frequently, the rendering of housing assistance for low-income families qualifies as a charitable undertaking yet an organization that provides such assistance but gives preference for housing to employees of a particular organization was found to be advancing private, not charitable, interests. The operation of a private school can be a charitable program but an organization that provides bus transportation for children to a school was held to be not tax-exempt because it is relieving the children's parents of their responsibility to transport their children to school.

Likewise, an organization primarily engaged in the testing of drugs for commercial pharmaceutical companies was ruled not to be engaged in scientific research but to be serving the private interests of the manufacturers. One more example: An association of professional nurses that operates a nurses' registry was ruled to be affording greater employment opportunities for its members and thus to be substantially operated for private ends.

Joint Ventures

Charitable organizations are increasingly involved in partnerships with individuals and/or other joint ventures with individuals or for-profit entities. Real estate ventures, with a charitable organization as the general partner in a limited partnership, is a common manifestation of this practice. The use of partnerships and similar vehicles are discussed in Chapter 16; the point here is the concern being voiced by the IRS in the private inurement context.

In a general partnership, all of the partners are subject to liability for the acts committed in the name of the partnership. However, in a limited partnership, which will have at least one general partner, the limited partners are essentially investors, with their liability confined to the extent of their investment. As investors, the limited partners are in that position to experience a return on their investment. Meanwhile, the general partner or partners in a limited partnership have the responsibility to operate the partnership in a successful manner—which includes seeing to it that the limited partners achieve an appropriate economic return, one worthy of the commitment of their capital.

It is in this structure and set of expectations that the IRS sees private inurement lurking. Cast in its worse light, a limited partnership with a charitable organization at the helm can be construed as the running of a business (the partnership) for the benefit of private interests (the limited partners). Of course, this is rarely the case, inasmuch as a partnership (general or limited) is basically a financing entity—a means to an end where, in this instance, a charitable organization is able to attract the funds of others for a legitimate purpose. Like the borrowing of money from a bank (where the charity pays interest), a charitable organization/general partner must pay the limiteds for its use of their money. But, because in the partnership structure the general partner is functioning in an active, not passive, manner, the IRS finds private benefit when the limited partners are paid but not when the bankers are paid.

Following some litigation, in which the IRS lost every case, the position of the IRS has evolved to this point: A charitable organization will lose its tax-exempt status if it participates as a general partner in a limited partnership, unless the purpose of the partnership is the advancement of charitable purposes; even where a charity passes that test, it will still forfeit tax exemption if it is not protected against the day-to-day duties of administering the partnership or if the payments to the limited partners are excessive.

Although there is much wrong with this IRS position, it is illustrative of the contemporary application of the private inurement rules. Despite the ferocity of its stance against charitable organizations in partnerships, however, the IRS has yet (since losing the string of cases) to deny or revoke exempt status to one that ends up in a limited partnership as general partner. That is, the IRS is (to date) always finding the partnership to be engaged in charitable purposes. Still, charitable organizations should be cautious when entering into any form of joint venture or partnership, in whatever capacity, so as to avoid conferring private benefit upon persons or otherwise being used to generate unwarranted benefits to persons in their private capacities.

Social Welfare Organizations

Social welfare organizations, like most forms of tax-exempt organizations, cannot be operated primarily for private gain. While the private inurement doctrine is not expressly applicable to these types of nonprofit entities, it does have its manifestations in this context. For example, homeowners' associations may be exempt as social welfare organizations only if they are engaged in the promotion of the common good and general welfare of a community, rather than operate for the benefit of a select group of individuals.

However, a closely approximate criterion of the social welfare organization is that it must not be operated primarily for the economic benefit or convenience of its members. Many cooperative entities fail to be social welfare organizations for this reason, in that, in the words of a federal court reviewing one, it is operated "primarily to benefit the taxpayer's membership economically." A federal appellate court denied social welfare status to a mutual assistance organization established by a church because its policies and practices benefit a "select few"—its members—rather than a larger public.

As is the case with membership associations in general, the rendering of services to members does not necessarily work a denial or loss of social welfare status. Correspondingly, an organization may be able to qualify as a social welfare organization where its services are equally available to members and nonmembers.

It was observed earlier that the private inurement proscription as applied to charitable organizations is not the same as the restriction on commercial practices. The same may be said with respect to social welfare organizations. At the same time, however, the federal tax law does expressly state that an exempt social welfare organization may not be organized or operated to carry on a business with the general public in a manner similar to organizations that are operated for profit. In addition, a social welfare organization (as well as a charitable organization) will lose or be denied tax-exempt status if a substantial part of its activities consists of the provision of commercial-type insurance.

Trade and Business Associations

The federal tax law governing the activities of tax-exempt trade, business, and professional associations (business leagues) expressly includes the proscription against the inurement of the net earnings of these organizations to individuals in their private capacities. At first glance, this rule may seem somewhat anomalous, given the fact that the purpose of these associations is to promote the common business interests of the membership. After all, is not the chief reason one joins an association to partake of the benefits it accords its membership?

Nonetheless, there is an important distinction between improving business conditions of a line of business (as described in Chapter 4, a business league's primary purpose) and performing services for members to the extent that private inurement results. Like the law with respect to social welfare organizations, the federal tax law prohibits these types of associations from carrying on *business activities for profit.*

Nonetheless, there is requirement of tax law applicable to business leagues that is often misunderstood and ignored. This is the rule that a tax-exempt business league may not perform *particular* services for individual persons. In practice, this prohibition is enforced only where these services are the primary function of an association; otherwise, the matter is one of unrelated income taxation. It can be difficult in a specific instance to distinguish between the performance of particular services and activities directed to the improvement of business conditions.

An activity of a business league is an exempt function where the activity benefits its membership as a group, rather than in their individual capacities. The benefit to the group occurs where the business league provides a product or service to its members for a fee, with the benefit not directly proportional to the fees. As one federal court stated, "the activities that serve the interests of individual . . . [members] according to what they pay produce individual benefits insufficient to fulfill the substantial relationship test, since those activities generally do not generate inherent group benefits that inure to the advantage of its members as members."

Labor and Like Organizations

Labor organizations, which frequently are unions, are much like business leagues. While trade associations and similar entities strive to promote conditions within lines of businesses, labor organizations operate to better the workings and economic conditions of employees. Thus, labor organizations are often membership groups, providing services to the membership. But, again, the federal tax law forbids the net earnings of a labor organization from inuring to the benefit of persons in their private capacity.

The private inurement constraint also is specifically applicable to social clubs, agricultural and horticultural organizations, voluntary employees' beneficiary associations, certain teachers' retirement fund associations, veterans' organizations, shipowners' protection and indemnity associations, and homeowners' associations.

Still other manifestations of the distinctions between public and private benefit are evident in the law pertaining to other types of tax-exempt organizations. Thus, the net earnings of local associations of employees must be devoted to charitable purposes. The same "reverse inurement" rule applies to domestic fraternal societies, which are also prohibited from paying life, sick, accident, or other benefits to their members.

In another twist on the prohibition of private benefits flowing from tax-exempt organizations, the law mandates that the economic benefits flowing out of employee benefit plans not discriminate in favor of highly compensated employees. This is particularly true with respect to voluntary employees' beneficiary associations and supplemental unemployment benefit trusts.

The federal tax law of other exempt organizations simply states that they may not be operated "for profit." This is the case with respect to cemetery companies and certain credit unions.

"Private Benefit" Tax-Exempt Organizations

There are, the foregoing notwithstanding, several types of tax-exempt organizations that have, as their tax-exempt function, the provision of "private" benefits. This is not to say that the law allows the net earnings of some tax-exempt organizations to inure to persons in their private capacity, for it does not. But there are tax-exempt organizations that serve to advance private ends.

The most notable of the "private benefit" tax-exempt organizations are those that provide economic benefits to employees, either in the case of difficulty or at retirement. For example, the funds underlying retirement, pension, and profit-sharing plans are tax-exempt organizations. Other employee benefit organizations are the voluntary employees' beneficiary associations (that provide life, sick, accident, and other benefits to their members and dependents), supplemental unemployment benefit trusts (that provide unemployment compensation benefits to employees), group legal service organizations (that fund prepaid legal services for employees), Black Lung Benefits Trusts (that fund employer liabilities for pneumoconiosis under federal and state Black Lung benefits laws), and multi-employer pension plan trusts (designed to improve retirement income security under private multi-employer pension plans).

Other private benefit programs can be undertaken by the tax-exempt fraternal and other organizations. For example, fraternal beneficiary societies that operate under the lodge system provide for the payment of life, sick, accident, or other benefits to their members and dependents, as do some veterans' organizations. Benevolent life insurance associations provide life insurance coverage to their members. Cemetery companies own and operate cemeteries for ultimate use by their members. Exempt credit unions provide financial services to their members, as do crop operations finance corporations. Other membership entities that function on behalf of their members are farmers' cooperatives, shipowners' protection and indemnity associations, and homeowners' associations.

The type of tax-exempt organization where private benefit is the most blatant—permissibly—is the social club. While, as noted, the private inurement doctrine expressly applies, the exempt social club is organized and operated for the pleasure and recreation of its membership, as is the case with entities such as country, eating, and sports clubs. Nonprofit fraternities and sororities are usually classified as social clubs for federal tax purposes. Indeed, a social club will lose its tax-exempt status if makes its facilities unduly available to the general public.

The private inurement doctrine, as specifically applicable to social clubs, has several manifestations. One emerges when an exempt club generates too much nonmember income that operates as a subsidy of the membership, such as in the form of reduced dues and improved facilities. Another instance of private inurement can arise when a club has more than one class of members and the dues payments of one class operate to subsidize the members of another class. And, in more conventional terms, private inurement can exist when a social club engages in undue dealings with its members, such as regular sales of liquor for consumption off the club's premises.

As the federal law of tax-exempt organizations evolves, the private inurement/private benefit constraint is becoming more stringent. Entire classes of organizations have lost their tax exemption as the result of this evolutionary process. Homeowners' associations ceased being exempt social welfare organizations (although Congress stepped in and provided them their own exemption category). Veterans' organizations that provide benefits to their members and dependents were likewise extricated from the social welfare exemption (although again Congress intervened). So-called "self-interest" organizations, those that provide sick and death benefits to members (such as individuals within a particular ethnic group) and their beneficiaries, are no longer exempt as social welfare organizations (and, in this instance, Congress has let that policy decision of the IRS stand).

--------------------- FOCUS ON THE CAMPAIGN TO ---------------------
CLEAN UP AMERICA

The Campaign to Clean Up America, being a charitable organization, is, of course, subject to the rule that its net earnings may not inure to the benefit of individuals in their private capacities. Being a public charity, however, the self-dealing rules do not apply; however, the concepts underlying these rules can often be used as helpful guides.

Application of the private inurement doctrine to the Campaign first requires an assessment of who its insiders are. As with most organizations, the most likely of insiders are its founders, directors, and officers. In the case of the Campaign, as with so many entities, the same individual can serve in two or all three capacities. You, as the founder of the Campaign, a director, and an officer (president) are obviously an insider (in the parlance of the self-dealing rules, a disqualified person). So, too, is your spouse, as a director and officer (maybe co-founder as well). Other directors and officers are insiders, as well as potential others, such as key employees and substantial contributors.

The other principal aspect of private inurement in the case of the Campaign lies in the transactions, if any, between the organization and its insiders. Thus, you and the other directors and/or officers may also function as employees and be paid a salary. To avoid private inurement, the compensation must be reasonable and not excessive. Because of the self-dealing taint of this type of compensatory arrangement, the IRS will likely give it more than passing scrutiny, so you and the other insiders wisely develop a substantive rationale for the salary amounts.

You happen to lease space in a building for use as an office for your business. You decide to sublease space to the Campaign for its offices, at least until the organization has the wherewithal to locate in independent quarters. The Campaign can pay you rent without endangering its tax exemption, as long as the rental rate is reasonable. Again, the arrangement may well be subject to strict scrutiny, so you must be prepared to justify the nonexcessiveness of the rental rates.

You are contributing money to the Campaign, as are a few others, but it needs more funding now. You can lend money to the Campaign, at interest. However, once again, the private inurement doctrine is in the picture, requiring that the interest rate be reasonable. And, once again, you must be able to justify the interest rate selected.

While the law theoretically tolerates it, it is not advisable for you or other insiders to rent from or borrow money from the Campaign. If it is done, however, the charges must be reasonable. Moreover, the other terms of the arrangement (self-dealing) must be reasonable as well, such as the rental term and/or the borrowing term, and in the case of the loan, the repayment terms and the security provided.

For the Campaign (and other public charities), since the self-dealing rules do not apply, there is no real limit on the types or number of transactions between it and its insiders. However, there are limits as a matter of practicality. Thus, while it is possible for the Campaign to lawfully employ every insider and each of his or her family members, the Campaign's lawyer advises prudence in that respect and a minimization of that employment practice. He recites to you and the other directors a litany of court cases where tax exemption was lost or denied because the nonprofit organization involved was a nest of self-dealing, including incestuous employment practices. You decide to avoid that fate.

During the course of its existence, the Campaign will purchase goods and services. It will likely pay fees to consultants (such as lawyers, accountants, and fund-raisers, and perhaps investment counselors and management consultants) and purchase equipment, furniture, supplies, and the like. In these respects, as noted at the outset, it is no different than a for-profit organization. However, the private inurement constraint is ever-present with respect to the Campaign and its nonprofit counterparts, so that when the consultants or vendors are insiders, the Campaign should always be in a position to justify both the relationship and the amounts paid. The law does not require "competitive bidding" in these respects but, for nonprofit organizations, a good rule of thumb is to minimize, if not avoid, self-dealing transactions. Even if legal, nothing can spoil a good fund-raising campaign than adverse publicity about intra-family business dealings.

For example, one of the programs of the Campaign is trash collection, using volunteers. To facilitate this program and at the same time to generate publicity about the organization, you decide that the Campaign will purchase plastic trash bags, bearing the name and logo of the Campaign, for distribution and use by volunteers in this program. It so happens that your brother-in-law (remember, your spouse is on the Campaign's board) owns a company that manufactures lawn maintenance supplies, including trash bags. So, the Campaign purchases the bags from his company. If the company gives the Campaign a discount, such as for purchasing in bulk, the acquisition of the bags from the company by the Campaign is not a transgression of the private inurement doctrine. But, if the bags are being sold to the Campaign at a price mark-up substantially in excess of the retail market price, private inurement could be occurring. Even if the purchase of the bags was for a fair price (or even at a discount), the launching of the Campaign and its programs, and its fund-raising program, could be hindered if an enterprising reporter discovered the facts and wrote a newspaper story strongly suggesting that the organization was being manipulated for private gain.

That, in essence, is what separates the Campaign and other nonprofit organizations from for-profit businesses: the absence of private gain. Charitable and like organizations are expected to serve the public, not private individuals. If the Campaign wishes to further an activity that would best be housed in a for-profit entity, it should explore the establishment of a for-profit subsidiary (see Chapter 15).

6

Tax Exemption:
The Art of Application

Under the federal income tax system, every element of gross income received by a person—whether a corporate entity or an individual—is subject to taxation, unless there is an express statutory provision that exempts from tax either that form of income or that type of person.

As discussed in Chapter 4, many types of nonprofit organizations are eligible for exemption from the federal income tax. However, the exemption is not forthcoming merely because an organization is not organized and operated for profit. Organizations are tax-exempt where they meet the requirements of the particular statutory provision that supplies the tax-exempt status.

RECOGNITION OF TAX-EXEMPT STATUS

Whether a nonprofit organization is entitled to tax exemption, on an initial or continuing basis, is a matter of law. It is the U.S. Congress that defines the categories of organizations that are eligible for tax exemption and it is up to Congress to determine whether an exemption from tax should be continued, in whole or in part. Except for state and local governmental entities, there is no constitutional right to a tax exemption.

Despite what many think, the IRS does not "grant" tax-exempt status (see Myth 5 in Chapter 3). Congress, by means of sections of the Internal Revenue Code that it has enacted, does that. Rather, the function of the IRS in this regard is to *recognize* tax exemption.

Consequently, when an organization makes application to the IRS for a ruling or determination as to tax-exempt status, it is requesting the IRS to recognize a tax exemption that already exists (assuming the organization qualifies), not to grant tax exemption. Similarly, the IRS may determine that an organization is no longer entitled to tax-exempt status and act to revoke its prior recognition of exempt status.

For most nonprofit organizations that are eligible for a tax exemption, it is not required that the exemption be recognized by the IRS. Whether a nonprofit organization seeks an IRS determination on the point is a management decision that takes into account the degree of confidence the individuals involved have in the eligibility for the exemption and the costs associated with the application process. Most organizations in this position elect to pursue recognition of tax-exempt status.

However, charitable organizations and employee benefit organizations must, to be tax-exempt, file (successfully) with the IRS an application for recognition of the exemption. By contrast, entities such as social welfare organizations, labor organizations, trade and professional associations, social clubs, and veterans' organizations need not file an application for recognition of tax-exempt status.

Unlike most requests for a ruling from the IRS (which are commenced by a letter to the IRS), a request for recognition of tax exemption generally is commenced by filing a form, entitled "Application for Recognition of Exemption." Charitable organizations file Form 1023; most other organizations file Form 1024. (In rare instances, neither form is used; it is done by letter.)

Subject only to the authority of the IRS to revoke recognition of exemption for good cause (such as a change in the law), an organization that has been recognized by the IRS as being tax-exempt can rely on the determination as long as there are no substantial changes in its character, purposes, or methods of operation. Should material changes occur, the organization should notify the IRS and may have to undergo a reevaluation of its exempt status.

The Application Procedure

The IRS has specific rules by which a ruling or determination letter may be issued to an organization in response to the filing of an application for recognition of its tax-exempt status. An organization seeking recognition of exemption must file an application with the office of the key district director of the IRS in relation to the district in which the principal place of business or principal office of the organization is located. The determination of exemption will be issued by that district director's office unless the application presents a matter of some controversy or an unresolved or novel point of law. In that case, the application will be sent for resolution to the National Office of the IRS in Washington, DC.

Organizations should allow at least three months for the processing of an application for recognition of tax exemption. There is a procedure for expedited consideration in extreme cases, although the IRS is reluctant to consider applications out of the order in which they are received.

A ruling or determination will be issued to an organization, as long as the application and supporting documents establish that it meets the particular statutory requirements. The application must include a statement describing the organization's purposes, copies of its governing instruments (such as, in the case of a corporation, its articles of incorporation and by-laws), and either a financial statement or a proposed multi-year budget.

The application filed by a charitable organization must also include a summary of the sources of its financial support, its fund-raising program, the composition of its governing body (usually board of directors), its relationship with other organizations (if any), the nature of its services or products and the basis for any charges for them, and its membership (if any).

The IRS is generally free to seek and obtain other information deemed to be necessary for a determination or ruling, and it frequently does so. The ability of the IRS to pursue additional information is not unlimited, however, and the courts have held that recognition of exemption must be granted once an organization makes the requisite "threshold showing."

If the application is not complete, the IRS will not retain it and ask for the remaining information but will return the application and all supporting documents to the organization and request that it file again, by submitting a complete application.

The proper preparation of an application for recognition of exemption involves far more than merely filling in the blanks of a government form. It is a process similar to the preparation of a prospectus in conformance with the federal securities laws requirements, in that every statement made in the application should be carefully considered. The prime objective should be to be accurate; it is essential that all material facts be fully and fairly disclosed. The determination as to which facts are material requires judgment.

The manner in which the answers to questions in the application are phrased can be extremely significant. In this regard, the exercise is more one of "art" than "science." Whoever prepares the form should be able to anticipate any concerns the contents of the application may cause and to see that the application is drawn properly, and yet be able to minimize if not eliminate the likelihood of conflict with the IRS. Too many organizations that are entitled to a particular tax exemption have been denied recognition of tax-exempt status because inartful phraseologies in the application have enabled the IRS to build a case that the organization cannot qualify for exemption.

In addition, proper preparation of the application for recognition of exemption is a useful exercise in forcing an organization to think through what it wants to do, how its activities will be financially supported, and other aspects of its organization and operation. Frequently, the language developed in preparing the application can be useful in other contexts, such as grant applications and fund-raising appeals. Sometimes, preparation of the application causes an organization to consider significant aspects of its organization and operation that it would otherwise ignore.

These considerations are even more important in the case of charitable organizations. That is because the information filed with the IRS pursuant to this procedure is used to make three sets of determinations: whether the organization will be recognized as tax-exempt, whether it will be eligible to receive deductible charitable contributions (and sometimes to what extent), and whether the organization will be a public charity or a private foundation.

It is not necessary that a nonprofit organization retain the services of a lawyer or other professional to help in the preparation of an application for recognition of exemption (see Myth 12 in Chapter 3). However, because of the complexities involved, it is a good idea to obtain the assistance of a professional who understands the process (see Myth 13), if only to review the documents before they are filed. In most instances, a lawyer will have been involved with the organization as part of the process of preparing the governing instruments.

An application for recognition of exemption should be regarded as an important legal document and prepared accordingly. Throughout an organization's existence, this document will likely be called upon for review. A nonprofit organization is required to keep a copy of this application, and supporting documents and related correspondence, available for scrutiny by anyone during regular business hours.

A nonprofit organization seeking a determination as to recognition of its tax-exempt status has the burden of proving that it satisfies all of the requirements of the particular exemption provision. If the application process is not initially successful, the organization has certain appeals rights within the IRS. If the organization fails to successfully navigate the administrative process, there are opportunities to pursue the matter in federal court.

The Application Itself

The purpose of this section is to provide some guidance as to preparation of an application for recognition of tax exemption. (The next section of this chapter will provide some sample answers, using the facts involving the hypothetical Campaign to Clean Up America.) Because it is the more complex of the two, the Form 1023 will be used for analysis. It is useful to have a copy of this form available while reviewing this portion of the text.

Form 1023 comes in a packet. This packet includes instructions for preparation of the form, the form itself (in duplicate), and some Forms 872-C (discussed next). Only one copy of Form 1023 need be filed with the IRS; the other copy may be used in drafting the application.

The application itself will require some attachments. It is good practice to identify these attachments in some way in the form itself, such as Exhibits A,

B, and the like. Sometimes the answers will be longer than the space provided on the form and the answers can be the subject of attachments.

Part I. Part I of Form 1023 requests certain basic information about the organization, such as its name, address, and date of formation. Every nonprofit organization must have an "employer identification number" (even if there are no employees) and this is obtained by filing Form SS-4 (see Chapter 2). Form SS-4 may be filed as soon as the organization is formed and organized or it may be filed with Form 1023. Thus, question 2 should be answered by inserting the number or the statement "Form SS-4 attached," as the case may be.

The contact person (question 4) may be either someone directly involved with the organization, such as an officer or director, or an independent representative of the organization, such as a lawyer or accountant. If such a representative is being used, he or she must be granted a power of attorney, which is filed with the application on Form 2848.

The organization must state the month in which its annual accounting period ends (question 5). The determination of a fiscal year should be given some thought; probably most organizations use the calendar year (in which case the answer is December). Whatever period is selected, the organization should be certain that the same period is stated on Form SS-4 and used when compiling its multi-year budget (Part III).

The date of formation is to be provided (question 6). If incorporated, for example, this date will be the date the state agency received the articles of incorporation. This date is significant in relation to the 15-month rule (see Part II).

The application requires the organization to select up to three "activity codes" that best describe or most accurately identify its purposes, activities, and other operations. These code numbers are found on the back of the Form 1023 package. The numbers are used for all types of exempt organizations, so caution should be exercised in selecting them as some codes are inappropriate for some organizations. For example, a nonprofit organization seeking recognition as a charitable entity would be ill-advised to select code number 483 ("support, oppose, or rate political candidates").

Part II. Part II of Form 1023 requires an applicant organization to identify its "type." As discussed in Chapter 2, the organization must be one of three types: nonprofit corporation, trust, or unincorporated association.

If a corporation, the attachments will be the articles of incorporation and bylaws, any amendments thereto, and the certificates of incorporation and amendment (if any) issued by the state. If an unincorporated association, the attachments will be the constitution and bylaws. If a trust, the attachments will be the trust document(s). For example, if the entity is a corporation, the articles of incorporation can be attached as Exhibit A and the bylaws as Exhibit B.

These attachments must be in the form of "conformed" copies. This does not mean, in the case of a corporation, a "certified" copy of the articles of incorporation. This requirement means that each of the documents must be accompanied by a certification from an appropriate individual (usually an officer or director) that the copy is a true, correct, and complete copy of the original, and that the individual is authorized to make the certification.

Part III. For most organizations, Part III of Form 1023 will be the most important portion of the application. It can also be the most difficult (and sensitive, in terms of potential trouble with the IRS) to prepare.

The organization must identify, in order of size, its sources of financial support (question 1). The answers will be something like the following: contributions from the general public, other contributions, grants, dues, other exempt function (fee-for-service) revenue, and investment income. Whatever sources of support are identified here, the organization should be careful to be consistent when preparing the multi-year budget and selecting the non-private foundation status, if any (see later discussion).

The organization must describe its actual and planned fund-raising program (question 2). Here the organization will summarize its actual use of, or plans to use, selective mailings, fund-raising committees, professional fund-raisers, and the like. Again, the organization should be certain to coordinate its discussion of financial support with that of its fund-raising plans. There are some questions in Form 1023 that can be answered in any reasonable way (that is, there is no "right" or "wrong" answer) and this is one of them. Thus, the organization can describe a very detailed fund-raising program or it can state that it has yet to develop a fund-raising program. If the organization has developed material for the solicitation of contributions or dues, it should attach copies (perhaps as Exhibit C).

The organization must provide a narrative of its purposes and activities (question 3)—perhaps the most important single portion of the form. Usually, this is an essay that is descriptive of the organization's programs and thus should, as noted, be carefully written. Good practice is to open with a description of the organization's purposes, followed by one or more paragraphs summarizing its program activities. This response should be as full as is reasonable and may occupy more space than is provided, in which case the response can be in the form of a separate submission (perhaps as Exhibit D).

This is the segment of the form that can generate many questions from the IRS once the application if filed. Moreover, some activities can generate additional questions to be answered as part of the application. Organizations, in preparing the application, often overlook Part VIII, entitled "Required Schedules for Special Activities." If an applicant organization engages in, or is planning to engage in, one or more of these special activities, the appropriate schedule(s) must be filed as part of the application.

As to the matter of follow-up questions, two types of activities will illustrate the point (and the fact that the IRS uses form sets of questions). If, for example, the applicant organization is to have a scholarship program, here are the questions it will likely have to answer (unless answered in Part VIII, Schedule 2): (1) describe the class of eligibles, or potential recipients, of the organization's grants, (2) indicate whether there are any restrictions or limitations on who may make application for a scholarship or who the organization will consider as possible grantees, (3) who makes the selection of eventual recipients from the class of eligibles (and if these people are related to the organization give complete details), (4) list and describe all criteria used by the selection committee in selecting recipients from the class of eligibles, (5) will any grants be made to spouses, children, descendants, spouses of children or descendants, or other persons disqualified in relationship to the organization, its directors or officers, (6) describe how the scholarship program is publicized to ensure that all eligible individuals are reasonably likely to be informed of the availability of the scholarship aid, (7) will all grants be limited to students attending qualified educational institutions, (8) will the organization provide aid to students both as grants and as loans, (9) if loans are to be made, describe the interest rates (if any) applicable to any loans to be given, how such interest rates are determined, and the terms of repayment of the loans, (10) explain the follow-up procedures in place to ensure that all scholarship funds will be used for the stated purposes, (11) explain the procedures that will be followed if a misuse of funds is discovered, (12) will funds be paid to the individual students or will they be paid directly to the school the students will be attending, (13) when did the organization begin giving scholarship aid, (14) how many scholarships have been given, and (15) provide a list of all grant recipients together with an indication of how much money was received by each recipient.

If, as the other example, the applicant organization is to have a research program, here are the questions it will likely have to answer: (1) describe the nature of the research engaged in or contemplated, (2) describe research projects completed or presently being engaged in, (3) how and by whom research projects are determined and selected, (4) whether the organization has or contemplates having contract or sponsored research and, if so, submit the names of past sponsors or grantors, the terms of the contract or grant, and copies of any executed contracts or grants, (5) summarize the disposition made or to be made of the results of the research, including whether preference has or will be given to any organization or individual, either as to results or timing of the release of results, (6) who will retain ownership or control of any patents, copyrights, processes, or formulae resulting from the research, (7) submit copies of publications or other media showing reports of the research activities, and (8) if the organization is engaged in medical research, is the research performed in connection with a hospital?

The names and addresses of the organization's officers and directors must be provided, along with the amount (if any) of their annual compensation (question 4). As to compensation, this includes all compensation, not just that for serving as an officer or director (or trustee). For example, an individual may simultaneously be a director, officer, and employee. Whatever the compensation is, it must be reasonable (see Chapter 5). Usually, there is insufficient room on the form to provide this information and thus it can be submitted on a separate attachment (perhaps as Exhibit E).

The balance of question 4 is self-explanatory. (In question 4d, the term "disqualified person" is discussed in Chapter 5.)

Question 5 can be very important for some organizations. As a general rule, it does not matter whether the charitable organization has a special relationship with, or is controlled by, another organization. For example, some charitable organizations are controlled by other types of tax-exempt organizations, such as social welfare organizations or trade associations (see Chapter 4), or are controlled by for-profit corporations (such as corporation-related foundations). Again, there usually is no "right" or "wrong" answer to this question. If there is an interlocking directorate, it is good practice to make reference to the provision in the governing instruments that describes the overlap of directors.

Some caution may be required in responding to the question as to whether the organization is an "outgrowth" of another. This can illuminate a problem, such as where the applicant organization is a corporation, the other organization is an unincorporated organization, and the other organization has been operating as a charitable entity albeit without recognition of tax-exempt status.

Question 6 can relate to the facts in question 5. Beyond the control question, however, some organizations are financially accountable to others, such as the recipient of a grant that may be required to periodically report on the progress of the funded project to the grantee.

Question 7a is self-explanatory. Often a new organization will simply answer that it does not have any assets at this time. Question 7b is somewhat perplexing, in that it does not make the slightest difference, with respect to tax exemption as a charitable entity, as to whether the applicant organization does or does not have, or plan to have, an endowment fund.

Question 8 is intended to identify situations where there may be private inurement, in the form of the siphoning off of the organization's funds, by means of a management contract. However, there is nothing inherently wrong with a management arrangement and the organization should not be concerned about disclosure of the terms of a bona fide arrangement.

While question 9b is relatively self-explanatory, question 9a brings the applicant organization into a sensitive area. There is nothing inherently inappropriate about a charitable organization charging a fee for its "benefits, services, or products." However, the IRS is on the lookout for commercial practices, so the focus is on *how* the charges are determined. The answer will largely be governed by the particular facts although an inappropriate response would be that the charges "are set to return a profit." The organization might say, if it is true, that the charges are determined so as to recover actual costs, alternatively, the answer may be that the charges are ascertained on the basis of cost.

Question 10 is self-explanatory. However, it relates to organizations that have a true membership, not merely arrangements where the concept of a "membership" is used as a fund-raising technique.

Question 11 is self-explanatory. Still, the applicant organization must be careful in formulating the response. (See Chapters 13 and 14.)

Question 12 is another instance where the answer does not affect tax-exempt status.

Question 13 can be of no importance or it can be of extreme importance, depending upon the circumstances. The basic rule is that the recognition of exemption will be retroactive to the date of formation of the organization where the application is filed with the IRS within 15 months from the end of the month in which it was established. (This is why the date inserted in response to question 6 of Part I can be of importance.) For example, if the organization is created on January 15, 1989, and the application for recognition of exemption is filed before April 30, 1990, the recognition of exemption (if granted) will be retroactive to January 15, 1989, irrespective of when the determination is made by the IRS. However, to continue with this example, if the application was filed on or after July 1, 1990, the recognition of exemption is effective only as of the date the application was received by the IRS.

As for tax-exempt status, the 15-month rule may not be of any particular importance because the organization can qualify as a tax-exempt social welfare organization until the date of its classification as a charitable organization. (Remember, social welfare organizations *do not* have to have a ruling recognizing their exempt status.) However, this alleviation of the tax-exemption problem does not help with respect to the posture of the organization as a charitable donee or as a nonprivate foundation (if the latter is applicable). Donors making gifts during the interim period will, upon audit, find their charitable deductions disallowed. Private foundations making grants during the interim period may be subject to taxation for failure to exercise "expenditure responsibility" (see Chapter 11). Thus, it is imperative that an organization desiring to be recognized as a charitable organization from the outset file a completed application for recognition of tax exemption prior to the expiration of the 15-month period.

Hopefully, then, the applicant organization can answer "yes" to question 13a. If not, an exception may be available. Or, the organization may be eligible for special relief (question 13c and d). Otherwise, the organization must agree that the determination of exemption will only have prospective effect (question 13e).

Part IV. Part IV of Form 1023 is the smallest part but the answers can be of very large consequence. This is where the public charity/private foundation rules come into play (see Chapter 11).

If the applicant charitable organization is a private foundation, the completion of Part IV is generally simple; the answer to question 1 is "yes." If the organization is seeking classification as a private operating foundation, it should so indicate in response to question 2 and complete Part VII.

However, if the applicant organization believes it can avoid private foundation status, it must select either a "definitive" ruling or an "advance" ruling. For new charitable organizations that are seeking to be classified as publicly supported entities, an advance ruling (selected by responding to question 3b) is the correct choice. This is because they lack the financial history to demonstrate actual public support, which is required before a publicly supported organization can receive a definitive ruling. If the applicant believes it will be supported principally by gifts and grants, it should check the first box of question 3b. The second box of question 3b is for organizations that are expecting support in the form of a blend of gifts, grants, and exempt function income. (Again, these distinctions are summarized in Chapter 11).

Either type of publicly supported organization must demonstrate its initial qualification for nonprivate foundation status by convincing the IRS that it will receive the requisite extent of public support. This is done by submitting (in what would be, in the sequence, Exhibit F) a proposed budget. This budget summarizes contemplated types of revenue (such as gifts, grants, exempt function revenue, and investment income) and types of expenses (such as expenditures for program, compensation, occupancy, telephone, travel, postage, and fund-raising), for each of five years. For this purpose, a year is a period consisting of at least eight months. (For new organizations, this budget is submitted in lieu of the financial statements reflected in Part V.) The five-year period is the "advance ruling period."

In designing the budget, the five years involved are the fiscal years of the organization. The applicant organization should be certain that the fiscal year used to develop the budget is the same period referenced in the response to question 5 of Part I. Also in this process, the applicant should be certain that the types of revenue stated in the budget correspond to the types of revenue summarized in the response to question 1 of Part III.

The advance ruling pertains only to the applicant organization's status as a publicly supported entity. That is, it is not an advance ruling as to tax-exempt status or charitable donee status. Thus, the advance ruling period is a probationary or conditional ruling, as to "public" status. Once the advance ruling period expires and the organization has in fact received adequate public support during the five-year period, that fact will be reported to the IRS, which will in turn issue a definitive ruling that it is a publicly supported charity. Just as the advance ruling is conditional, the definitive ruling is permanent (unless upset by a subsequent loss of qualification or change in the law).

The publicly supported charitable organization must, during and after the expiration of the advance ruling period (on an ongoing basis), continue to show that it qualifies as a publicly supported charity, assuming it wants to retain that status. This is done by reporting the financial support information as part of the annual information return (see Chapter 7) on a matrix that is the same as that contained in section B of Part VI.

It does not matter which type of publicly supported organization the charitable entity is at any point in its existence; the principal objective is to, at any one time, qualify under one category or another. Thus, an organization can "drift" from one classification of publicly supported organization to another throughout its duration. Likewise, a charitable organization can, without harm, select one category of publicly supported organization when it completes Part IV and only satisfy the requirements of the other category as of the close of the advance ruling period.

The IRS, private foundations, and major donors do not care why the organization is publicly supported—they simply want to have the assurance that it is.

If an organization selects a category of publicly supported charitable organization when it prepares Part IV, only to find that it did not meet either set of requirements for publicly supported status at the close of the advance ruling period, it will be categorized as a private foundation, unless it can demonstrate that it is eligible for otherwise avoiding private foundation status. This can be done if the organization qualifies as an entity such as a church, school, hospital, or supporting organization (see below).

If the organization is classified as a private foundation following the close of its advance ruling period, it will have to pay the excise tax on its net investment income (see Chapter 11) for each of the years in the advance ruling period (and thereafter). For the IRS to be able to assess a tax retroactively for five years, the taxpayer must agree to waive the running of the statute of limitations which otherwise would preclude the IRS from reaching that far back. The waiver is granted by the execution of Form 872-C (in duplicate), which is part of the Form 1023 package.

An applicant organization that qualifies as a church, school, hospital, supporting organization, or the like is eligible to receive a definitive ruling at the outset. This is because its financial support is not the factor used in classifying it as a "public" entity. Instead, its public status derives from what it does programmatically.

An organization can receive a definitive ruling that it is publicly supported if it has been in existence at least two years and received the requisite public support during those years. The organization in this situation would submit a completed Part V for each of these years. It would also complete section B of Part VI.

An organization that seeks to be categorized as a supporting organization (see Chapter 11) must complete section C of Part VI.

Every organization that is requesting a definitive ruling must evidence its selection of nonprivate foundation status by completing section A of Part VI. By the way, this section graphically displays the various options open to a charitable organization desiring to avoid private foundation status.

Other Parts. Parts V–VIII of Form 1023 have been discussed in the previous section. Together, these parts of the form, if properly completed, amount to a rather complete portrait of the applicant organization. It is important to devote some time and thinking to the preparation of the form. It is a public document and, during the course of the organization's existence, copies may be requested by prospective donors or grantors, or representatives of the media.

A ruling from a governmental agency is only as good as the facts on which it is based. Therefore, if the material facts of a charitable organization change, the determination letter granting recognition of tax-exempt status may be voided. In such an instance, it is necessary to contact the IRS to have the matter reviewed, to assure ongoing tax-exempt status.

FOCUS ON THE CAMPAIGN TO CLEAN UP AMERICA

The Campaign to Clean Up America, desiring to be a charitable organization, and a publicly supported one, must complete and file a Form 1023. The following answers to the questions in the form are designed to illustrate the form and content of these answers for any applicant organization. Not all of the questions are given answers, where the answers are particularly fact specific.

Part I, Question 7

The appropriate activity codes for the Campaign to Clean Up America are 354 (preservation of scenic beauty), 125 (giving information or opinion), and 402 (activities aimed at combatting community deterioration).

Part III, Question 1

The Campaign to Clean Up America would answer question 1 of Part III as follows:

The sources of financial support of the Campaign to Clean Up America will be, in order of size, (1) contributions from the general public, (2) grants from private foundations, (3) other contributions and grants, (4) incidental exempt function revenue, (5) incidental unrelated income, and (6) miscellaneous investment income.

Part III, Question 2

The Campaign would answer question 2 of Part III as follows:

The fund-raising program of the Campaign to Clean Up America is in the process of formulation. The Campaign will commence its fund-raising program with selective mailings and other attempts to reach the general public (such as brochures, flyers, and newspaper advertisements). The Campaign will endeavor to secure gifts of money and property, including charitable bequests. The Campaign will soon commence a planned giving program and will likely, in the future, begin a capital campaign. The Campaign is in the process of retaining the services of a professional fund-raising consultant but an agreement has not been executed as yet. A copy of the first fund-raising letter that has been developed is attached as Exhibit C.

Part III, Question 3

The Campaign would answer question 3 of Part III as follows:

As the name of the organization indicates, the purpose of the Campaign to Clean Up America is to rid the cities, towns, suburbs, and other areas of the United States of trash, debris, and other litter. It is the vision of those who have formed the organization that the beauty of the landscapes of this country should not be tarnished, or hidden, by accumulations of garbage and other trash.

It is the Campaign's belief that much of the solution to the nation's trash problem lies in individuals' attitudes and mindsets. An area that is clean is less likely to be trashed than one that is already littered. A community where its occupants are sensitized to the litter accumulation problem is less likely to be full of trash than the one where its occupants have subconsciously repressed the ugly sights. A community whose members are willing to rid the area of trash, and keep it that way, will be a far more beautiful place to live and work, and be proud of, than one that is constantly strewn with litter.

Therefore, the focus of the Campaign will always be on the prevention of littering and the pick-up of litter where it is found. As to the latter, the Campaign will, on a community-by-community basis, organize teams of volunteers who will pick up trash so as to keep their community clean and scenic. It will supply these teams with the equipment necessary to achieve this end, including rakes, shovels, gloves, trash bags, and safety signs to alert traffic that Clean Up America teams are at work in their community. If funding permits, the Campaign will provide members of these teams with "Clean Up America" tee-shirts, to both stimulate spirit in their volunteer work and advertise the program of the Campaign.

The Campaign will provide these teams with information as to organizational techniques, safety matters, and ideas for coordinating their efforts with local governmental officials. This latter aspect will also be of importance in organizing means of trash disposal. The Campaign will also provide the teams with practical guidelines on matters such as trespassing, personal safety, and similar aspects that involve considerations of law.

The Campaign will endeavor to prevent littering from occurring in the first instance through public education programs. These will consist of the distribution of literature, media advertising, and community meetings. The public education aspect of the Campaign's program will be intertwined with its fund-raising program. Essentially, the public education component of the Campaign's efforts will be directed to ways to sensitize individuals to the problem of litter accumulation, in the hope that they will not litter, be moved to dispose of litter caused by others, and join a Campaign volunteer team to make and keep their community trash-free.

It is the belief of the Campaign that a community that is physically attractive (litter-free) is a community that will have other desirable attributes that contribute to a better way of life for its members.

The Campaign will undoubtedly engage in some attempts to influence legislation, mostly at the local level, such as laws to toughen the fines for littering and to force trucks to travel with their loads covered. However, any such activities will be insubstantial in relation to total activities.

The Campaign may engage in some activities that may constitute unrelated business. For example, the Campaign may sell trash bags (bearing its name and an anti-litter message) to the general public. Again, any unrelated business activities will be insubstantial in relation to total activities.

Part III, Question 7b

The Campaign would answer question 7b of Part III as follows:

The Campaign to Clean Up America intends to hold some of the contributions it receives in an endowment fund, to provide a source of stable funding for its programs.

Part III, Question 10

The Campaign would answer question 10 of Part III "no." However, in the future, it may formally organize community groups, perhaps in the nature of chapters, that would be members of the corporation. Still, such a development is so speculative at this point that there is no need to reference it in the application. But if the Campaign became a membership corporation, it would have to amend its articles of incorporation and bylaws accordingly, and notify the IRS of the development, because the change would be a material one in its character and method of operation.

At the same time, the Campaign can use the "membership" concept in its fundraising, without being a formal membership corporation and without having to answer "yes" to question 10 and complete the balance of it. For example, the Campaign can have, without creating true memberships, recognition levels for donors, such as "founding members," "sustaining members," and "associate members."

Part III, Question 11

The Campaign would answer "yes" to question 11 of Part III and then simply cross-reference to the answer to question 3 of Part III. It would not, however, file Form 5768 (see Chapter 13).

Part IV

The Campaign would answer "no" to question 1 of Part IV. It would also check the first box in question 3b and enclose with its Form 1023 two executed copies of Form 872-C.

Part V

The Campaign would not file any financial statement of Part V. Instead, it would provide a five-year budget, showing its (public) financial support and its anticipated expenditures.

Remainder of Form 1023

Given the facts, the Campaign to Clean Up America does not have to complete Parts V–VIII. Therefore, the Form 1023 illustrates that a straightforward application for recognition of tax exemption for a charitable organization can merely utilize the first four pages of the form.

The attachments to the Form 1023 can be as important, if not more important, than the contents of the form itself, particularly if the statement of activities (the response to question 3 of Part III) is submitted as a separate exhibit. A review of the attachments to accompany the Form 1023 submitted on behalf of the Campaign to Clean Up America serves as a basic checklist for all of these submissions:

- Form SS-4 (application for an identification number)
- Form 2848 (power of attorney)
- Form 8718 (user fee form)
- A check in payment of the user fee
- Conformed copy of organizing document (e.g., articles of incorporation)
- Conformed copy of rules of operation (e.g., bylaws)
- Form 872-C (in duplicate)
- Other attachments, such as copies of solicitations for financial support (question 2, Part III), statement of activities (question 3, Part III), list of directors and officers (question 4, Part III), copies of any assignments of income or assets (question 4e, Part III), any management agreement (question 8, Part III), any schedule of membership fees and dues (question 10a, Part III), any descriptive literature for prospective members (question 10b, Part III), and any documents or other attachments that may be required in responding to the questions in Part VIII.
- A cover letter to the IRS, stating exactly what is being requested. If expedited consideration of the application is being requested, this is the place to include that statement. It is also a good practice to include a request for an administrative hearing in the event the IRS decides to (initially at least) rule adversely with respect to the organization.

GROUP EXEMPTION

An underutilized procedure allows a charitable (and other) organization to be tax-exempt without having to file an application for recognition of tax exemption. This can be accomplished by tax exemption on a "group" basis.

For this procedure to be available, there must be a "group." A group consists of a "central" (or parent) organization and at least one "subordinate" (or affiliated) organization. An affiliated organization is a chapter, local, post, or like entity that is affiliated with and subject to the general supervision or control of a central organization, which is usually a state, regional, or national organization. (The term "affiliated" is not defined in this context but usually entails some intermixture of funding or governance.) In this way, an organization is recognized as exempt by reason of, in addition to its qualifying activities, its relationship with the parent organization.

The group exemption concept contemplates that the parent organization responsibly and independently evaluate the tax-exempt status of its subordinate organizations from the standpoint of the organizational and operational tests applicable to them. The parent organization must annually certify to the IRS those organizations that are part of the group. Private foundations and foreign organizations may not be part of one of these groups.

A central organization may be involved in more than one group exemption arrangement, such as a charitable parent organization having both charitable and social welfare organization affiliates. Also, a central organization may be a subordinate organization with respect to another central organization, such as a state organization that has subordinate units and that itself is affiliated with a national organization. While all of the subordinate organizations in the group must have the same category of tax-exempt status, the tax-exempt status of the central organization may be different from that of the subordinates.

EXEMPTIONS FROM FILING

There are a few charitable organizations that are exempted from filing an application for recognition of exemption with the IRS. That is, these entities are considered tax-exempt as charitable organizations, even though they do not file a Form 1023. These are:

- A church, interchurch organization, local unit of a church, a convention or association of churches, or an integrated auxiliary of a church
- An organization that is not a private foundation (see Chapter 11) and normally has gross receipts of not more than $5,000 in each tax year
- An organization that is a subordinate organization covered by a group exemption but only if the central organization timely submits a notice covering the subordinates

7

Tax Exemption Is Not a Paperwork Exemption

Nonprofit organizations have not, for the most part, escaped the burdens of governmental regulation that are manifested in the flow of returns, reports, and other paperwork demanded by federal, state, and sometimes local governments. Tax exemption may mean that an organization does not have to file a tax return; it will likely, nonetheless, have to file an information return that can be just as complex as a tax return, if not more so.

In this chapter, the current basic reporting requirements for most nonprofit organizations are reviewed. This summary only covers the basics, particularly when it comes to state and local requirements. Some reporting requirements are unique to certain types of nonprofit organizations. Other nonprofit organizations (churches are the best example) may be exempt from one or more reporting requirements that most others have to face. One set of reporting obligations has already been discussed in Chapter 6—those in connection with the process of applying for recognition of tax-exempt status.

Some nonprofit organizations have to comply with reporting requirements that are not directly imposed by government. For example, a nonprofit organization that is the recipient of a grant probably has to periodically report to the grantor. Another illustration is the nonprofit organization that is under a group exemption (see Chapter 6) and annually reports to the central organization for the purpose of preparing combined information returns. Still another example is the nonprofit organization that is reporting to one or more of the so-called "voluntary watch-dog agencies."

INFORMATION RETURN

Nearly all nonprofit organizations that are tax-exempt under federal law are required to file an annual information return with the IRS. For most organizations, this annual information return is Form 990; private foundations file Form 990-PF; black lung benefit trusts file Form 990-BL; and religious and apostolic organizations file Form 1065 (the partnership information return).

Some nonprofit organizations must annually file a tax return. Thus, political organizations file Form 1120-POL and homeowners' associations file Form 1120-H. Nonprofit corporations that are not tax-exempt file the regular corporate tax return, Form 1120. Trusts that do not file Form 990 generally file Form 1041.

Annual Returns

The general annual return for tax-exempt organizations (Form 990) must reflect the organization's items of "support and revenue" (such as gifts, grants, dues, program service revenue, other public support, revenue from the sales of assets, rents, and investment income). For this purpose, the term "gifts" does not (according to the form's instructions) include the value of donated services or items such as the free use of materials, equipment, or facilities. The return differentiates between "direct" and "indirect" public support—the former being amounts received from individuals, corporations, trusts, estates, foundations, and other tax-exempt organizations, while the latter is amounts received from federated fund-raising agencies and similar fund-raising organizations. "Program service revenue" is revenue derived from the performance of services that are related to the organization's tax-exempt purposes, such as tuition received by a school, patient fees paid to a hospital, or revenue from admissions to a conference or sales of publications.

Unrelated income and related expenses must be reflected on the annual information return as well as on the unrelated income tax return (see below).

The return also must reflect disbursements (such as grants made, compensation, other employee benefits, professional fund-raising fees, legal and accounting fees, occupancy, travel, conferences, and supplies). Expenses must also be categorized by function, namely, program services, management and general, and fund-raising (see Chapter 9). Expenses that relate to more than one functional category may be allocated on a reasonable basis. The four largest (as measured by total expenses incurred) program services and related expenses must be identified.

The return includes a balance sheet showing assets, liabilities, and net worth. The names, addresses, time expended, and compensation must be shown for the directors and officers.

The return includes a list of questions about the organization's activities, including these inquiries: (1) has the organization engaged in any activities not previously reported to the IRS; (2) have any changes been made in the organizing or governing documents not reported to the IRS; (3) was there a liquidation, dissolution, termination, or substantial contraction during the year; (4) is the organization related to any other exempt or nonexempt organization; and (5) did the organization receive donated services or the use of materials, equipment, or facilities at no charge or at substantially less than fair rental value?

The annual information return filed by a charitable organization must include the following information (in Schedule A of Form 990): (1) the compensation of the five highest paid employees; (2) the total number of other employees paid over $30,000; (3) the compensation of the five highest paid persons for professional services; (4) the total number of others receiving over $30,000 for professional services; (5) a description of any legislative or political campaign activities (see Chapters 13 and 14); (6) an explanation of any acts of self-dealing between the organization and its directors and officers (see Chapter 11); (7) the reason for its nonprivate foundation status and, if applicable, details as to the extent of its public support (again, see Chapter 11); (8) if a school, certain information concerning its policies that may involve discrimination; (9) certain information concerning legislative activities if it has elected to come within the special lobbying rules for public charities (see Chapter 13); and (10) information with respect to direct or indirect transfers to, and other direct or indirect transactions and relationships with, tax-exempt organizations other than charitable ones (such as lobbying and political campaign entities).

This annual return further requires the organization to provide its address, identification number, accounting method, and its group exemption number (if applicable), as well as the federal tax law provision describing its tax exemption.

The annual information return for private foundations (Form 990-PF) must include the following items: (1) an itemized statement of the foundation's support, expenses, assets, and liabilities; (2) a reporting of capital gains and losses; (3) a calculation of the excise tax on net investment income; (4) information concerning any legislative or political campaign activities; (5) information concerning any acts of self-dealing, mandatory payout, excess business holdings, jeopardy investments, or taxable expenditures; (6) a list of all directors, officers, highly paid employees, and contractors; (7) a list of the five highest paid persons for professional services; (8) computation of the minimum investment return and distributable amount; (9) calculation of the limitation on grant administrative expenses; (10) an itemized list of all grants made or approved, showing the amount of each grant, the name and address of each recipient, any relationship between a grant recipient and the foundation's managers or substantial contributors, and a concise statement of the purpose of each grant; (11) the address of the principal office of the foundation and (if different) of the place where its books and records are maintained; and (12) the names and addresses of the foundation's managers that are substantial contributors or that own 10 percent or more of the stock of any corporation of which the foundation owns 10 percent or more, or corresponding interests in partnerships or other entities.

A private foundation must also divulge on the Form 990-PF a schedule of relevant statistical information, as to its principal direct charitable activities and program-related investments, such as the number of organizations and other beneficiary served, conferences convened, or research papers produced. The foundation must also provide information demonstrating conformance with the public inspection requirements, including a copy of the newspaper notice.

Fund-Raising Aspects

As discussed in Chapter 9, the Form 990 is an integral part of the federal government's process of participation in the regulation of fund-raising for charitable purposes. There are some aspects of this that warrant mention here.

Form 990 gives special attention to "special fund-raising events and activities." In computing "total revenue" (but not, as discussed below, "gross receipts"), an organization need only use net income from these events and activities.

Fund-raising events and activities include dinners, dances, carnivals, raffles, bingo games, and door-to-door sales of merchandise. These undertakings are not exempt functions but are engaged in solely or primarily to raise funds for the organization's programs. Here, the organization is offering goods or services of more than nominal value in return for a payment higher than the direct cost of the goods or services provided. The payment is not a deductible gift. (If only "nominal value" is involved, the payment is a deductible gift, the receipts are reported elsewhere on the return as contributions, and the undertaking is not a "special fund-raising event or activity.") If, in the course of a fund-raising event or activity, a purchaser pays more than the value of the goods or services furnished, the excess is a contribution (and reported as such) and the amount paid that is equal to the value of the goods or services is reported as gross revenue from the event or activity.

An organization must attach a schedule to the return, describing and providing financial detail for the three largest (as measured by gross receipts) special events conducted. Summary information must be provided for the other events.

Some or all of the dollar limitations applicable to Form 990 when filed with the IRS may not apply when using the form in place of state or local report forms. Examples of federal law dollar limitations that do not meet some state requirements are the $25,000 gross receipts minimum that gives rise to an obligation to file with the IRS (see next section), the short reporting format for organizations that report total revenue of $25,000 or less (see next section), and the $30,000 minimum for listing professional fees in Schedule A of the Form 990 (see previous discussion).

Exceptions

Form 990 must be filed by nearly all charitable organizations that have annual gross receipts that are normally in excess of $25,000. Organizations with less gross receipts should merely file the identification portion of the return. This entails no more than giving the IRS the organization's name and address, and an indication, by marking a box on the first page of the return, that its gross receipts are under the $25,000 threshold. (Technically, this filing is not required but if it is not made the IRS does not know whether the organization is not filing because it does not have to or because it is avoiding the requirement.) All private foundations *must file* Form 990-PF.

The $25,000 filing threshold is frequently misunderstood. Generally, an organization's annual gross receipts are the total amount it received during its annual accounting period, without subtraction of any costs or expenses. However, the form allows an organization to, in computing its "total revenue," net certain income items and related expenses, namely, receipts (and associated expenses) in the form of rents, revenue from assets sales, revenue from special fund-raising events, and certain other gross sales. Thus, an organization's "gross receipts" can be more than $25,000, even though its "total revenue" as shown on the return is less than $25,000. It is all rather confusing, compounded by the fact that the concept of "normally" here means a three-year average. This exception does not necessarily excuse an organization from filing an information return in any year in which its gross receipts for the year are less than $25,000.

In fact, an organization can have more than $25,000 in gross receipts in a year and still be excused from filing an information return. The rules on this point are as follows: an organization's gross receipts are considered to be $25,000 or less if the organization is (1) up to one-year-old and has received, or donors have pledged to give, $37,500 or less during its first tax year; (2) between one- and three-years-old and averaged $30,000 or less in gross receipts during each of its first two tax years; or (3) three-years-old or more and averaged $25,000 or less in gross receipts for the immediately preceding three tax years (including the year for which the return would be filed).

The annual information return reporting requirement does not apply to (1) a church (including an interchurch organization of local units of a church); (2) an integrated auxiliary of a church; (3) a convention or association of churches; (4) a financing, fund management, or retirement insurance program management organization functioning on behalf of the foregoing organizations; (5) certain other entities affiliated with a church or convention or association of churches; (6) state institutions; (7) certain schools and mission societies; and (8), as noted, organizations that normally receive less than $25,000 annually.

Just because an organization is exempt from filing an annual information return does not always mean a return should not be filed, as a matter of good management practice. Preparation of the return may be a good idea, as a discipline for keeping good financial records—and as preparation for when a return becomes mandatory because gross receipts are over the filing threshold. In addition, filing the return starts the statute of limitations running—a protection against audits for years long passed.

If an organization's total revenue is $25,000 or less and its gross receipts are normally more than $25,000, it must (unless excepted) file Form 990 but need not complete all items on the form. There is a box on the first page of the return that should be marked to indicate this filing status.

PUBLICITY AND PENALTIES

Failure to file the information return in a timely way, without reasonable cause or an exception, can give rise to a $10 per day penalty, payable by the organization for each day the failure continues, with a maximum of $5,000. An additional penalty can be imposed at the same rate with the maximum for the individual(s) responsible for the failure to file, without reasonable cause. Other fines and imprisonment can be imposed for willful failure to file returns or for filing fraudulent returns and statements with the IRS.

A tax-exempt organization must make its three most recent annual information returns available for inspection by anyone at its principal office during regular business hours. (This requirement does not cause disclosure of the names or addresses of donors.) If an organization regularly maintains one or more regional or district offices having at least three employees, this inspection requirement applies to each office. The penalty for failure to provide copies of the annual information returns for inspection is $10 per day, in the absence of reasonable cause, with a maximum penalty per return of $5,000.

A copy of a private foundation's annual return must be made available to anyone for inspection at its principal office during regular business hours. Notice of the availability of the return must be published in a newspaper having general circulation in the county in which the principal office of the foundation is located. Failure to properly publicize the availability of the annual return can result in the same sanction as the failure to file it.

Forms 990 and 990-PF are also available for public inspection and copying at the IRS. However, the IRS is not permitted to disclose certain portions of otherwise disclosable returns and attachments, including the list of contributors required to accompany Form 990. A request for inspection of a return must be in writing and must include the name and address of the organization that filed it. A request to inspect a return should indicate the type (number) of the return and the year(s) involved. The request should be sent to the District Director (Attention: Disclosure Officer) of the district in which the person making the request desires to inspect the return. If inspection at the IRS National Office in Washington, DC, is desired, the request must be sent to the Commissioner of Internal Revenue, Attention, Freedom of Information Reading Room, 1111 Constitution Avenue, NW, Washington, DC 20224.

There is still another dimension to this matter of filing annual information returns. Organizations that are eligible to receive tax-deductible contributions are listed in an IRS publication titled *Cumulative List of Organizations Described in Section 170(c) of the Internal Revenue Code* (Publication 78). This list is frequently relied upon by donors and their advisors in planning charitable giving. The IRS may remove an organization from this listing if its records show that it is required to file Form 990 but it does not file a return or otherwise advise the IRS that it is not required to file. (Even if this happens, contributions to the organization remain deductible.)

The annual information return embodies the functional method of accounting for the reporting of expenses. This accounting method requires not only the identification, line by line, of expenses (including program expenses, such as publications and conferences, and professional expenses, such as the fees paid to lawyers and accountants) but also the allocation of expenses by function, namely, the categories of "program service," "management and general," and "fund-raising." (The law also requires an allocation of any expenses for legislative activities.) Organizations must identify their sources of program-service revenue and have the option of distinguishing between revenue that is restricted and unrestricted.

The annual information return is now also used to elicit information about a charitable organization's fund-raising program and results.

The Form 990 is due on or before the 15th day of the fifth month following the close of the tax year. Thus, the information return for an organization with a fiscal year the same as the calendar year should be filed by May 15 of each year.

UNRELATED INCOME TAX RETURNS

A tax-exempt organization with unrelated business taxable income (see Chapter 12) must file—in addition to an annual information return—a tax return. It is on this return that the source or sources of unrelated income, and accompanying expenses, are reported and any tax computed. There is an exemption from taxation for the first $1,000 of annual net unrelated income.

Form 990-T also contains special schedules concerning rental income, unrelated debt-financed income, investment income of social clubs and certain other tax-exempt organizations, and income from controlled organizations.

This return is also due on or before the 15th day of the fifth month following the close of the organization's tax year.

An addition to tax for failure to file this tax return in a timely manner may be imposed.

MATERIAL CHANGES

A nonprofit organization that has been recognized by the IRS as a tax-exempt organization must report to the IRS any material changes in its purposes, character, or methods of operation. The purpose of this requirement is to enable the tax agency to determine if the change or changes may lead to revocation or alteration of the entity's tax-exempt status. A determination by the IRS that an organization is exempt is like any other government agency ruling—the ruling is only as valid as the material facts on which it is based and if the facts materially change, the ruling may change as well.

The key word here is *material*. A material change would be a substantial alteration in the organization's statement of purpose, a major new program undertaking, or a significant structural change (such as the creation of a membership). This often involves judgment, perhaps best made with the advice of a lawyer or accountant. If in doubt, it may be best to send the information to the IRS. Sometimes, it is not necessary to request a review of the original ruling; it may be enough to simply submit the changes and not ask for anything. In any event, all changes (such as amendments to bylaws or alterations in program activities) are to be reported to the IRS as part of the preparation and filing of the annual information return (see above). So, the government should get the changes sooner or later—it is just a question of when.

DONEE RETURNS

In many instances, a charitable organization that sells, exchanges, or otherwise disposes of gift property within two years after the date of receipt of the property must file an information return with the IRS (Form 8282).

The purpose of this return basically is to enable the IRS to compare a charity's selling price of property with the value claimed by the donor in computing a charitable contribution deduction. This filing requirement is part of the package of rules concerning the need for appraisals of gift property and other aspects of the charitable deduction substantiation rules (see Chapter 8).

STATE ANNUAL REPORTS

Most states require organizations created under their laws and/or operating in their jurisdictions to file annual reports with the appropriate governmental agency. This requirement is usually applicable to nonprofit organizations. These are not tax returns but are corporate annual reports, filed most frequently with the state's secretary of state. Sometimes these reports are due irrespective of whether the entity is formally a corporation.

Some states have additional filing requirements, such as those for charitable trusts. This type of filing is usually made with the office of the state's attorney general. States may also require information and/or tax returns, like federal Forms 990 and 990-T.

This is one of these areas of the law where it is difficult to generalize. Each organization must, on its own or with professional assistance, determine what reports and returns may be required of the state, county, and/or other governmental jurisdiction in which it is located.

However, the matter may be even more complex. Some nonprofit organizations have operations in more than one state. This can lead to additional filing requirements.

An organization is a "domestic" organization to the state in which it is formed. In all other states, the organization is a "foreign" entity. As noted previously, the domestic organization may have reporting obligations under the law of the home state. However, the organization may also have reporting obligations under the law of the states in which it is a foreign organization "doing business" in those states. The concept of "doing business" is not particularly definitive but it includes the maintenance of an office.

Where an organization is doing business in a state other than the domestic state, it must first obtain from that jurisdiction a certificate of authority to conduct operations in that state. This will require the naming of a registered agent in that state and probably will require the filing of an annual report in that state.

Thus, a nonprofit organization that has multistate operations will likely have a registered agent and file an annual report in each state in which it is operational. These requirements are in addition to those that may be required under the states' charitable solicitation acts (discussed next).

CHARITABLE SOLICITATION ACTS

As discussed in Chapter 9, many states are heavily into the practice of regulating fund-raising by charitable organizations by means of the enforcement of charitable solicitation acts. As noted, some counties and cities are involved in this process as well.

Annual reporting is a mainstay of charitable fund-raising regulation. A charitable organization engaging in the solicitation of contributions is generally required to file a report with every state in which it seeks funds. (A similar reporting requirement is applicable to professional fund-raisers and professional solicitors.) As noted in Chapter 9, a charitable organization fund-raising throughout the country is expected to file reports with nearly 40 states, not to mention the tens of counties and towns that want reports as well.

Worse, some states treat the process of raising funds for charitable purposes as being a form of "doing business" in the state. When this occurs, the state insists that the charity, in addition to complying with the state's charitable solicitation act, obtain permission to do business in the state. As noted, that latter requirement means that the charity must appoint a registered agent in the state and thereafter begin filing annual reports as a foreign corporation. Fortunately, only a few states take this extreme position. If all states were to do so, a charitable organization engaging in fund-raising in each of the states would have to register and report under 40 charitable solicitation acts and 51 (including the District of Columbia) nonprofit corporation acts.

OTHER REPORTING

Depending upon state law, a nonprofit organization may have to report to a state in relation to its exemption from or compliance with state income, sales, and/or property (tangible or intangible, personal or real) taxation.

If a nonprofit organization is an employer, it must file all of the federal and state forms concerning payment of compensation. Pertinent federal forms include Form W-2 (wage and tax statement), Form W-3 (transmittal of income and tax statements), Form W-2P (statement for recipients of annuities or pensions), Form 1096 (annual summary and transmittal of federal information returns), Form 940 (employer's annual federal unemployment tax return), Form 941 (employer's quarterly federal tax return, used to report the withholding of federal income taxes and Social Security taxes), and Form 5500, 5500-C, or 5500-R (reporting on employee benefit plans).

A nonprofit organization generally must file an information return (Form 1099) with the IRS when paying more than $600 a year to another person. This is not the case, however, for some charitable organizations that make payments to individuals for information about the commission of crimes.

——————— FOCUS ON THE CAMPAIGN TO ———————
CLEAN UP AMERICA

The Campaign to Clean Up America fully expects to annually receive gross receipts in excess of $25,000, so it will be obligated to prepare and file with the IRS an annual information return (Form 990). The Campaign will be a publicly supported charitable organization (see Chapter 11) and thus not a private foundation, so it will not be filing the annual return for foundations (Form 990-PF). There are no present plans to have unrelated business income (see Chapter 12), so there is no current obligation to file a tax return (Form 990-T).

The Campaign to Clean Up America will be soliciting contributions throughout the United States, so it will be registering with each of the states that have a charitable solicitation act (see Chapter 9). For some of these states, this means that the Campaign will have to obtain a certificate of authority to do business as a foreign corporation. However, at the present, the Campaign does not intend to actually do business in any other state.

The state in which the Campaign is organized (Michigan) has an annual report requirement, so the Campaign will be obligated to annually file that report.

At this time, the Campaign has no employees, so the federal and state reporting requirements associated with a payroll are not applicable . . . for now. The Campaign will be using consultants (a lawyer, an accountant, and a fund-raising professional), so the compensation paid to them will have to be annually reported to the IRS (Form 1099).

8
The Basic Charitable Giving Rules

The basic concept of the federal income tax charitable contribution deduction is that individual taxpayers who itemize deductions and corporate taxpayers can deduct, subject to varying limitations, an amount equivalent to the value of a contribution to a qualified donee. A *charitable contribution* for income tax purposes is a gift to or for the use of one or more "qualified donees."

Charitable gifts are also the subject of federal gift tax and estate tax deductions.

A PERSPECTIVE

Donors and the charitable organizations they support commonly expect gifts to be in the form of outright transfers of money or perhaps property. For both parties (the donor and the charitable donee), a gift is usually a unilateral transaction, in a financial sense, with the donor parting with the contribution and the charity acquiring it. The advantages to the donor in these instances are confined to the resulting charitable deduction and the emotional enhancement derived from making the gift.

There are, however, forms of charitable giving that provide far greater financial and tax advantages to the donor. This type of giving is frequently referred to as *planned giving* or as *deferred giving*. This type of giving is discussed in Chapter 17.

TYPES OF CHARITABLE GIVING

There are three categories of charitable giving, each providing some form of emotional and/or financial satisfaction to the donor. These are *impulse giving, interest giving,* and *integrated giving.*

Impulse Giving

Impulse giving is just that—the donor is responding on impulse to an appeal for a charitable gift. The gift is made in immediate response to a compelling plea (for example, children ravaged by war, hunger, or disease; suffering animals; or an impending cure for a deadly disease), usually in response to a direct mail, television, radio, telephone, door-to-door, or street corner solicitation.

The impulse gift almost always is cash and is usually a relatively small amount. The donor may not have donated previously to the organization, probably has no expectation of becoming involved with the organization's programs or administration, and has likely not thought about any subsequent gifts. The gift may have been prompted by the receipt of a premium. In many of these instances, a charitable contribution deduction is not particularly important or (because the donor does not itemize deductions or because the donee is not a charitable entity) is not available.

Interest Giving

Interest giving is the result of a donor's ongoing authentic interest in a charitable organization's program. The donor usually has some unique relationship with the charitable organization—it is the donor's church, synagogue, or like religious institution; school, college, or university from which he or she graduated; a hospital in the community; or some other charitable organization with programs having some special appeal to the donor.

This type of giving is usually done on a periodic basis (for example, weekly in church or annually in response to an annual fund effort). While the gift is often made using cash, the amount is generally greater than is the case with impulse giving. Also, in interest giving, there is a greater possibility that the gift will be made using property—probably securities or real estate.

Integrated Giving

Integrated giving is the most sophisticated form of charitable giving because, unlike the other two categories of giving, the gift is deliberately integrated with the donor's overall financial, tax, and/or estate plans.

The integrated gift is most often from a donor who has a substantial relationship with the charitable organization and necessarily involves a large contribution. The integrated gift is less likely to involve outright gifts of cash or property and more likely to entail gifts utilizing trusts, contracts, and/or wills. For the integrated contributor, the ensuing charitable deduction is of major importance and is an integral part of the transaction.

ACTUAL PRACTICE

These three categories of charitable giving are generalizations. In actual practice, the lines of demarcation between them are often blurry. The labels are somewhat arbitrary and are not meant to suggest that the impulse donor lacks an authentic interest in the recipient charity or that the integrated donor is motivated solely by personal financial aspects. In practice, one category of charitable gift can lead to another; impulse giving can evolve into interest giving, just as interest giving can give rise to integrated giving.

It is a significant role of the fund-raising professional to cause these types of progressions in giving. Any fund-raising (development) program worthy of that name is predicated upon upgrading a donor from an impulse donor to an interest donor, and perhaps to an integrated donor. For example, a direct mail program may result in a donor's first time gift (as part of a donor acquisition effort) but the organization is generally interested in the donor giving regularly, that is, becoming an interest donor (as part of a donor renewal effort). Many planned giving programs (integrated gift programs) are built upon the conversion of interest donors to integrated donors.

The economic advantages resulting from a charitable gift can be manifold: (1) a federal, state, and/or local tax charitable contribution deduction, (2) avoidance of capital gains taxation, (3) creation of or increase in cash flow, (4) betterment of tax treatment of income, (5) free professional tax and investment services, (6) transfer of property within the family between generations, and (7) receipt of benefits (usually services) from the charitable donee.

For the impulse donor, none of these advantages may be involved, although the charitable deduction may be a possibility. In the case of the interest donor, the charitable deduction is usually a factor and capital gains tax avoidance may be an element of the transaction. This type of donor may receive some benefits from the donee (such as a magazine, discount, or token gift in return). But only in the instance of the integrated donor are all of the economic advantages realized—plus the satisfaction of making a major gift to a charitable organization.

WHAT CONSTITUTES A GIFT?

In the literature concerning nonprofit organizations, much time and attention is devoted to the matter of charitable giving.

The federal tax law on this subject is contained in the Internal Revenue Code (IRC) and in the interpretation of that law found in court opinions, Treasury Department and IRS regulations, and IRS public and private rulings. The IRC is rather specific on such components of the law of charitable giving as qualification of charitable donees, percentage limitations on a year's deductibility, gifts of particular types of property (such as inventory and works of art), and eligibility of various planned giving vehicles.

Despite this extensive treatment of this aspect of the law, there is a glaring omission in the developed rules concerning charitable giving. Oddly, this omission exists at the threshold. That is, the law is very scarce regarding the definition of the word *gift*. This is highly significant because there must be a *gift* in order to have a *charitable gift*.

Integral to the concept of the charitable contribution deduction is the fundamental requirement that the cash or property transferred to a charitable donee be transferred as a *gift*. Just because cash is paid, or property is transferred, to a charity does not necessarily mean that the payment or transfer is a gift. Consequently, when a university's tuition, a hospital's health-care fee, or an association's dues are paid, there is no gift and thus no charitable deduction for the payment.

There is some law, most of it generated by the federal courts, as to what constitutes a gift, although the IRC and the tax regulations are essentially silent on the subject. Basically, a "gift" has two elements: it involves a transfer that is *voluntary* and is motivated by something other than "consideration" (namely, something being received in return for a payment). Where payments are made to receive something in exchange (education, health care, etc.), the transaction is more in the nature of a purchase. The law places more emphasis on the second element than on the first. Thus, the income tax regulations state that a transfer is not a contribution when made "with a reasonable expectation of financial return commensurate with the amount of the transfer." A corollary of this simple rule is that a single transaction can be partially a gift and partially a purchase, so that when a charity is the payee only the gift portion is deductible.

Years ago, the U.S. Supreme Court observed that a gift is a transfer motivated by "detached or disinterested generosity." The High Court has also characterized a gift as a transfer stimulated "out of affection, respect, admiration, charity, or like impulses." (This is the factor frequently referred to as "donative intent.") One federal court of appeals put the matter more starkly, recently succinctly observing that this is a "particularly confused issue of federal taxation." Not content with that, this appellate court went on to portray the existing IRC structure on this subject as "cryptic," with the indictment that "neither Congress nor the courts have offered any very satisfactory definition" of the terms "gift" and "contribution."

These concepts have been revisited many times in recent years. One example of this has been the availability of a charitable deduction for the transfer of money to a college or university, where the transferor is granted preferential access to good seating at the institution's athletic events. The IRS has refused to regard these payments as gifts, finding that the payment results in receipt of a "substantial benefit." (The IRS concedes that there can be a gift of the portion of a payment that is in excess of the value of the benefits received in return.) The IRS struggled with this issue in the early 1980s, when it was popular for homes to be auctioned with benefits accruing to a charitable organization. The IRS ruled that those who purchase tickets from a charity are not making gifts. Other recent manifestations of this phenomenon include the various tax shelter programs involving gifts of artwork and the use of premiums and other items of property to donors in response to their contributions.

The IRS, for years, has been advising the charitable community that, when a "donor" receives some benefit or privilege in return for a payment to charity, the payment may not, in whole or in part, constitute a deductible charitable gift. The IRS position is that charitable organizations must advise individuals and corporations when a payment is not deductible or only partially deductible but the requirement lacks any sanctions. For example, if a charity sponsors a dinner as a fund-raising event, charging $75 dollars for a ticket, where the fair market value of the dinner to the patron is $50, the charity is supposed to advise the purchasers of the tickets that the deductible gift is $25, not $75.

As part of passage of the Revenue Act of 1987, Congress passed a law requiring noncharitable organizations that solicit gifts to disclose in their fund-raising literature that the contributions are not deductible (see Chapter 9). The report of the House Committee on Ways and Means accompanying its version of the tax legislation contains a discussion of the nondeductibility of payments to charitable organizations. The Committee wrote that it "is concerned that some charitable organizations may not make sufficient disclosure, in soliciting donations, membership dues, payments for admissions or merchandise, or other support, of the extent (if any) to which the payors may be entitled to charitable deductions for such payments."

This discussion focuses on "memberships" in a charitable entity, typically a museum or library, where the "members" receive benefits of some monetary value, such as free admission to events where others are charged, merchandise discounts, and free subscriptions. The Committee cautioned that some or all of these membership payments are not deductible as charitable contributions.

The Committee's analysis also references payments to a charity that are not deductible charitable gifts at all, such as the sale of raffle tickets and the auctioning of property or services. (However, those who donate property to a charity to be used by it in an auction are entitled to a charitable deduction, within the limits described below.) This legislative history states that, however, the portion of the winning bid at a charity auction that is in excess of the fair market value of the item or service received may be deductible. This discussion notes that some charities wrongfully imply that all such payments are fully deductible, while "many other charities carefully and correctly advise their supporters of the long-standing tax rules governing the deductibility of payments made to a charitable organization in return for, or with the expectation of, a financial or economic benefit to the payor."

The Committee wrote that it "anticipates" that the IRS "will monitor the extent to which taxpayers are being furnished accurate and sufficient information by charitable organizations as to the nondeductibility of payments to such organizations where benefits or privileges are received in return, so that such taxpayers can correctly compute their Federal income tax liability." Moreover, the Committee expects the charitable community to do its part, noting its anticipation that groups representing the community will further "educate their members as to the applicable tax rules and provide guidance as to how charities can provide appropriate information to their supporters in this regard."

There should be no doubt that the Ways and Means Committee has fired a warning shot in this regard. If these abuses (mostly innocent) continue, it is quite likely that the federal tax law will be revised to mandate disclosure of the nondeductibility of payments made to charitable organizations. It will be interesting to see what guidance is disseminated by and within the charitable community.

In the meantime, it is odd that the statutory law can be so explicit on the consequences in tax law of making a charitable gift, yet be so skimpy in defining the threshold word *gift*.

QUALIFIED DONEES

Qualified donees are charitable organizations (including educational, religious, and scientific entities), certain fraternal organizations, and most veterans' organizations. (These and other types of tax-exempt organizations are described in Chapter 4.) As to charitable organizations, contributions to both private and public charities (see Chapter 11) are deductible, although the law favors gifts to the latter.

Federal, state, and local governmental bodies are, under the tax law, charitable donees. However, other law may preclude a governmental entity from accepting charitable gifts. In many instances, a charitable organization can be established to solicit deductible contributions for and make grants to governmental bodies. This is a common technique for public schools, colleges, universities, and hospitals.

In some instances, an otherwise nonqualifying organization may be the recipient of a deductible charitable gift, where the gift property is used for charitable purposes or received as agent for a charitable organization. An example of the former is a gift to a trade association that is earmarked for a charitable fund within the association. An example of the latter is a gift to a title-holding corporation that operates a property for charitable purposes.

GIFT PROPERTIES

Aside from the eligibility of the gift recipient, the other basic element in determining whether a charitable contribution is deductible is the nature of the property given. Basically, the distinctions are between outright giving and planned giving (see Chapter 17), and between gifts of cash and gifts of property. In many instances, the tax law of charitable giving differentiates between personal property and real property, and tangible property and intangible property (the latter being stocks and bonds). The value of a qualified charitable contribution of an item of property often is its fair market value.

The federal income tax treatment of gifts of property is dependent upon whether the property is *capital gain property.* The tax law makes a distinction between long-term capital gain and short-term capital gain (although generally such net gain of either type is taxed as ordinary income). Property that is neither long-term capital gain property nor short-term capital gain property is *ordinary income property.* Short-term capital gain property is generally treated the same as ordinary income property. These three terms are based on the tax classification of the type of revenue that would be generated upon sale of the property. In general, therefore, the operative distinction is between capital gain property (really long-term capital gain property) and ordinary income property.

Capital gain property is property that is a capital asset that has appreciated in value, which if sold would give rise to long-term capital gain. To result in long-term capital gain, property must be held for the long-term capital gain holding period, generally 12 months. (For property acquired after June 22, 1984 and before January 1, 1988, the long-term capital gain holding period is six months.) Most forms of capital gain property are stocks, bonds, and real estate.

The charitable deduction for capital gain property is often equal to its fair market value or at least is computed using that value. Gifts of ordinary income property generally produce a deduction equivalent to the donor's cost basis in the property. The law provides exceptions to the basis-only rule, such as in the instance of gifts by a corporation out of its inventory.

PERCENTAGE LIMITATIONS

The deductibility of charitable contributions for a particular tax year is confined by certain percentage limitations, which for individuals are a function of the donor's *contribution base.* An individual's contribution base is essentially his or her adjusted gross income. There are five of these percentage limitations. Again, the limitations are dependent upon several factors, principally the nature of the charitable recipient and the nature of the property donated. The examples will assume an individual donor with a contribution base (adjusted gross income) each year in the amount of $100,000.

First, there is a percentage limitation of 50 percent of the donor's contribution base for contributions of cash and ordinary income property to public charities and private operating foundations. A donor may, in any one year, make deductible gifts of cash to public charities up to a total of $50,000. If an individual makes contributions to one or more public charities (or operating foundations) that exceed the 50 percent limitation, the excess generally may be carried forward and deducted in 1 to 5 subsequent years. Thus, if a donor gave $60,000 to public charities in year 1, (and made no other charitable gifts), he or she would be entitled to a deduction of $50,000 in year 1 and $10,000 in year 2.

Another percentage limitation is 30 percent of contribution base for gifts of capital gain property to public charities and private operating foundations. A donor may, in any one year, contribute up to $30,000 in qualifying stocks, bonds, real estate, and like property to one or more public charities and receive a charitable deduction for that amount. Any excess (more than 30 percent) is subject to the carryforward rule described previously. Thus, if a donor gave $50,000 in capital gain property to public charities in year 1 (and made no other charitable gifts that year), he or she would be entitled to a charitable contribution deduction of $30,000 in year 1 and $20,000 in year 2.

A donor who makes gifts of cash and capital gain property to public charities (and/or private operating foundations) in any one year generally must use a blend of these percentage limitations. For example, if a donor in year 1 gives $50,000 in cash and $30,000 in appreciated capital gain property to a public charity, his or her charitable deduction in year 1 is comprised of the $30,000 of capital gain property and $20,000 of cash (thereby capping the deduction with the overall 50 percent ceiling); the other $30,000 of cash is carried forward for deductibility in year 2 (or years 2 through 5, depending upon the donor's circumstances).

A donor of capital gain property to public charities and/or private operating foundations may use the 50 percent limitation, instead of the 30 percent limitation, where the amount of the contribution is reduced by all of the unrealized appreciation in the value of the property. This election is usually made in situations where the donor wants a larger deduction in the year of the gift and the property has not appreciated in value to a great extent. As discussed later in the chapter, this election can be useful in avoiding a problem in relation to the alternative minimum tax.

The fourth and fifth percentage limitations apply to gifts to private foundations and certain other charitable donees (other than public charities and private operating foundations). These other charitable donees are generally veterans' and fraternal organizations. For contributions of cash and ordinary income property to private foundations and these other entities, the deduction may not exceed 30 percent of the individual donor's contribution base. The carryover rules apply to this type of gift. Thus, if a donor gives $50,000 in cash to one or more private foundations in year 1, his or her charitable deduction for that year (assuming no other charitable gifts) is $30,000, with the balance of $20,000 carried forward for potential deductibility in subsequent years.

These rules also blend with the percentage limitations applicable with respect to gifts to public charities. For example, if in year 1 a donor gave $65,000 to charity, of which $25,000 went to a public charity and $40,000 to a private foundation, his or her charitable deduction for that year would be $50,000, consisting of $30,000 of the gift to the private foundation and $20,000 of the gift to the public charity; the remaining $10,000 of the gift to the foundation and the remaining $5,000 of the gift to the public charity would be carried forward and made available for deductibility in year 2.

The fifth percentage limitation is 20 percent of the contribution base in the case of gifts of capital gain property to private foundations and other charitable donees (other than public charities and private operating foundations). There is no carryforward for any excess deduction in the case of these gifts. For example, if a donor gives appreciated securities, having a value of $30,000, to a private foundation in year 1, his or her charitable deduction for year 1 (assuming no other charitable gifts) is $20,000; the remaining $10,000 would never be deductible. In this situation, the wise donor would elect to contribute $20,000 of the securities in year 1 and postpone the gift of the remaining $10,000 in securities until year 2. Or, if the value of the stock may substantially decline and an immediate charitable deduction is of prime concern, the donor could in year 1 donate $20,000 of the securities to the private foundation and donate $10,000 of the securities to a public charity.

Deductible charitable contributions by corporations in any tax year may not exceed 10 percent of pretax net income. Excess amounts may be carried forward and deducted in subsequent years, up to five. For gifts by corporations, the federal tax laws do not differentiate between gifts to public charities and private foundations. As an illustration, a corporation that grosses $1 million in a year and incurs $900,000 in expenses in that year (not including charitable gifts) may generally contribute to charity and deduct in that year an amount up to $10,000 (10 percent of $100,000); in computing its taxes, this corporation would report taxable income of $90,000. If the corporation instead gave $20,000 in that year, the numbers would stay the same, except that the corporation would have a $10,000 charitable contribution carryforward.

A corporation on the accrual method of accounting can elect to treat a contribution as having been paid in a tax year if it is actually paid during the first 2½ months of the following year. Corporate gifts of property are generally subject to the deduction reduction rules discussed next.

DEDUCTION REDUCTION RULES

A donor (individual or corporate) that makes a gift of ordinary income property to any charity (public or private) must confine the charitable deduction to the amount of the cost basis of the property. That is, the deduction is not based on the fair market value of the property; it must be reduced by the amount that would, if sold, have been gain (ordinary income). As an example, if a donor gave to a charity an item of ordinary income property having a value of $1,000 for which he or she paid $600, the charitable deduction would be $600.

Any donor who makes a gift of capital gain property to a public charity generally can, as noted above, compute the charitable deduction using the property's fair market value at the time of the gift, irrespective of basis and with no taxation of the appreciation (the capital gain inherent in the property). However, a donor who makes a gift of capital gain tangible personal property (e.g., a work of art) to a public charity must reduce the deduction by all of the long-term capital gain that would have been recognized had the donor sold the property at its fair market value as of the date of contribution, where the use by the donee is unrelated to its tax-exempt purposes.

Generally, a donor who makes a gift of capital gain property to a private foundation must reduce the amount of the otherwise allowable deduction by all of the appreciation element in the gift property. However, an individual is allowed full fair market value for a contribution to a private foundation of certain publicly traded stock made before 1995.

"TWICE BASIS" DEDUCTIONS

As a general rule, when a corporation makes a charitable gift of property from its inventory, the resulting charitable deduction is confined to an amount equal to the donor's basis in the donated property. In most instances, this basis amount is rather small, being equal to the cost of producing the property. However, under certain circumstances, corporate donors can receive a greater charitable deduction for gifts out of their inventory. Where the tests are satisfied, the deduction can be equal to cost basis, plus one-half of the appreciated value of the property.

Nonetheless, this charitable deduction may not, in any event, exceed an amount equal to twice the property's cost basis.

There are five special requirements that have to be met for this twice-basis charitable deduction to be available. These are:

1. The donated property must be used by the charitable donee for a related use.
2. The donated property must be used solely for the care of the ill, the needy, or infants.
3. The property may not be transferred by the donee in exchange for money, other property, or services.
4. The donor must receive a written statement from the donee representing that the use and disposition of the donated property will be in conformance with these rules.
5. Where the donated property is subject to regulation under the Federal Food, Drug, and Cosmetic Act, the property must fully satisfy the applicable requirements of that statute on the date of transfer and for 180 days prior thereto.

For these rules to apply, the donee must be a public charity. That is, it cannot be a private foundation, including a private operating foundation. Further, an "S corporation"—the tax status of many small businesses—cannot utilize these rules.

ALTERNATIVE MINIMUM TAX

The alternative minimum tax is intended to cause an individual or corporate taxpayer, no matter how sophisticated his, her, or its financial affairs are structured from a tax point of view, to pay some tax. The alternative minimum tax is a flat tax of 21 percent, payable on the economic value of a variety of "tax preference items," less certain adjustments. This tax is to be paid when it is greater than the regular income tax.

In 1986, Congress decided to lower overall tax rates and absorb the resulting revenue losses by taxing the wealthy and corporations, and by eliminating many deductions, credits, and the like. In this environment, the alternative minimum tax was toughened.

One of the tax preference items used to construct the alternative minimum income tax base is an amount equal to the appreciation element inherent in the contributed long-term capital gain property, to the extent it is included in the allowable charitable contribution deduction for regular income tax purposes. This is the *appreciated property charitable deduction.* For example, a donor gave $100,000 in appreciated securities to a public charity in a tax year and claimed an income tax deduction in that amount, having made no other charitable gifts that year; the securities had a cost basis of $10,000, so the donor has a tax preference item for alternative minimum tax purposes of $90,000.

However, this tax preference rule is inapplicable where the contributed appreciated property, normally subject to the previously described 30 percent limitation, is the subject of the elective 50 percent limitation.

In computing the alternative minimum tax, the individual taxpayer first computes the regular income tax, in the process determining the presence (if any) of the 13 tax preference items. Second, adjusted gross income is determined. Third, the (six) deductions that are allowed in computing the alternative minimum tax are ascertained and subtracted from adjusted gross income. Fourth, this amount and the total of the tax preference items are combined to total "gross minimum taxable income." Fifth, to determine "net minimum taxable income," the alternative minimum tax exemption is subtracted from gross minimum taxable income. This exemption is $40,000 for joint taxpayers and $30,000 for single taxpayers; these exemptions are phased out at 25 cents per dollar once gross minimum taxable income exceeds $150,000 for couples and $112,500 for singles. The exemption disappears for married couples with adjusted gross income at $310,000 and for singles with adjusted gross income at $232,500. Sixth, the net minimum taxable income is multiplied by the 21 percent rate, to arrive at the alternative minimum tax.

The alternative minimum tax will not trouble most donors of appreciated property. When the tax applies in this context, usually it involves a donor with a large income and highly appreciated gift property. As to situations where there may be other tax preference items, some mitigating factors are present—most notably the elimination, as the result of tax law revision in 1986, of some tax preference items that would otherwise trigger the alternative minimum tax.

Also, there are three important things a taxpayer can do to eliminate the alternative minimum tax when making charitable gifts: (1) stage the gifts (such as shares of stock) to avoid even the threat of the alternative minimum tax, (2) make remainder interest gifts instead of outright gifts (see Chapter 17), or (3) use the 50 percent limitation election (for basis-only gifts) rather than the 30 percent limitation in computing the charitable contribution deduction for the year.

PARTIAL INTEREST GIFTS

Most charitable gifts are of all interests in property, that is, by giving, the donor parts with all right, title, and interest in the property. But it is possible to make a deductible gift in the form of a contribution of less than a donor's entire interest in the property. This is a gift of a *partial interest.*

As a general rule, charitable deductions for gifts of partial interests in property, including the right to use property, are denied. But, the exceptions, which are many, are gifts made in trust form (using a so-called "split-interest trust"); gifts of an outright remainder interest in a personal residence or farm; gifts of an undivided portion of one's entire interest in property, gifts of a lease on, option to purchase, or easement with respect to real property granted in perpetuity to a public charity exclusively for conservation purposes; and a remainder interest in real property that is granted to a public charity exclusively for conservation purposes.

Contributions of income interests in property in trust are basically confined to the use of charitable lead trusts. Aside from the charitable gift annuity and the above-described gifts of remainder interests, there is no charitable deduction for a contribution of a remainder interest in property unless it is in trust and is one of three types: a charitable remainder annuity trust, a charitable remainder unitrust, or a pooled income fund. (The concept of "partial interest" gifts, more popularly known as "planned giving," is the subject of Chapter 17.)

Defective charitable split-interest trusts may be reformed to preserve the charitable deduction where certain requirements are satisfied.

GIFTS OF INSURANCE

One underutilized type of charitable giving involves life insurance. To secure an income tax deduction, the gift must include all rights of ownership in a life insurance policy. Thus, an individual can donate a fully paid-up life insurance policy to a charitable organization and deduct (for income tax purposes) its value. Or, an individual can acquire a life insurance policy, give it to charity, pay the premiums, and receive a charitable deduction for each premium payment made.

It is crucial, however, for the policy of insurance to be valid that the charitable organization be able to demonstrate that it has an insurable interest in the life of the donor of the policy. From an income tax deduction standpoint, it is not enough for a donor to simply name a charitable organization as a beneficiary of a life insurance policy. There is *no income tax charitable contribution deduction* for this philanthropic act. However, although the life insurance proceeds become part of the donor's estate, there will be an offsetting estate tax charitable deduction.

APPRAISAL RULES

The law contains requirements relating to the proof of most charitable deductions for contributions of property claimed by an individual, a closely held corporation, a personal service corporation, a partnership, or a S corporation. These requirements, when applicable, must be complied with if the deduction is to be allowed.

The requirements apply to contributions of property (other than money and publicly traded securities) if the aggregate claimed or reported value of the property (and all similar items of property for which deductions for charitable contributions are claimed or reported by the same donor for the same tax year whether or not donated to the same donee) is in excess of $5,000. The phrase "similar items of property" means property of the same generic category or type, including stamps, coins, lithographs, paintings, books, nonpublicly traded stock, land, or buildings.

For this type of gift, the donor must obtain a "qualified appraisal" and attach an "appraisal summary" to the return on which the deduction is claimed. However, in the case of nonpublicly traded stock, the claimed value of which does not exceed $10,000 but is greater than $5,000, the donor does not have to obtain a qualified appraisal but must attach a partially completed appraisal summary form to the tax or information return on which the deduction is claimed.

A *qualified appraisal* is an appraisal document that (1) relates to an appraisal that is made no more than 60 days prior to the date of the contribution of the appraised property, (2) is prepared, signed, and dated by a "qualified appraiser" (or appraisers), and (3) does not involve a prohibited type of appraisal fee (see below).

Certain information must be included in the qualified appraisal:

1. A sufficiently detailed description of the property
2. The physical condition of the property (in the case of tangible property)
3. The date (or expected date) of contribution
4. The terms of any agreement or understanding concerning the use or disposition of the property
5. The name, address, and social security number of the appraiser
6. The qualifications of the qualified appraiser or appraisers
7. A statement that the appraisal was prepared for tax purposes
8. The date or dates on which the property was valued
9. The appraised fair market value of the property on the date (or expected date) of contribution
10. The method of valuation used to determine the fair market value
11. The specific basis for the valuation
12. A description of the fee arrangement between the donor and the appraiser

The qualified appraisal must be received by the donor before the due date (including extensions) of the return on which the deduction for the contributed property is first claimed or, in the case of a deduction first claimed on an amended return, the date on which the return is filed.

A separate qualified appraisal is required for each item of property that is not included in a group of similar items of property. One qualified appraisal is required for a group of similar items of property contributed in the same tax year, as long as the appraisal includes all of the required information for each item. However, the appraiser may select any items the aggregate value of which is appraised at $100 or less, for which a group description—rather than a specific description of each item—is adequate.

The appraisal summary must be on IRS Form 8283, signed and dated by the donee and qualified appraiser (or appraisers), and attached to the donor's return on which a deduction with respect to the appraised property is first claimed or reported. The signature by the donee does not represent concurrence in the appraised value of the contributed property.

Certain information must be included in the appraisal summary:

1. The name and taxpayer identification number of the donor
2. A sufficient description of the property
3. A summary of the physical condition of the property (in the case of tangible property)
4. The manner and date of acquisition of the property
5. The basis of the property
6. The name, address, and taxpayer identification number of the donee
7. The date the donee received the property
8. The name, address, and taxpayer identification number of the qualified appraiser (or appraisers)
9. The appraised fair market value of the property on the date of contribution
10. A declaration by the appraiser

The rules pertaining to separate appraisals, summarized above, also apply with respect to appraisal summaries. However, a donor who contributes similar items of property to more than one charitable donee must attach a separate appraisal summary for each donee.

If the donor is a partnership or S corporation, it must provide a copy of the appraisal summary to every partner or shareholder who receives an allocation of a deduction for a charitable contribution of property described in the appraisal summary. The partner or shareholder must attach the appraisal summary to that partner's or shareholder's return.

A *qualified appraiser* is an individual who includes on the appraisal summary a declaration that (1) he or she holds himself or herself out to the public as an appraiser, (2) because of the appraiser's qualifications as described in the appraisal, he or she is qualified to make appraisals of the type of property being valued, and (3) he or she understands that a false or fraudulent overstatement of the value of the property described in the qualified appraisal or appraisal summary may subject the appraiser to a civil penalty for aiding and abetting an understatement of tax liability, and consequently the appraiser may have appraisals disregarded.

In addition, an individual is not a qualified appraiser if the donor had knowledge of facts which would cause a reasonable person to expect the appraiser to falsely overstate the value of the donated property. Also, the donor, donee, or certain other related persons cannot be a qualified appraiser of the property involved in the transaction. (In formulating these rules, the government did not include in the criteria certain professional standards or the establishment of a registry of qualified appraisers.) More than one appraiser may appraise donated property, as long as each appraiser complies with the requirements.

Generally, no part of the fee arrangement for a qualified appraisal can be based on a percentage (or set of percentages) of the appraised value of the property. If a fee arrangement is based in whole or in part on the amount of the appraised value of the property that is allowed as a charitable deduction, it is treated as a fee based on a percentage of the appraised value of the property. (In certain circumstances, this rule does not apply to appraisal fees paid to a generally recognized association that regulates appraisers.)

RECORD-KEEPING RULES

A corporate or individual donor must keep some record of contributions of money to charity. Preferably, this record will be a cancelled check or a receipt. Otherwise, the record must be "written" and "reliable." The record must show the name of the donee, the date of the contribution, and the amount of the contribution.

A letter or other communication from the recipient charity acknowledging receipt of the contribution, and showing the date and amount of the contribution, constitutes a "receipt." A donor has the burden of establishing "reliability" of a written record other than a check or receipt. Factors indicating that such other written evidence is "reliable" include the contemporaneous nature of the writing that evidences the contribution, the regularity of the donor's record-keeping procedures, and—in the case of a contribution of a "small amount"—any other written evidence from the charity evidencing the making of a gift that would not otherwise constitute a "receipt" (such as an emblem or a button).

As for contributions of property other than money to charity, a corporate or individual donor must obtain a receipt from the recipient charitable organization and a reliable written record of specified information with respect to the donated property.

This receipt must include the name of the donee, the date and location of the contribution, and a detailed description of the property (including the value of the property). However, a receipt is not required in instances where the gift is made in circumstances where it is impractical to obtain a receipt.

Also, the donor of property that has appreciated in value must maintain a "reliable written record" of specified information for each item of property. This information must include (1) the name and address of the charitable donee, (2) the date and location of the contribution, (3) a detailed description of the property (including the value of the property) and, in the case of securities, the name of the issuing company, the type of security, and whether or not it is regularly traded on a stock exchange or in an over-the-counter market, (4) the fair market value of the property at the time of the gift, the method utilized in determining the value, and a copy of the signed report of any appraiser, (5) the cost or other basis of the property if it is "ordinary income property" or other type of property where the deduction must be reduced by the gain (see above), (6) where the gift is of a "remainder interest" or an "income interest" (see Chapter 17), the total amount claimed as a deduction for the year due to the gift and the amount claimed as a deduction in any prior year or years for gifts of other interests in the property, and (7) the terms of any agreement or understanding concerning the use or disposition of the property, such as any restriction on the charity's right to use or dispose of the property, a retention or conveyance of the right to the income from the donated property, or an earmarking of the property for a particular use.

Additional rules apply with respect to charitable gifts of property other than money for which the donor claims a deduction in excess of $500. In this situation, the donor is required to maintain additional records, regarding the manner of acquisition of the property and the property's cost or other basis if it was held for less than six months prior to the date of gift. For property held for six months or more preceding the date of contribution, the cost or other basis information must be maintained by the donor if it is available.

REPORTING RULES

A charitable organization donee, that sells or otherwise disposes of gift property within two years after receipt of the property, generally must file an information return (Form 8282) with the IRS. A copy of this information return must be provided to the donor and retained by the donee.

This information return must include the following: (1) the name, address, and taxpayer identification number of the donor and the donee, (2) a detailed description of the property, (3) the date of the contribution, (4) the amount received on the disposition, and (5) the date of the disposition.

A donee that receives a charitable contribution valued in excess of $5,000 from a corporation generally does not have to file a donee information return.

——————————— Focus on Campaign to ——————————— Clean Up America

The Campaign to Clean Up America, as a "qualified donee," desires to be financially supported largely by charitable contributions. At the outset, these gifts are likely to be cash and in relatively small amounts. However, as the organization grows and its programs take hold in communities, larger gifts of cash should result, as well as gifts of property. The Campaign will be embarking on a gift solicitation program, relying at the beginning principally on a direct mail effort and perhaps a telemarketing program.

The Campaign is in the process of preparing literature generally describing the deductibility of contributions of cash and property to it. For the larger gifts, the Campaign will be in the position to generally advise donors as to the appraisal, substantiation, and record-keeping requirements.

The Campaign hopes to receive gifts from corporations out of their inventory (such as trash bags and trash collection equipment) and will be developing the requisite documentation to support the deductibility of those gifts.

The Campaign will be looking for ways to integrate its general charitable giving program with its planned giving program (see Chapter 17). Its fund-raising activities will be fully registered with the pertinent states (Chapter 9).

9

Charity under Siege: The Regulation of Fund-Raising

Those who manage and advise nonprofit organizations are often unaware of all of the law—federal, state, and local—that is applicable to the organizations and the individuals involved.

In no instance is this phenomenon more pronounced than the field of fund-raising regulation. The sheer magnitude of contemporary regulation by state governments of charitable gift solicitation is substantially unappreciated, even unknown in many cases. The role of the federal government in this regard is the best kept secret when it comes to the regulation of some aspect of nonprofit organizations' functions. Governmental regulation of fund-raising is becoming so pervasive and onerous, and yet so misunderstood and even ignored despite the rapidity of its growth, that it is next to impossible to place this body of law in some meaningful context. It is, however, the aspect of governmental regulation that is the most widespread and sidestepped, and growing to the point that it is threatening the very meaning of philanthropy itself.

FUND-RAISING REGULATION AT THE STATE LEVEL

Most government regulation of fund-raising has been at the state level. Many states (nearly 40 at this time) have laws or statutes on this subject— charitable solicitation acts. Many counties, cities, and towns compound the process by enforcing similar ordinances. And, as discussed below, the federal government is rapidly becoming more involved in the regulation of fund-raising for charity.

Among the many misunderstandings of this aspect of the law is the scope of its application. A fund-raising charitable organization should comply with the charitable solicitation act (if any) in effect in the state in which it is principally located. However, the fact that these laws also frequently mandate compliance by those who assist charities in fund-raising endeavors (such as professional fund-raisers and commercial co-venturers) is not fully appreciated. Even more difficult for some to grasp is that the fund-raising charity is expected to adhere to the law in each state in which it is soliciting funds. Thus, a charitable organization that is fund-raising nationally, must—under the strict interpretation of the law—be in compliance with about 40 statutes. Those who administer the county and city ordinances in this area usually expect the national charities to comply with them as well. Again, those who aid charities in the fund-raising process must comply with the laws of each of the states in which the charity is seeking contributions.

What does "compliance" with these laws mean? This varies from state to state, but essentially it means that a charity must obtain permission from the appropriate regulatory authorities before commencing a fund-raising effort. The permission is usually termed a "permit" or "license," acquired as the result of filing a "registration." Most states also require a filing fee, a bond, and the registration of professional fund-raisers and others. Thereafter, the registration is usually updated annually, by the filing of a report on the fund-raising program, including financial information.

This process would be amply difficult if the registration and reporting requirements were uniform. The staff time and expense required to obtain, maintain, and disseminate the information throughout the states can be considerable. But there is very little uniformity, as charities must constantly face differing registration and reporting forms, accounting methods, due dates, and other substantial variances in this regulatory scheme.

It is not possible to briefly summarize the states' charitable solicitation acts. Nonetheless, a summary of the prototype solicitation statute developed under the auspices of the National Association of Attorneys General provides an insight as to the scope of some of these laws.

Definitions

The model state fund-raising regulation statute, like many of them that have been enacted, opens with a series of definitions. The fund-raising professional is termed a *fund-raising counsel.* A fund-raising counsel is "a person who for compensation plans, manages, advises, consults, or prepares material for, or with respect to, the solicitation in this state of contributions for a charitable organization, but who does not solicit contributions and who does not employ, procure, or engage any compensated person to solicit contributions." A bona fide salaried officer, employee, or volunteer of a charitable organization is not a fund-raising counsel, nor are lawyers, investment counselors, or bankers.

A paid solicitor is "a person who for compensation performs for a charitable organization any service in connection with which contributions are, or will be, solicited in this state by such compensated person or by any compensated person he employs, procures, or engages, directly or indirectly, to solicit." Similarly, there is an exclusion from this definition for officers, employees, and volunteers of charitable organizations.

Other terms defined in this package are *charitable organization, solicit, solicitation, charitable purpose, contribution, commercial co-venturer,* and *charitable sales promotion.*

Regulation of Charitable Organizations

As to charitable organizations, the model law is generally in conformance with the pre-existing regulatory approach in this field.

Every charitable organization (unless exempt) desiring to solicit contributions in the state must, in advance of the solicitation, file a "registration statement" with the appropriate state agency. This requirement applies where the charity is to solicit on its own behalf, have funds solicited for it by another organization, or be the recipient of gifts generated as the result of the services of a commercial co-venturer or paid solicitor.

Where the organization is in compliance, the state issues a certificate of registration, thereby enabling the solicitation to proceed. The statement must be filed in every year in which the charitable organization is soliciting in the state. A registration fee is levied.

A charitable organization is also required to file an annual financial report. However, an organization with gross support and revenue not exceeding a certain amount (not prescribed) is excused from filing an annual financial report. The financial information may be provided by submitting a copy of the annual information return filed with the IRS (see Chapter 7). Where the gross support and revenue of a charitable organization exceeds a certain amount (again, not prescribed) the organization must submit audited financial statements.

Churches, other religious organizations, and charitable organizations closely affiliated with them are exempt from the registration requirements. Also exempt are organizations that engage in small annual solicitations (that is, do not receive gifts in excess of a certain amount (not prescribed) or do not receive gifts from more than 10 persons), but only if all of their functions (including fund-raising) are carried on by persons who are not paid for their services.

Every charitable organization engaged in a solicitation in the state must disclose, at the point of solicitation, its name, address, telephone number, a "full and fair" description of the charitable program that is the subject of the campaign, and the fact that a financial statement is available upon request. As discussed later, where the services of a paid solicitor are utilized, additional disclosures at the point of solicitation are required.

Regulation of Fund-Raising Counsel

This prototype law differentiates between fund-raising counsel "who at any time has custody of contributions from a solicitation" and fund-raising counsel who does not. A fund-raising counsel who has custody of contributions is required to register with the state, post a bond, and comply with an accounting requirement and a "pre-solicitation contract" filing requirement.

The registration is annual, for a fee, and on an application that contains such information as the state may require. The bond amount is not specified in the model law. Within ninety days following the completion of a solicitation campaign, and on the anniversary of the commencement of a campaign longer than one year, the fund-raising counsel must account in writing to the charitable organization for all income received and expenses paid.

Every contract between a charitable organization and a fund-raising counsel must be in writing, and filed by the fund-raising counsel prior to the performance by the fund-raising counsel of any material services. The contract must be adequately explicit to enable the state regulator to identify the services the fund-raising counsel is to provide.

A fund-raising counsel who does not have custody of contributions is required to comply only with the presolicitation contract filing requirement.

Regulation of Paid Solicitors

A paid solicitor is required to annually register with the state prior to any activity, on an application containing such information as the state may require, and pay a fee (unspecified). At that time, the solicitor must post a bond (again, in an unspecified amount).

Prior to the commencement of a solicitation campaign, the paid solicitor must file with the state a copy of the contract between it and the charitable organization. Also, before the start of the solicitation campaign, the paid solicitor must file with the state a "solicitation notice." This notice must include a "copy of the contract . . . , the projected dates when soliciting will commence and terminate, the location and telephone number from where the solicitation will be conducted, the name and residence address of each person responsible for directing and supervising the conduct of the campaign, a statement as to whether the paid solicitor will at any time have custody of contributions, and a full and fair description of the charitable program for which the solicitation campaign is being carried out."

Every contract between a paid solicitor and a charitable organization must be in writing and must "clearly state the respective obligations" of the parties. The contract must state a fixed percentage of the gross revenue (or reasonable estimate of it) from the solicitation campaign that the charitable organization will receive. The stated minimum percentage may not include the expenses of the solicitation paid by the charity.

The model law imposes a "point-of-solicitation" requirement, for which paid solicitors are responsible. Under this rule, prior to an oral request for a contribution or contemporaneously with a written request for a contribution, there must be disclosed to the potential donor the fact that the solicitor is a paid solicitor and that the charitable organization will receive a percentage of gross receipts as stated in the contract. The disclosures must be "clear" and "conspicuous." In the case of an oral solicitation (such as by telephone), a written receipt must be sent to each contributor, within five days of the gift, including a clear and conspicuous disclosure of the point-of-solicitation items.

Within 90 days after the completion of a solicitation campaign, and on the anniversary of the commencement of a solicitation campaign longer than one year, the paid solicitor is required to file with the state a financial report for the campaign.

A paid solicitor is required to maintain certain information during each solicitation campaign and for at least three years thereafter. This information is the name and address of each contributor, the date and amount of each contribution, the name and residence of each employee or other person involved in the solicitation, and all expenses incurred in the course of the solicitation campaign.

All monies collected by a paid solicitor must be deposited in a bank account in a timely manner and the account must be in the name of the charitable organization involved. The charitable organization must have sole control over withdrawals from the account.

Special rules are applicable to situations where paid solicitors represent that tickets to an event will be donated for use by another. These rules include limitations on solicitations for donated tickets and record-keeping requirements.

Regulation of Commercial Co-Venturing

Every charitable sales promotion must be the subject of a written contract between the charitable organization and the commercial co-venturer. A copy of the contract must be filed with the state at least 10 days prior to the commencement of the promotion.

The model law defines a "commercial co-venturer" as a "person who for profit is regularly and primarily engaged in trade or commerce other than in connection with soliciting for charitable organizations or purposes and who conducts a charitable sales promotion." A *charitable sales promotion* is defined as "an advertising or sales campaign, conducted by a commercial co-venturer, which represents that the purchase or use of goods or services offered by the commercial co-venturer will benefit, in whole or in part, a charitable organization or purpose."

The charitable sales promotion contract must include a statement of the goods or services to be offered to the public, the geographic area where the promotion will occur, the starting and concluding dates of the promotion, the manner in which the name of the charitable organization will be used (including the representation to be made to the public as to the amount or percent per unit of goods and services purchased or used that will benefit the charitable organization), a provision for a final accounting on a per unit basis by the commercial co-venturer to the charitable organization, and the date by when and the manner in which the benefit will be conferred on the charitable organization.

The commercial co-venturer is required to disclose in each advertisement for the charitable sales promotion the amount per unit of goods or services purchased or used that will benefit the charitable organization or purpose. This amount may be expressed as a dollar amount or percentage.

The final accounting must be retained by the commercial co-venturer for three years and be made available to the state upon request.

Other Provisions

The prototype statute provides that all documents required to be filed (principally registration statements, applications, and contracts) are matters of public record.

True records must be maintained by every charitable organization, fund-raising counsel, commercial co-venturer, and paid solicitor required to register. These records, which must be retained for at least three years, must be available to the state authorities for inspection.

The prototype law authorizes the state to enter into reciprocal agreements with other states or the federal government for the purpose of exchanging information or receiving information filed by a charitable organization in another state in lieu of the information required to be filed by the organization under the particular state's law.

The state agency is authorized to conduct investigations and enjoin solicitations. Certain civil penalties can be imposed for failure to adhere to the law. Under various circumstances, a registration can be revoked, cancelled, or suspended.

Constitutional Law Considerations

The matter of fund-raising regulation for charitable organizations is more than the states' charitable solicitation acts and the rules governing the deductibility of charitable gifts. This aspect of the law also involves fundamental principles of constitutional law.

Foremost is the doctrine of free speech, protected at the federal level by the First Amendment and at the state level by the Fourteenth Amendment. There are two forms of free speech: "pure" free speech and "commercial" free speech. The former may be regulated by the state by only the narrowest of means; the latter may be regulated by the state by any means that is "reasonable." Fund-raising by charitable organizations is a form of pure free speech.

Thus, the courts have held that, while government has legitimate interests in regulating this field, it may not do so by broad and arbitrary classifications. As the Supreme Court has written, government can regulate charitable fund-raising but "must do so by narrowly drawn regulations designed to serve those interests without unnecessarily interfering with First Amendment freedoms." As the High Court has observed in other contexts: "Broad prophylactic rules in the area of free expression are suspect. Precision of regulation must be the touchstone . . ."

One of the most significant clashes between governmental police power to regulate for the benefit of its citizens and rights of free speech involves the application of percentage limitations on fund-raising costs as a basis for determining whether a charity may lawfully solicit funds in a jurisdiction. Many aspects of this head-on conflict were resolved by the Supreme Court in 1980, when it held that a municipal ordinance that prohibits solicitations by charitable organizations that expend more than 25 percent of their receipts for fund-raising and administrative expenses (known as an absolute percentage limitation) is unconstitutionally overbroad in violation of free speech considerations. Subsequently, the Court addressed the so-called "rebuttable percentage limitation," where fund-raising expenses in excess of a percentage are presumed to be unreasonable, with the charity given the opportunity to rebut the presumption, and found that it too was contrary to charities' rights of free speech. These free speech rights also apply when charities obtain outside fund-raising assistance.

Both the absolute percentage limitation and the rebuttable percentage limitation can also suffer from another constitutional law violation: denial of due process. Laws regulating the fund-raising activities of charitable organizations must afford those subject to them with their due process rights as prescribed in the Fifth and Fourteenth Amendments to the U.S. Constitution.

Also, a charitable solicitation act must be in conformance with the guarantee of equal protection of the laws as provided by the Fourteenth Amendment to the U.S. Constitution. This means that such a law may not contain an inappropriately discriminatory classification of organizations. An equal protection argument can be raised in connection with the exceptions from coverage provided in a charitable fund-raising regulation law.

A cardinal doctrine of administrative law is that a governmental agency may issue regulations but must do so in the context of a policy established by a legislative body that has fixed standards for the guidance of the agency in the performance of its functions. A charitable solicitation act may run afoul of this doctrine (borne of the separation-of-powers principle), where the executive regulatory agency is granted too wide a range of discretionary authority so that it is exercising legislative power.

The State's Police Power

Before leaving the matter of state regulation of charitable fund-raising, it is appropriate to consider one other aspect of the law in this area. Many ask: How is it that the states can regulate this field the way they do, often crossing state lines (such as via radio and television) and involving the federal system (such as by use of the mails)? The answer lies in the "police power" that every state and municipality inherently possess.

The police power enables a state or political subdivision to regulate— within the bounds of constitutional law principles—the conduct of its citizens and others, to protect the safety, health, and welfare of its people. A state can enact and enforce, in the exercise of its police power, a charitable solicitation act that requires a charity planning on fund-raising in the jurisdiction to first register with the appropriate regulatory authority and subsequently to render periodic reports as to the results of that solicitation.

The rationale is that charitable solicitations may be reasonably regulated in order to protect the people from deceit, fraud, unreasonable annoyance, or the unscrupulous obtaining of money under a pretense that the money is being collected for a charitable purpose. Consequently, the laws that regulate charitable solicitations are by no means constitutionally deficient per se. They are, instead, utilizations of the states' police power. At the same time, these laws must, like all legislation, conform to certain basic legal standards or face challenges in the courts.

FEDERAL REGULATION OF FUND-RAISING

As reflected in Chapter 3 (Myth 10), the federal government is becoming greatly involved in the process of regulating fund-raising for charitable purposes. Once the province of the states, regulation of fund-raising is now also being conducted at the federal level, largely through the tax law. (Other agencies, such as the U.S. Postal Service and the Federal Election Commission, may also be involved.) However, federal level involvement in this area of law is, all too often, ignored or, worse, unknown.

Fund-Raising Disclosure

Congress specifically brought the IRS into the fund-raising regulation business when it legislated certain fund-raising disclosure rules. These rules are not applicable to charitable organizations, although the legislative history accompanying them strongly hints that this type of law may be extended to charities if they persist in securing payments from individuals that are not gifts (such as dues or payments made for raffle tickets or at auctions) under circumstances where the payors think that the payments are gifts and try to deduct them as charitable contributions. The fund-raising disclosure rules are thus applicable to all types of tax-exempt organizations, other than charitable ones, including political organizations (see Chapter 4), except organizations that have annual gross receipts that are normally no more than $100,000.

Under these rules, each fund-raising solicitation by or on behalf of a noncharitable organization must contain an express statement, in a "conspicuous and easily recognizable format," that gifts to it are not deductible as charitable contributions for federal income tax purposes. A fund-raising solicitation is any solicitation of gifts made in written or printed form, by television or radio, or by telephone (although there is an exclusion for letters or calls not part of a coordinated fund-raising campaign soliciting more than 10 persons during a calendar year). Despite the clear reference in the statute to "contributions and gifts," the IRS interprets this rule to mandate the disclosure when any tax-exempt organization (other than a charity) seeks funds, such as dues from members.

Failure to satisfy this disclosure requirement can result in imposition of penalties. The penalty is $1,000 per day (maximum of $10,000 per year), albeit with a reasonable cause exception. However, in an instance of an "intentional disregard" of these rules, the penalty for the day on which the offense occurred is the greater of $1,000 or 50 percent of the aggregate cost of the solicitations that took place on that day—and the $10,000 limitation is inapplicable. For these purposes, the days involved are those on which the solicitation was telecast, broadcast, mailed, otherwise distributed, or telephoned.

Exemption Application Process

Organizations are required, to be tax-exempt as charitable entities and to be charitable donees, to secure a determination letter to that effect from the IRS. This application process requires the organization to reveal some information about its fund-raising program.

This aspect of federal fund-raising regulation is discussed in Chapter 6. As discussed there, the application process requires a discussion of the applicant's fund-raising program (Form 1023, Part III, response to questions 1 and 2), and should entail some reference to fund-raising costs in the financial statements or in the proposed budgets submitted with the application.

Reporting Requirements

Among the overlooked aspects of federal regulation of the charitable solicitation process is that being accomplished by means of the annual reporting obligations imposed on charitable organizations (see Chapter 7).

The annual information return (Form 990) requires charitable organizations to use the functional method of accounting as the means to report their expenses (Part III of the return). This approach to the accounting for an organization's expenses requires not only the identification, line by line, of expenses but also an allocation of expenses by function, namely, the categories of program services, management and general, and fund-raising.

Proper compliance with the requirements of the functional method of accounting obligates organizations to maintain detailed records as to their fund-raising (and other) expenses, since the fund-raising component of each line-item expenditure must be separately identified and reported. This requirement that the fund-raising elements of all expenditures be separately identified may reveal some indirect fund-raising costs that, when combined with direct fund-raising expenses, result in the reporting of considerably higher total outlays for fund-raising. This, in turn, could have adverse repercussions as respects the organization's status under state charitable solicitation acts, particularly those that seek to place limits on allowable fund-raising expenses. This approach to the reporting of expenses raises other pertinent accounting issues, not the least of which is the basis to be used in making these allocations among functions and whether the state regulators will accept reports containing the allocations as being in compliance with the states' reporting requirements.

The instructions accompanying the return define the term *fund-raising expense* as "all expenses, including allocable overhead costs, incurred in: (a) publicizing and conducting fundraising campaigns; (b) soliciting bequests, grants from foundations or other organizations, or government grants . . . ; (c) participating in federated fundraising campaigns; (d) preparing and distributing fundraising manuals, instructions, and other materials; and (e) conducting special fundraising events that generate contributions . . ." The IRS does not differentiate, when using the term *professional fund-raiser,* between fund-raising counsel and solicitors, in that it defines the phrase *professional fund-raising fees* to mean "the organization's fees to outside fund-raisers for solicitation campaigns they conducted, or for providing consulting services in connection with a solicitation of contributions by the organization itself."

There are least four other areas of disclosure, mandated by the annual information return, pertaining to fund-raising. First, the return (in Part II) requires organizations to separately identify their sources of "program service revenue." Second, organizations have the option of distinguishing between the reporting of revenue that is restricted and revenue that is unrestricted (in Part I). Third, organizations must report their receipts from and expenses of "[s]pecial fund-raising events and activities," with information separately provided for each type of event. These events include dinners, dances, carnivals, raffles, bingo games, and door-to-door sales of merchandise.

As to special fund-raising events, the IRS observes in the return's instructions that "[i]n themselves, these activities only incidentally accomplish an exempt purpose" and that "[t]heir sole or primary purpose is to raise funds (other than contributions) to finance the organization's exempt activities." "This is done," the instructions continue, "by offering goods or services of more than nominal value (compared to the price charged) in return for a payment higher than the direct cost of the goods or services provided." Thus, an activity that only generates contributions (such as a direct mail campaign) is not a "special fund-raising event." However, a special fund-raising event can generate both contributions and revenue, such as when a purchaser pays more than the value of the goods or services furnished.

The contents of the annual information return pertain to the relationship between the federal government and the state regulatory agencies with respect to the regulation of fund-raising for charity. These levels of government are coordinating their respective roles. The IRS has taken a significant step toward implementation of this process by stating, in its summary of its adoption of the present return, that "[s]tates are encouraged to use this return as the basic form satisfying State reporting requirements" and adding that "[a]ny additional information needed by a particular State could be provided by that State's own supplemental schedules and by requiring every filer to complete all parts of Form 990 to be filed with the State." More states than ever before use Form 990 as the form for providing financial information in compliance with the states' charitable solicitation acts; for some reason, the IRS wants to know the states in which the return is filed and expects the organizations to report that information (in Part VII).

The instructions accompanying the annual information return suggest that fund-raising is a form of "doing business" requiring separate registration under the states' nonprofit corporation acts.

Unrelated Income Rules

One of the ways in which the IRS is regulating the charitable fund-raising process is through the unrelated income rules. These rules are the subject of Chapter 12.

It would be a substantial understatement to say that charitable organizations do not regard their fund-raising activities as unrelated business endeavors. Yet the fund-raising practices of charities and the unrelated business rules have been enduring a precarious relationship for years. The IRS is more frequently using the unrelated income rules to characterize the receipts from certain fund-raising activities as unrelated income.

It must be conceded that many fund-raising practices possess all of the technical characteristics of an unrelated business. (See the above discussion concerning special fund-raising events.) Reviewing the basic criteria for unrelated income taxation, some fund-raising activities are trades or businesses, regularly carried on, and not efforts that are substantially related to the performance of tax-exempt functions. Further, applying some of the tests often used these days by the IRS and the courts, there is no question that some fund-raising endeavors have a commercial counterpart and are being undertaken in competition with that counterpart and are being undertaken with the objective of realizing a profit. Some fund-raising activities are sheltered by law from consideration as businesses, such as an activity in which substantially all of the work is performed for the organization by volunteers; carried on primarily for the convenience of the organization's members, students, patients, officers, or employees; or which consists of the sale of merchandise, substantially all of which has been received by the organization as gifts.

As the functional accounting rules (see above) indicate, the law regards program activities and fund-raising activities as separate matters. Even a simple undertaking such as a car wash or a bake sale is an unrelated business—saved from taxation only because it is not regularly carried on or conducted wholly by volunteers. Some fund-raising activities—such as the mailing of greeting cards, charitable sales promotions, affinity card programs, and "membership" arrangements—are currently undergoing close scrutiny by the IRS, the courts, and/or Congress.

Some of these rules may go beyond the question of unrelated income and raise issues pertaining to eligibility for tax-exempt status. Fund-raising charitable groups may be facing a new wave of regulation, with their tax exemption or taxation of income as the federal government's leverage.

Lobbying Restrictions

At this writing, the Treasury Department and the IRS are writing regulations that will define the term *fund-raising costs* and spell out rules by which to distinguish those costs from (that is, allocate between) the expenses of administration and program. These regulations are being drawn as part of the effort to promulgate rules implementing the elective lobbying restrictions for public charities (see Chapter 13).

Under these lobbying rules, certain percentages are applied to the organization's outlays for program but not fund-raising expenditures. Thus, it becomes necessary for an organization endeavoring to comply with these rules to distinguish between its fund-raising costs and its other costs. The amounts against which these percentages are applied are called *exempt purpose expenditures*. But exempt purpose expenditures do not include amounts paid or incurred to or for (1) a separate fund-raising unit of the organization, or an affiliated organization's fund-raising unit, or (2) one or more other organizations, if the amounts are paid or incurred primarily for fund-raising.

Therefore, to adhere to these rules, an electing public charity must determine its direct and indirect fund-raising costs, assuming that there is understanding as to the scope of the term *fund-raising* in this context.

Public Charity Classifications

A charitable organization is classified as either a *public* or a *private* charity (see Chapter 11). One of the ways to avoid private foundation status is to be a publicly supported organization. And one of the ways to be a publicly supported organization is to qualify as a *donative* charity. In turn, one of the ways to achieve that classification is to meet a *facts-and-circumstances* test, where the amount of public support normally received by the organization may be as low as 10 percent of its total support. A variety of criteria may be utilized to demonstrate compliance with this test.

One of the criteria is the extent to which the charitable organization is attracting public support. This element is satisfied where the organization can demonstrate an active and ongoing fund-raising program. The tax regulations state that an entity may satisfy this aspect of the test "if it maintains a continuous and bona fide program for solicitation of funds from the general public, community, or membership group involved, or if it carries on activities designed to attract support from governmental units or other [publicly supported] organizations . . . ."

Consequently, the IRS may be monitoring the extent of a charitable organization's fund-raising efforts, to ascertain whether they qualify as an entity other than a private foundation.

Other Aspects of Federal Regulation

Federal tax law prohibits a private educational institution from qualifying as a charitable entity if it has racially discriminatory policies. Under guidelines promulgated by the IRS, school must adhere to an assortment of record-keeping requirements. This includes the rule that every private school must maintain, for at least three years, copies of all materials used by or on behalf of it to solicit contributions. Failure to maintain or to produce the required reports and information creates a presumption that the school has failed to comply with the guidelines and thus has a racially discriminatory policy as to students—which could result in loss or denial of tax-exempt status.

10

Compensating the Nonprofit Employee

Nonprofit organizations frequently have employees, just as their for-profit counterparts usually do. Employees are compensated, irrespective of whether they work for a nonprofit or for-profit employer.

There is a tendency in our society to expect employees of nonprofit organizations to work for levels and types of compensation that are less than what would be paid if their employers were for-profit organizations. Somehow, the nonprofit characteristics of a tax-exempt organization are being, in this context, ascribed to its employees—hence the reference in the chapter title to the "nonprofit" employee. At times, this outcome is unavoidable given the budgetary constraints of some nonprofit organizations. In other cases, the problem is a manifestation of the phenomenon of the nonprofit mentality, where the employees passively feel they must accept low compensation. More positively, some may work for nonprofit organizations in furtherance of the organizations' programs, willingly sacrificing for the cause what might otherwise bring greater pay. By contrast, on occasion nonprofit organization employees are better compensated than their for-profit entity counterparts. However, in many instances, it is likely that employees of nonprofit organizations are simply undercompensated.

A 1987 study supports some of these conclusions. The analysis concludes that those who work for nonprofit organizations (expected to be about 8.6 million in 1990 and 9.3 million in 1995) "display few characteristics that set them off from other service workers." Overall, the study concludes that workers in the nonprofit sector earn less than four-fifths as much as their for-profit counterparts. However, nonprofit employee earnings often exceeded those of their for-profit counterparts in a number of services, such as in health and social services, and research and development. The researchers thus question the conclusion of others that "lower pay is acceptable to nonprofit employees because of a variety of intrinsic job benefits that nonprofit employees receive."

Many nonprofit organizations, particularly the larger ones (such as universities, hospitals, major charities, and trade associations), require sophisticated and talented employees. These individuals are not likely to want to be "nonprofit" employees, thus placing nonprofit organizations and for-profit organizations in competition for the same pool of talented persons. This forces competition not only in salaries but also in fringe benefits and retirement programs.

Whatever the mode of compensation—be it salaries, bonuses, commissions, fringes, and/or retirement benefits—most nonprofit organizations are constrained by the private inurement doctrine (see Chapter 5). What this means is that all compensation, no matter how determined or whatever the form, must, for the employer to be tax-exempt, be "reasonable."

CURRENT COMPENSATION

A nonprofit organization may pay a salary or wage. This is a form of "current," as opposed to "deferred" (see below), compensation. Generally speaking, the payments must be "reasonable," largely using community standards, taking into account the comparability of the value of services being rendered and pertinent experience. (In a sense, the same rule applies with respect to for-profit employers, in that, to be deductible as a business expense, cash compensation must be "ordinary and necessary.") For this purpose, reasonable current compensation includes appropriate salary increases based on merit and appropriate cost-of-living adjustments.

In the instance of private foundations, the matter becomes one of potential self-dealing (see Chapter 11). Unreasonable (excessive) compensation is a form of self-dealing that can lead to penalty taxes.

Nonprofit organizations may pay bonuses. Again, a bonus is also subject to the standard of "reasonableness." A bonus is likely to be more closely scrutinized than regular current compensation, because it is *additional* compensation and thus more susceptible than regular compensation to be excessive compensation (and therefore a form of inurement of net earnings). The sensitivity is increased where a bonus is paid to one who is an "insider" with respect to the nonprofit organization.

In many respects, commissions are subject to the same rules as bonuses, in that both are forms of incentive compensation. However, commissions and other forms of percentage-based compensation can result in heightened inquiry because, by nature, they are computed using percentages and thus get close to the concept of private inurement. Thus, the IRS will carefully scrutinize compensation programs of nonprofit organizations that are predicated on an incentive feature whereby compensation is a function of revenues received, is guaranteed, or is otherwise outside the boundaries of conventional compensation arrangements.

For example, the IRS has developed criteria for assessing compensation arrangements based upon a percentage of a tax-exempt organization's gross revenues. The factors the IRS uses in this regard are whether:

- the compensation actually paid was reasonable
- the agreement was completely negotiated at arms' length
- the service provider participated in or had any control over the conduct of the organization
- the "contingent" payments serve a "real discernible business purpose" of the exempt organization (that is, independent of any purpose to benefit the service provider)
- the amount of compensation is dependent upon the accomplishment of the objectives of the compensatory arrangement
- actual operating results reveal any evidence of abuse or unwarranted benefits to the service provider
- there is a "ceiling or reasonable maximum limit" in the compensation agreement to avoid a "windfall benefit" to the service provider based upon factors "which had no direct relationship to the level of services provided"

In conclusion, all forms of current compensation paid by tax-exempt organizations are subject to the rule of reasonableness, with the tax exemption of the employer on the line.

FRINGE BENEFITS

Federal tax and other law does not prohibit the payment of fringe benefits by nonprofit organizations. A "fringe benefit" basically is a form of noncash compensation to the employee, although it may well entail a cash outlay by the employer. Once again, a fringe benefit (or a package of them) must be reasonable to preserve the tax exemption of the employer.

Typically, an employer will pay for fringe benefits such as health insurance, major medical insurance, disability insurance, and perhaps travel insurance. For the most part, nonprofit organizations can pay for one or more of these benefits without tax law difficulties.

Other common forms of fringe benefits paid (either directly or by reimbursement) by employers are entertainment costs, costs of an automobile, moving expenses, costs of attending conventions and/or educational seminars, costs of parking, club memberships, and costs of certain professional fees (such as physicians' charges for physicals, financial planning fees, and stress management expenses).

These latter types of fringe benefits are likely to cause problems for the tax-exempt organizations that pay them. Some entities may be able to pay moving expenses, continuing education expenses, and perhaps automobile and parking expenses, without attracting too much investigation. However, generally, a nonprofit organization will be suspect, in the eyes of legislators and regulators (and perhaps the general public), if its employees are granted fringes such as country club memberships, financial planning services, or an entertainment allowance. Golden parachutes are not frequent in the nonprofit world.

DEFERRED COMPENSATION

It is becoming more common for nonprofit organizations to provide "deferred compensation" to their employees. Colleges, universities, and hospitals have paved the way in this area. Yet, many tax and other issues are resulting from this practice. As with current compensation, deferred compensation is subject to the rule of reasonableness.

Deferred compensation embraces retirement plans and profit-sharing plans. (Yes, a nonprofit organization can maintain a profit-sharing plan; the words "excess of revenue over expenses" are used instead of "profit.") These plans are usually subject to the law laid down by the Employee Retirement Income Security Act, amended from time to time, and related Internal Revenue Code provisions.

Deferred compensation plans are divided into qualified and nonqualified plans.

Qualified Plans

A qualified plan is a plan that satisfies a variety of tax law requirements, as to coverage, contributions, other funding, vesting, nondiscrimination, and distributions.

For for-profit organizations, it is desirable for a plan to be qualified, to enable employer contributions to the plan to be deductible as business expenses. This, of course, is not of relevance to tax-exempt organizations. Other advantages of a qualified plan are that the income and capital gains from the assets underlying the plan are not subject to the federal income tax, in that they are held in a tax-exempt trust (see Chapter 4), and that employees are usually not taxed until the benefits of the plans are actually received.

Qualified plans are either *defined benefit* plans or *defined contribution* plans, the latter also referred to as *individual account* plans. A pension plan may fall into either category.

Defined Benefit Plans. A defined benefit plan is established and maintained by an employer primarily to systematically provide for the payment of a definitely determinable benefit to the employees over a period of years, usually life, following retirement. Retirement benefits under a defined benefit plan are measured by and based on various factors, such as years of service rendered by the employee and compensation earned by the employee. The determination of the amount of benefits and the contributions made to the plan are not dependent upon the profits of the employer. Under a defined benefit plan, the benefits are established in advance by a formula and the employer contributions are determined within federal tax law limits, by an actuary using a variety of interest and mortality factors.

Defined Contribution Plans. A defined contribution plan provides an individual account for each participant and bases benefits solely upon the amount allocated to the participant's account, as adjusted by investment gains or losses, and forfeitures allocated to the account.

This type of plan defines the amount of contribution to be added to each participant's account. This may be done in one of two ways: by directly defining the amount the employer will contribute on behalf of each employee or by leaving to the employer's discretion the amount of contribution but defining the method of allocation. The individual accounts are adjusted, at least annually, to reflect in a proportionate fashion, investment gains and losses.

Ordinarily, the total plan assets are completely allocated to the individual accounts. If a participant terminates his or her employment before becoming vested, the account balance is forfeited and is applied either to reduce future employer contributions or is allocated to accounts of other participants. When a participant becomes eligible to receive a benefit, his or her benefit equals the amount that can be provided by the account balance. The benefit may be paid in the form of a lump-sum distribution, a series of installments, or an annuity for the lifetime of the participant or for the joint lifetimes of the participant and other beneficiary.

Where the undertaking is to set aside periodic contributions according to a predetermined formula, the plan is referred to as a "money purchase pension plan." Contributions are generally expressed as a percentage of covered payroll, with the rate sometimes varying with the employee's age at entry into the plan. A "target benefit plan" is a money purchase plan that sets a targeted benefit to be met by actuarily determined contributions. Special antidiscrimination rules apply to target benefit plans.

Another type of defined contribution plan is a *profit-sharing* plan. A profit-sharing plan is established and maintained by an employer to provide for participation in profits by employees or their beneficiaries. The plan must have a definite, predetermined formula for allocating contributions made under the plan among the participants and for distributing the funds accumulated under the plan after a fixed number of years, the attainment of a stated age, or upon the prior occurrence of some event, such as layoff, illness, disability, retirement, death, or severance of employment. A plan cannot qualify as a profit-sharing plan unless the employer's contributions are contingent upon the existence of the necessary profits. A profit-sharing plan may, but is not required, to have a definite, predetermined formula for computing the amount of annual employer contributions.

Other defined contribution plans (some of which are profit-sharing plans) include stock bonus plans, employee stock ownership plans, thrift plans, simplified employee pension plans (which can be a form of inoIvidual retirement accounts), and so-called cash or deferred arrangements.

THE FUNDING MECHANISM

The usual method of funding a pension or profit-sharing plan is through a tax-exempt trust. A "trusteed" plan uses a trust to receive and invest the funds contributed under the plan and to distribute the benefits to participants and/or their beneficiaries. The law requires that, in order for a trust forming part of a pension, profit-sharing, or like plan to constitute a qualified trust, the following conditions must be met:

1. The trust must be created or organized in the United States and must be maintained at all times as a U.S. domestic trust
2. The trust must be part of a pension, profit-sharing, or like plan established by the employer for the exclusive benefit of the employees and/or their beneficiaries
3. The trust must be formed or availed for the purpose of distributing to employees and/or their beneficiaries the corpus and income of the fund accumulated by the trust in accordance with the plan
4. It must be impossible under the trust instrument at any time before all liabilities, with respect to employees and their beneficiaries, are satisfied for any part of the trust's corpus or income to be used for, or diverted to, purposes other than for the exclusive benefit of employees and/or their beneficiaries
5. The trust must be part of a plan that benefits a nondiscriminatory classification of employees under applicable IRS guidelines and provides nondiscriminatory benefits
6. If the trust is part of a pension plan, the plan must provide that forfeitures cannot be applied to increase the benefit of any participant.

The tax advantages of a qualified plan can be obtained without the use of a trust through an "annuity plan," under which contributions are used to purchase retirement annuities directly from an insurance company. An annuity contract is treated as a qualified trust if it would, except for the fact that it is not a trust, satisfy all the requirements for qualification. In that case, the person holding the annuity is treated as if he or she was the trustee.

A segregated asset account of a life insurance company can be used as an investment medium for assets of a qualified pension, profit-sharing, or annuity plan. Insurance companies establish special funds to hold plan investments; trusts are not required.

Another form of a nontrusteed plan is the use of a custodial account. Under this approach, the employer arranges with a bank or other qualified institution to act as custodian of the plan funds placed in the account. Although a custodial account is not a trust, a qualifying custodial account is treated for tax purposes as a qualified trust.

Nonqualified Plans

Nonqualified plans are used as means to provide supplemental benefits and/ or to avoid the technical requirements imposed upon qualified plans. However, the advantages of nonqualified plans for many employers (particularly for-profit ones) have been substantially eroded by recently enacted laws. Also, the employer's deduction is deferred until the amount attributable to the contribution is includible in the employees' income. Yet, nonqualified plans are of great importance to nonprofit employers.

The federal tax consequences of nonqualified plans vary, depending upon whether the plan is funded or unfunded. Where the plan is funded, contributions by an employer to a nonexempt employees' trust are includible in an employee's gross income in the first tax year in which the rights of the individual having the beneficial interest in the trust are transferable and are not subject to a substantial risk of forfeiture. Unfunded plans are contractural promises to pay for which the employer is not setting aside any dollars into an annuity contract or trust. The tax consequences to an employee under an unfunded arrangement are determined by application of the doctrines of constructive receipt or economic benefit.

Funds in these plans can be deemed taxable to employees and accessible by creditors of the employer.

457 Plans

Congress, in 1986, extended rules for the provision of nonqualified unfunded deferred compensation to employees of nonprofit organizations. The programs covered by these rules are called "457 plans" (named after the section of the Internal Revenue Code that authorizes them). Prior to 1986, 457 plans were available only to employees of state and local governments.

A 457 plan is available to employees of tax-exempt organizations (and, still, governmental agencies). Compliance with the rules for 457 plans enables employees to defer the taxation of income; otherwise, the deferred amount is immediately taxable. Also, these plans are "unfunded," so that the deferred amounts (and the resulting earnings) remain the property of the employer and thus are subject to the creditors of the employer.

In a 457 plan, the most compensation that can be deferred in a year is the lesser of $7,500 or one-third of the employee's or other participant's gross income. Under certain circumstances, catch-up deferrals are permitted, up to $15,000 annually. Distributions cannot be made before the earlier of the discontinuance of employment or the occurrence of an unforeseeable emergency. Distributions payable upon death must be paid within 15 years or within the life expectancy of a surviving spouse.

The law requires, as to distributions, that 457 plans satisfy certain minimum distribution requirements and imposes a penalty excise tax equal to 50 percent of the amount that should have been distributed; for lifetime distributions, at least two-thirds of the total amount payable must be paid during the life expectancy of the participant and any amount not distributed during the life of the participant must be distributed at death at least as rapidly as required by the method that was used during the participant's life; and in the case of distributions that do not begin until after the participant's death, the entire amount payable must be paid during a period that does not exceed 15 years or, if the beneficiary is the surviving spouse, the life expectancy of that spouse.

Amounts in a 457 plan cannot be rolled over (that is, transferred without taxation) to a qualified plan or to an individual retirement account. However, a transfer from one 457 plan to another will not trigger a tax.

403(b) Plans

Another form of deferred compensation in the nonprofit organizations context is the tax-sheltered (or tax-deferred) annuity. This is an annuity paid out of a "403(b) plan" (again, a plan named after the section of the IRC that authorizes it). A tax-sheltered annuity is treated as a defined contribution plan.

Tax-sheltered annuity programs are available only to employees of charitable (including educational and religious) organizations, as well as employees of public educational institutions. Essentially, the law is that if amounts are contributed by an employer toward the purchase of an annuity contract for an employee, then, to the extent that the amounts do not exceed the "exclusion allowance" (see below) for the tax year of the employees, the employee is not required to include the amounts in gross income for the tax year. These "plans" are usually funded through an individual annuity contract purchased by the employee or a group annuity contract held by the employer where a separate account is maintained for each participant. As an alternative, funding may be through a custodial account arrangements.

Contributions to a 403(b) plan—usually made on a salary reduction basis—are excluded from the employees' taxable income, with certain limitations. Generally, elective (employee) contributions may not exceed $9,500 annually. The funds held under these programs are generally permitted to appreciate without any tax obligation.

Amounts contributed by an employee to a 403(b) plan are not required to be included in the gross income of the employee to the extent that the amounts do not exceed the employee's "exclusion allowance" for the year. The exclusion allowance for a year is (1) the product of (a) 20 percent of an employee's includible compensation times (b) his or her years of service with the employer as of the close of the taxable year over (2) the aggregate of the amount contributed by the employer for annuity contracts and excludable from the gross income of the employee for any prior year. The minimum exclusion allowance is the lesser of $3,000 or the employee's includible compensation. Thus, all of an eligible employee's includible compensation may be contributed to a 403(b) plan on an excludible basis, up to $3,000.

Tax-sheltered annuity plans are generally subject to less federal law regulation. However, various provisions of the Employee Retirement Income Security Act are applicable, as are many of the nondiscrimination, distribution, and other limitations (including restrictions on loans) of qualified plans.

Distributions from a 403(b) plan are generally taxed in the same way as are periodic distributions from qualified plans.

CONCLUSION

Most nonprofit organization employers offer some type of compensatory arrangements beyond basic current compensation, such as fringe benefits and deferred compensation (including retirement plans), for their employees. The type and extent of the plan(s) and the benefits provided are subject to many factors, including the budgetary constraints on the employer. As competition for talent escalates between for-profit and nonprofit employers, the costs to the nonprofit employers go up, as does the intricacy of the law. (The law, however, prevents one form of competition over benefits, in that tax-exempt organizations may not maintain the qualified cash or deferral arrangements known as "401(k) plans.")

The law in this field has become quite complex, with Congress repeatedly visiting the subject in recent years. The enactment of the Employee Retirement Income Security Act in 1974 brought a vast amount of new statutory law on the subject, for nonprofit and for-profit employers alike. In 1986 alone, Congress, as noted above, extended the 457 plan rules to nonprofit employment and made it clear that tax-exempt organizations can maintain qualified profit-sharing plans. Congress, Treasury, and the

IRS will assuredly add more law in this field in the coming years—much of it of direct applicability in the nonprofit organizations context.

Focus on the Campaign to Clean Up America

Being a new organization, the Campaign to Clean Up America is not in a position to maintain a large payroll, replete with large salaries, an array of fringe benefits, a profit-sharing plan, and a retirement plan.

However, the Campaign will have employees and they will be fairly paid—subject, as is always the case in this setting, to adequate funding. There will hopefully soon be some of the basic fringe benefits, such as health insurance. There will be additional benefits, including sick and vacation leave. There will be cost-of-living adjustments, merit increases, and perhaps bonuses.

Certainly, as the Campaign matures, a retirement program will be installed. This may be the traditional tax-sheltered annuity (403(b)) program or, depending upon developments in the law and cash flow, a deferred compensation (457) plan.

Part III

Tax-Exempt Organizations Can Be Taxable . . . and So Can Their Managers

11

Be Public, Not Private

One of the great myths about tax-exempt organizations is that they are not taxable (see Chapter 3). The truth is, they can be taxable and, in some situations, subject to heavy taxation. Moreover, the individuals involved can be personally taxable. In no instance is the degree of taxation more stringent than in the case of private foundations.

WHAT IS A "PRIVATE FOUNDATION"?

Before delving into the various taxes imposed upon private foundations, it is necessary to first understand what a private foundation is (or is not).

The term *private foundation,* while used generically in the nonprofit organization community for decades, was not defined in the Internal Revenue Code until 1969. At that time, Congress was on an anti-foundation rampage, legislating against them in every way it could think of. Congress wanted to be certain that each charitable organization that is not clearly "public" (as explained below) is treated as a private foundation, so it wanted that term to be as all-encompassing as possible. Indeed, it was searching for a way to cast the net so wide that it could not write a definition of the term "private foundation." Instead, it wrote a definition as to what a private foundation *is not.*

Therefore, under the federal tax law, every charitable organization—be it a church, university, hospital, or local community group—is presumed to be a private foundation. This means that every charitable organization must either rebut that presumption (and thus become public) or exist as a private foundation.

Despite the intricacies of the tax law definition of the term *private foundation,* the concept of such an entity is simple. A true private foundation generally has three fundamental characteristics. One, its financial support came from one source: usually an individual, family, or company. Two, its annual expenditures are funded out of earnings from investment assets, rather than from an ongoing flow of contributions. In this regard, a private foundation is much the same as an endowment fund. Three, a private foundation makes grants to other organizations for charitable purposes, rather than operate its own programs. As to this last characteristic, a hybrid entity (a blend between a private foundation and a public charity) is the *private operating foundation,* which, although it conducts its own programs, has most of the other features of a private foundation.

There is no advantage to private foundation status. Indeed, the range of disadvantages is multitudinous: (1) the necessity to comply with a battery of onerous rules, such as prohibitions on self-dealing, insufficient grants for charitable purposes, excess business holdings, jeopardizing investments, and certain types of grants, (2) a tax on net investment income, (3) greater reporting responsibilities, (4) narrower limitations on gift deductibility, and (5) the practical fact that private foundations are highly unlikely to make grants to other private foundations.

As will be seen, the word "private" in this setting means funding from a single source. The term has nothing to do with the composition of an organization's board of directors or trustees. Some believe that an advantage to private foundation status is an ability to function "in private," that is, without scrutiny from outsiders; classification as a private foundation can have the opposite results.

Frequently, a lawyer or other professional helping a new charitable organization through the tax law maze can provide no greater service than enabling the organization to avoid private foundation status.

AVOIDING PRIVATE FOUNDATION STATUS

Essentially, there are three types of charitable organizations that are not private foundations and thus are *public charities.*

These types of organizations are the "institutions" of the charitable world, the so-called "publicly supported" charities, and the supporting organizations. Put another way, to avoid categorization as a "private" charity, an organization must either demonstrate "public" involvement, "public" financial support, or an operating relationship with a "public" organization.

Institutions

Federal tax law identifies certain institutions within the philanthropic sector that are—by reason of that classification alone—exempted from the private foundation rules and taxes.

These entities are (1) churches, or conventions or associations of churches, (2) operating educational institutions, such as universities, colleges, and schools, (3) operating health care providers (including hospitals) and certain medical research organizations, and (4) governmental units, whether federal or state.

The pathway to public charity status is rarely achieved by qualifying an entity as one of these institutions. A lawyer practicing full-time in the representation of nonprofit organizations may never have the opportunity to create a (bona fide) church, university, or hospital. So this approach is of little utility in tax planning.

At the same time, these exceptions from private foundation classification are extremely important, since the objectives Congress sought in creating the private foundation rules would not be advanced by treating these institutions as private foundations.

Publicly Supported Organizations

As noted, one of the chief characteristics of a private foundation is that it is (was) funded from one source. By contrast, one way for an organization to be a public charity is to be funded from many sources (the public). Therefore, it is axiomatic that an organization is not a "private foundation" if it is publicly supported.

There are two types of publicly supported organizations. The law has not assigned either of them a name, so for our purposes they will be categorized as *donative* charities and *fee-based* charities. These classifications are, at best, inexact, as most publicly supported charities receive a blend of gifts, grants, and fee-for-service revenue (as well as investment income). But these distinctions will serve to make the point.

The donative charity is one that "normally" receives a "substantial part" of its support from one or more governmental units in the form of grants and/or as direct or indirect contributions from the "general public."

Most donative organizations derive at least one-third of their financial support (the so-called "support ratio") from qualifying sources (eligible governmental and/or public support). For these purposes (except for new entities), the measuring period for determining the requisite support is the organization's most recent four fiscal periods—the meaning of the term "normally."

Contributions from individuals, trusts, corporations, or other legal entities constitute public support to the extent that the total amount of contributions from any donor (including related parties) during the support computation period does not exceed an amount equal to 2 percent of the organization's total support (excluding exempt function revenue) for the period. Therefore, while the total amount of support by a donor is included in full in the denominator of the support ratio (fraction), generally only the amount determined by application of the 2 percent limitation is included in the numerator of the support ratio. The 2 percent limitation generally does not apply to support received from other donative organizations, nor to support from governmental units. That is, in general, support from these two sources is—in its entirety—public support. Investment income received by the organization is included in the denominator of the support fraction but not in the numerator.

Donors who have a defined relationship to one another (such as husband and wife) must share a single 2 percent limitation. Multiple contributions from any one source are aggregated over the measuring period.

In constructing the support ratio, an organization must exclude from both the numerator and the denominator of the support fraction amounts received from the exercise or performance of its tax-exempt functions. However, an organization will not be treated as meeting this support test if it receives almost all of its support from receipts from related activities (fee-for-service or "exempt function" revenue) and an insignificant amount of its support from governmental units and/or the general public.

An example may clarify these rules. Assume that a charitable organization received gifts and grants during its most recent four accounting periods in the total amount of $250,000 (year one, $25,000; year two, $50,000; year three, $75,000; and year four, $100,000), along with $35,000 in investment income and $10,000 in exempt function revenue. Thus, the denominator of the support ratio is $285,000 ($250,000 in gifts and $35,000 in investment income); the numerator of the support ratio therefore must (if the organization is to qualify as a donative one) be at least $95,000; and the two percent amount is $5,700. Consequently, in this illustration, for the organization to qualify as a donative one, the numerator of the support fraction must, as noted, be at least $95,000, with that numerator generally consisting of gifts and grants where no more than $5,700 is from any one source.

In this illustration, if an individual gave $10,000 to the organization (for example, $5,000 in year one and $5,000 in year two), the $10,000 would be part of the denominator amount of $285,000 but only $5,700 of the $10,000 would be a part of the numerator amount (public support). By contrast, if the $10,000 was in the form of a grant from a donative organization or a governmental agency, all of the $10,000 would be a part of both the numerator and the denominator of the support fraction.

In this example, assuming the other gift support ($240,000) is from the "public," the numerator of the support fraction is $245,700 ($240,000 plus $5,700) and the denominator of the fraction is the $285,000, so that the public support ratio is 86 percent ($245,700 / $285,000). Thus, this organization qualifies as a donative charitable organization as of this stage of its existence and, therefore, is not a private foundation.

Special rules accord donative charity classification to organizations that meet a so-called "facts and circumstances" test (such as by having a public governing board, publicly available facilities or programs, and at least 10 percent of public support) or that constitute "community trusts."

The fee-based charitable organization is an entity that normally receives more than one-third of its support from (1) gifts and grants, (2) membership fees, and/or (3) gross receipts from the performance of exempt functions. Amounts that are eligible for the numerator of this support fraction are those that are derived from so-called "permitted sources," which are governmental agencies, the three basic types of institutions described above, donative charities, and persons who are not "disqualified persons" (described next). The denominator of this support fraction also includes any net income from unrelated activities (see Chapter 12).

To qualify as a fee-based charitable organization, the organization also must normally receive no more than one-third of its support in the form of investment income.

There is some commonality with the donative organization rules and the fee-based organization rules, in that both measure support over the most recent four years and both utilize a one-third support fraction.

However, there are also some major differences, such as the fact that exempt function revenue can count as public support for the fee-based organization. There is, nonetheless, this limitation: These receipts are eligible for inclusion in the numerator of the support fraction to the extent that the receipts, from any one source, do not exceed the greater of $5,000 or 1 percent of the organization's support for the year involved.

There is a limitation on the eligibility of gifts and grants under the rules pertaining to fee-based charitable organizations, derived from the point noted previously that public support cannot come from "disqualified persons." While disqualified persons include an organization's directors and officers, and members of their families, the term also includes any person (be it an individual, trust, estate, corporation, or other entity) that contributes or bequeaths an aggregate amount of more than $5,000, where that amount is more than 2 percent of the total contributions and bequests received by the organization (known as "substantial contributors").

To illustrate these rules for fee-based organizations, assume the same facts as in the example concerning the donative charity, except that, for purposes of this illustration, also assume the organization has only been in existence for the four fiscal periods. (As noted, the two percent amount is calculated, for purposes of donative organizations, by utilizing as the base the most recent four years' support, while, for purposes of fee-based organizations, the base is the organization's support over the totality of its existence.)

Therefore, under this example, the base by which the two percent is calculated for purposes of fee-based organizations is $250,000; the two percent amount is thus $5,000. The denominator of the support fraction is $295,000; for the organization to avoid being categorized as a private foundation, the numerator of the support fraction must be at least $98,334. Assume that the $10,000 in exempt function revenue is not limited by the one percent rule, so that it fully qualifies as public support.

No part of the contribution of the $10,000 can count as public support since it is from a substantial contributor (that is, the gift is in excess of $5,000 and of the two percent threshold). If the balance of the gifts is from permitted sources, the numerator is $250,000 ($240,000 in public contributions and $10,000 in exempt function revenue), so that the public support ratio is 85 percent ($250,000 / $295,000). This organization thus qualifies as a fee-based charitable organization as of this stage of its existence and, therefore, is not a private foundation.

Supporting Organizations

Another category of charitable organization that is deemed not to be a private foundation is the *supporting organization.*

A supporting organization is an entity that is sufficiently related, structurally or operationally, to one or more of the institutions or publicly supported organizations referenced above. (For simplicity, these qualified supported organizations will be referred to as "public charities.") A supporting organization must be organized, and at all times operated, exclusively for the benefit of, to perform the functions of, or to carry out the purposes of one or more public charities.

The supporting organization must be operated, supervised, or controlled by or in connection with one or more public charities. Thus, the relationship must be one of three types: (1) operated, supervised or controlled by, (2) supervised or controlled in connection with, or (3) operated in connection with.

The distinguishing feature of the first of these relationships is the presence of a substantial degree of direction by one or more public charities over the policies, programs, and activities of the supporting organizations—a relationship comparable to that of a subsidiary and a parent.

The distinguishing feature of the second of these relationships is the presence of common supervision or control by the persons supervising or controlling both the supporting organization and the public charity or public charities to ensure that the supporting organization will be responsive to the needs and requirements of the supported organization(s)—the "brother-sister" relationship.

The distinguishing feature of the third of these relationships is that the supporting organization is responsive to and significantly involved in the operation of one or more public charities. In amplification of this requirement, there is a "responsiveness test" and an "integral part test"—and two ways to meet each test.

A supporting organization may not be controlled directly or indirectly by one or more disqualified persons, other than those who are only foundation managers.

While most supported organizations are charitable entities, it is possible to structure a relationship where the supported organization is a tax-exempt social welfare, agricultural, labor, or trade or professional organization.

Special Rules for New Organizations

As the foregoing indicates, some charitable organizations can avoid private foundation classification solely by reason of their tax status as one of the institutions or as a supporting organization. Others achieve this end by demonstrating the requisite extent of public support.

Of course, a newly created organization lacks a financial history by which to ascertain public support. In these instances, the IRS will act only on the basis of a proposed budget.

Where an organization's nonprivate foundation status is based upon its classification as to what it is programmatically (for example, a church, university, college, school, hospital, or supporting organization), the IRS will issue a "definitive ruling." However, where the nonprivate foundation classification is predicated on the organization's prospective ability to function as a publicly supported organization (that is, one of the institutions, a donative charitable organization, or a fee-based charitable organization), the IRS will issue an "advance ruling."

The advance ruling protects the organization from classification as a private foundation during the entity's "advance ruling period." The advance ruling period is measured by the organization's first five fiscal periods, with the first year not counted as a full year where it consists of less than eight months.

Planning Considerations

A charitable organization that desires to avoid classification as a private foundation is likely to have to engage in some financial planning to that end. For the institutions, that is not the case, just as it is not the case for those organizations that intend, from the outset, to be classified as supporting organizations.

But, for those organizations that desire to be regarded as publicly supported (essentially the donative and fee-based charities), the matter may be somewhat more complicated. Also, the planning may be different for the advance ruling period than for the period following.

An organization that can expect to receive nearly all of its support in the form of many relatively small gifts will have no trouble in achieving either donative or fee-based status. Likewise, an organization that is essentially dues-based will be a fee-based entity, although not a donative entity. An organization that anticipates most of its financial support as exempt function revenue must look to the category of fee-based organization, rather than the category of donative organization, for relief from the private foundation rules, while the reverse is probably the case for the organization that is relying largely on government grants (not contracts) for support.

Many organizations, during their formative years, rely on just a few sources of financial support (for example, one or more private foundations and/or makers of large gifts). For these entities, compliance with either the donative organization rules or the fee-based organization rules—particularly during the advance ruling period—can be difficult (if not impossible). Under the fee-based organization rules, these sources of support are likely to be "substantial contributors," so that none of their support is eligible for treatment as public support. In these circumstances, the outcome will be more favorable where the donative organization rules are applied, inasmuch as at least the amount from each of these sources up to the 2 percent threshold can count as public support.

Compliance with either the donative organization rules or the fee-based organization rules at any time (including as of the close of the advance ruling period) is all that is required. An organization is not locked in to one set of these rules or the other.

Some Additional Options

A charitable organization may not be able to satisfy the requirements of the rules pertaining to the institutions, the publicly supported (donative or fee-based) organizations, or the supporting organizations. There still remain alternatives to private foundation status or ways to alleviate some of the stringencies of the private foundation rules.

"FACTS AND CIRCUMSTANCES" RULE

There are some organizations that generically are not private foundations, yet nonetheless come within the broad reach of that term as defined in the federal tax law. These organizations include museums, libraries, and other entities that have substantial endowment funds. Some of these organizations may be able to qualify as other than a private foundation by means of the "facts and circumstances" test.

To meet this test, an organization must demonstrate that (1) the total amount of public support (measured using the donative organization formula) received by it is at least 10 percent of its total support, (2) it has a continuous and bona fide program for the solicitation of funds from the general public, governmental units, and/or other public charities, and (3) it has other attributes of a "public" organization.

These other characteristics include the composition of the organization's governing board (that is, whether it is representative of the general public), the extent to which its facilities or programs are publicly available, its membership dues rates, and whether its activities are likely to appeal to persons having some broad common interest or purpose.

The higher the percentage of public support, the lesser is the burden of establishing the publicly supported nature of the organization through the other factors.

BIFURCATION

Sometimes, an organization that is, or would be, a private foundation can avoid that consequence by bifurcating (splitting) into two entities. That is, each of the two organizations may be able to qualify as a nonfoundation, where they could not do so if combined.

An organization may have within it a function that, if separately evaluated, would qualify as one of the above institutions, a donative publicly supported organization, or a fee-based publicly supported organization. This function could be spun off into a separate organization and qualified as a public entity. The organization, with its remaining activities, could then become qualified as a supporting organization with respect to its offspring. In this way, one private organization becomes two public organizations.

PRIVATE OPERATING FOUNDATION

Generally, the program activity of a private foundation is the making of grants. The more a charitable organization engages in programs itself (rather than funding those of others), the greater the likelihood that it is something other than a private foundation.

Because of this inherent distinction between grant-making and program administration, a hybrid entity has evolved, one that has some of the characteristics of a private foundation and some of a public charity. This is the private operating foundation that devotes most of its earnings and much of its assets directly for the conduct of its charitable, educational, or similar purposes.

To be a private operating foundation, the organization must meet an "income" test. This requires a foundation to annually expend an amount equal to substantially all of the lesser of its adjusted net income or its "minimum investment return" directly for the active conduct of its exempt activities. For these purposes, the term "substantially all" means at least 85 percent. The minimum investment return is equal to 5 percent of the foundation's assets that are not used for charitable purposes. Thus, for example, to pass this test, an organization with $100,000 of investment (noncharitable) assets (such as securities) would have to expend at least $4,250 ($85\% \times 5\% \times \$100,000$) for that year, unless an amount equal to 85 percent of its adjusted net income is less than $4,250, in which case it would have to timely expend the actual income amount.

In addition, to qualify as an operating foundation, an organization must satisfy at least one of three other tests: (1) the "assets" test, requiring that at least 65 percent of its assets be devoted directly to the active conduct of its charitable activities; (2) the "endowment" test, requiring that the organization normally expend its funds directly for the active conduct of its charitable activities in an amount equal to at least two-thirds of its minimum investment return ($2/3 \times 5 = 3 \ 1/3$); or (3) the "support" test, requiring that (a) at least 85 percent of its support (other than investment income) be normally received from the general public and/or at least five tax-exempt organizations (that are not disqualified persons), (b) no more than 25 percent of its support is derived from any one exempt organization, and (c) no more than one-half of its support is normally received from gross investment income.

Because of these rules, a private operating foundation is not subject to the minimum payout requirements imposed upon "standard" private foundations (see below). Moreover, contributions to a private operating foundation are deductible to the full extent permitted for gifts to public charities (see Chapter 8). That is, the percentage limitations that restrict the deductibility of contributions to "standard" private foundations are inapplicable in the case of gifts to private operating foundations.

EXEMPT OPERATING FOUNDATIONS

Not content with the complexity introduced with the hybrid form of private foundation known as the operating foundation, Congress has created a hybrid of a hybrid, this one known as the *exempt operating foundation.* The word exempt in this context, however, does not mean exempt from federal income taxes (which foundations generally are anyway).

While exempt operating foundations are presumably otherwise private operating foundations, they enjoy two characteristics that the others do not. One is that grants to them are exempt from the expenditure responsibility requirements otherwise imposed upon grantor foundations (see below). The other is that exempt operating foundations do not have to pay the tax on foundations' net investment income (see below).

To be an exempt operating foundation, an organization must (in addition to satisfying the requirements to be a private operating foundation) meet three tests. It must have been publicly supported (under the donative charity or fee-based charity rules) for at least ten years or have qualified as an operating foundation as of January 1, 1983. It must have a board of directors that, during the year involved, consists of individuals at least 75 percent of whom are not so-called "disqualified individuals" and is broadly representative of the general public (presumably, using the facts and circumstances test rule). Third, an exempt operating foundation must not have an officer who is a disqualified individual at any time during the year involved.

To be an exempt operating foundation, an organization must have a ruling from the IRS to that effect. However, one of the anomalies of the law in this area is that an organization that is able to qualify as an exempt operating foundation is also able to qualify under the facts and circumstances test—and thereby avoid all of the private foundation rules!

FACING THE INEVITABLE

Failing compliance with any of the foregoing rules, a charitable organization will be classified as a *private foundation*. This means that the organization is subject to a battery of stringent requirements that are not applicable to any other type of tax-exempt organization, charitable or otherwise.

Nonetheless, facts and/or the law can change. Thus, an organization may, later in its existence, shift from a private foundation to a private operating foundation (or perhaps to an exempt operating foundation). Or, a private foundation can terminate its private foundation status and become a public charity.

The point is that the private/public status of a charitable organization can be changed at any time. The same is true, by the way, with respect to nonprivate foundations, which can change the nature of their public charity status at any time, if the facts warrant. For example, a donative charity can switch to a fee-based charity (or vice-versa) very easily, and a supporting organization can convert to a publicly supported charity (or vice-versa).

THE ONEROUS RULES

For some pages now, we have been talking about a battery of stringent and onerous rules imposed by law only upon private foundations. What are these rules?

There are many. Taking them in no particular order, they are:

- Rules concerning "self-dealing"
- Rules forcing a minimum payout (grant-making) amount
- Rules limiting the extent of holdings of businesses
- Rules pertaining to the nature of investments
- Rules concerning the nature and scope of program
- Rules imposing a tax on net investment income

- Rules making it quite unlikely that one private foundation will make a grant to another private foundation
- Rules forcing more detailed annual reporting (see Chapter 7)
- Rules making charitable giving to private foundations less attractive (see Chapter 8)

The term *self-dealing* means a transaction between, directly or indirectly, a private foundation and a disqualified person. Generally, these transactions include sales or exchanges of property; leases of property; lending of money or other extensions of credit; furnishings of goods, services, or facilities; payments of unreasonable compensation; and transfers to, or uses by or for the benefit of, disqualified persons of the income or assets of a private foundation. There are many exceptions to the self-dealing rules.

A private foundation must annually expend for charitable purposes an amount equal to 5 percent of the value of its investment assets. This is known as the *distributable amount,* determined by calculating the foundation's "minimum investment return." Consequently, a private foundation must achieve at least a 5 percent return on its principal or it must use part of its assets to satisfy this minimum payout requirement. The amounts expended must constitute "qualifying distributions," which essentially are grants for charitable purposes (including "set-asides") and reasonable administrative expenditures. These rules thus require valuation of the investment assets (which do not include assets used for charitable purposes) and place limits on the extent to which grant administrative expenses can be qualifying distributions.

Generally, a private foundation, and its disqualified persons, may not hold more than 20 percent of a business enterprise. This means voting stock in a corporation, units in a partnership, and other forms of holdings in a business enterprise. Allowable holdings are termed "permitted holdings" and holdings that are not allowable are "excess business holdings." However, if effective control of a business is in unrelated parties, a private foundation and its disqualified persons may hold as much as 35 percent of a business enterprise. For these purposes, the term "business enterprise" does not include a so-called "functionally related business" or a business at least 95 percent of the income of which is derived from passive sources.

A private foundation may not invest any amount in a manner as to jeopardize the carrying out of any of its charitable purposes. The law does not define this term but it basically means highly speculative investments. These rules do not apply to *program related investments.*

A private foundation is expected to avoid making "taxable expenditures." Generally, a taxable expenditure is an amount paid or incurred to carry on propaganda, influence legislation, influence the outcome of a public election, make a variety of grants to individuals, make a variety of grants to organizations where the foundation failed to properly exercise "expenditure responsibility," or for any other noncharitable purpose. Again, these rules entail a range of exceptions, involving such matters as voter registration drives, eligible scholarship and fellowship grants, and the making available of the results of nonpartisan, analysis, study, or research. (It is because of these rules that most private foundations are forced to confine their grant-making to public charities, and not to other types of organizations or to individuals.)

A private foundation must pay an excise tax equal to 2 percent of its net investment income for each year. "Net investment income" means interest, dividends, rents, royalties, capital gain, and the like, less allowable deductions. As noted, certain operating foundations are excused from the payment of this tax.

THE TAXES

This part of the book summarizes the many instances in which ostensibly tax-exempt organizations are in fact taxable. Those tax-exempt organizations that are classified as private foundations, and their managers, are subject to many of these taxes—all considered excise (not income) taxes.

The private foundation rules are underlain with a series of sanctions in the form of these excise taxes. These are known as the "initial" taxes and the "additional" taxes. The additional taxes are payable when an offense has occurred, one or more initial taxes are imposed, and the offense is not timely corrected.

In the case of an instance of self-dealing, the initial tax is 5 percent of the amount involved, payable by the disqualified person who participated in the wrongful act. If that tax is imposed, a foundation manager who participated in the act is subject to a tax (not to exceed $10,000) in the amount of 2 ½ percent of the amount involved, where he or she knew the act was one of self-dealing and where the participation was willful and not due to reasonable cause. The additional tax on the self-dealer is 200 percent of the amount involved. The additional tax (not to exceed $10,000) on the participating foundation manager, who refused to agree to part or all of the correction, is 50 percent of the amount involved. Two or more individuals may be jointly and severally liable for these taxes.

If a private foundation (that is not an operating foundation) fails to satisfy the payout requirements, it must pay a tax equal to 15 percent of the undistributed income. The additional tax is 100 percent of the undistributed amount.

As to excess business holdings, a private foundation must annually pay a tax equal to 5 percent of the holdings. The additional tax is 200 percent of these holdings.

If a private foundation makes a jeopardizing investment, it must pay a tax equal to 5 percent of the investment. If that tax is imposed, a foundation manager who participated in the investment is subject to a tax (not to exceed $5,000) equal to 5 percent of the investment, where he or she knew that the investment was a jeopardizing one and where the participation was willful and not due to reasonable cause. The additional tax on the foundation is 25 percent of the amount of the investment. The additional tax (not to exceed $10,000) on the manager, who refused to agree to part or all of the removal from jeopardy, is 5 percent of the amount of the investment. Two or more individuals may be jointly and severally liable for these taxes.

The initial tax on a private foundation for the making of a taxable expenditure is 10 percent of the amount involved. An initial tax (not to exceed $5,000 per taxable expenditure) is also imposed upon every foundation manager who agreed to the making of a taxable expenditure, where he or she knew it was a taxable expenditure, where the making of the taxable expenditure was willful, and where it was not due to reasonable cause. The additional tax on the private foundation is 100 percent of the expenditure. The additional tax (not to exceed $10,000 per expenditure) on a manager of a private foundation, where he or she refused to agree to part or all of the correction, is 50 percent of the amount of the taxable expenditure. Again, two or more individuals may be jointly and severally liable for these taxes.

CONCLUSION

There is no advantage to classification as a private foundation. Private foundation status should be avoided whenever possible. This classification brings a battery of stringent rules to restrict the operations of a charitable organization and decrease the tax advantages of charitable giving to it. Private foundation categorization means that the organization, and in many instances its directors or officers, are subject to very onerous taxes. These tax rules are very technical and it is all too easy for an innocent misstep to lead to heavy taxation. Probably the most useful thing a lawyer or other tax professional can do for a charitable organization is to lead it (if at all possible) to public charity status.

——————— Focus on the Campaign to ——————— Clean Up America

The Campaign is organized and will be operated to function as a charitable organization that is not a private foundation. Because of the nature of its programs (see Chapter 6), it does not qualify as one of the institutional charities. Lacking any formal relationship to another nonprofit organization, it does not qualify as a supporting organization.

Because of its funding—principally grants and contributions—the Campaign is to be qualified as a donative publicly supported charity. This status will be under the general rules; that is, the "facts and circumstances" test will be inapplicable.

Being a new organization, the Campaign is ineligible for a definitive ruling as to its publicly supported organization status. However, it is entitled to an advance ruling as to that status.

12

When Possible, Make It Related

The previous chapter summarized the complexity of a series of laws levying a variety of taxes in an array of situations on many persons. This chapter reviews a body of law where the tax structure as such is very simple but where the rules leading to imposition of the tax are infinitely complex.

THE TAXES

Since 1950, the law of tax-exempt organizations has divided the activities of exempt entities into two categories: those that are related to the performance of tax-exempt functions and those that are not. The latter grouping of activities, termed *unrelated activities,* is subject to tax. That is, the gross revenues associated with such activities are taxable, taking into account the deductible expenses generated by those activities.

For organizations that are incorporated, the net revenue from unrelated activities is subject to the regular federal corporate income tax. Organizations that are not corporations (such as trusts) have their unrelated activities subject to the federal tax on individuals. Unlike the private foundation rules (see Chapter 11), the existing law concerning related and unrelated activities does not impose any taxes upon the directors and officers of nonprofit entities.

Therefore, to decide what activities of an otherwise tax-exempt organization are taxable, one must first ascertain which are related to exempt functions and which are not. The judgments that go into answering this inquiry are at the heart of the greatest controversy in law facing nonprofit organizations today. The existing legal structure on the point is at once simple and intricate; it is under immense challenge.

THE UNRELATED INCOME RULES

The treatment of unrelated activities represents one of the most dynamic and controversial aspect of federal tax law facing tax-exempt organizations. Although the rules were enacted in 1950, it was not until the early 1970s that this body of tax law emerged as the most important to nonprofit organizations.

Introduction

The unrelated income rules were significantly rewritten by Congress in 1969. The original concept underlying these rules was that of the *outside* business owned and perhaps operated by a tax-exempt organization. However, in 1969, Congress significantly expanded the reach of these rules by authorizing the IRS to evaluate activities conducted by nonprofit organizations internally—so-called *inside* activities.

The objective of the unrelated business income tax is to prevent unfair competition between tax-exempt organizations and for-profit, commercial enterprises. The rules are intended to place the unrelated business activities of an exempt organization on the same tax basis as the nonexempt business with which it competes.

To be tax-exempt, a nonprofit organization must be organized and operated primarily for exempt purposes (see Chapter 4). The federal tax law allows a tax-exempt organization to engage in a certain amount of income-producing activity that is unrelated to exempt purposes. Where the organization derives net income from one or more unrelated business activities, known formally as *unrelated business taxable income,* it is subject to tax on that income. An organization's tax exemption will be denied or revoked if an inappropriate portion of its activities is not in furtherance of one or more exempt purposes.

Business activities may preclude initial qualification of an otherwise tax-exempt organization as a charitable or other entity. This would occur through failure to satisfy the *operational test,* that looks to see whether the organization is being operated principally for exempt purposes. Likewise, an organization will not meet the *organizational test* if its articles of organization empower it, as more than an insubstantial part of its functions, to carry on activities that are not in furtherance of its exempt purpose.

A nonprofit organization may nonetheless satisfy the operational test even when it operates a trade or business as a substantial part of its activities, as long as the trade or business is in furtherance of the organization's exempt purpose and the organization is not operated for the primary purpose of carrying on an unrelated trade or business. If the organization's primary purpose is carrying on a trade or business for profit, it is expressly denied exemption on the grounds that it is a *feeder organization,* notwithstanding the fact that all of its profits are payable to one or more tax-exempt organizations.

The law in this area is on the brink of revision. The House Subcommittee on Oversight, a unit of the House Committee on Ways and Means, held five days of hearings on the subject in 1987. Specific alterations in this body of law are coming and they may be sweeping. Ironically, however, a large part of the impetus for these hearings was the charge by the business community of unfair competition. The difference between the circumstances in the 1950s and those in the 1980s is that the competing activities of nonprofit organizations in the 1950s were of the unrelated variety, while in the 1980s, the competing activities are those that are, under existing law definitions, related to exempt functions.

Prior to enactment of the unrelated income rules, the law embodied the so-called *destination of income* test. Pursuant to this standard, the law merely required that, for an organization to be tax-exempt, the net profits of the organization be used in furtherance of tax-exempt purposes. That is, the test did not consider the source of the profits, thereby tolerating forms of unfair competition.

Thus, in adopting these rules in 1950 and in amplifying them in 1969, Congress has not prohibited commercial ventures by nonprofit organizations nor has it levied taxes only on the receipts of businesses that bear no relation at all to the tax-exempt purposes of nonprofit organizations. Instead, it struck a balance between, as the Supreme Court phrased it in 1986, "its two objectives of encouraging benevolent enterprise and restraining unfair competition."

Essentially, for an activity of a tax-exempt organization to be taxed, three tests must be satisfied. First, the activity must constitute a "trade or business." Second, the activity must be "regularly carried on." Third, the activity must not be "substantially related" to the tax-exempt purposes of the organization. However, there are many exceptions to these rules that exempt from taxation certain forms of activity and types of income.

The unrelated income rules are in a peculiar state of affairs these days. Despite the intricacies of the statutory scheme, the courts are simultaneously developing additional and sometimes different criteria for assessing the presence of unrelated business. It is out of the latter context that the doctrine of *commerciality* is emerging. The result: considerable confusion as to what the law in this area is and extensive judgmental leeway on the part of the courts and the IRS in applying it.

Affected Tax-Exempt Organizations

Nearly all types of tax-exempt organizations are subject to the unrelated income rules. They include religious organizations (including churches), educational organizations (including universities, colleges, and schools), health care organizations (including hospitals), scientific organizations, and other charitable organizations. Beyond the realm of charitable entities, the rules are applicable to social welfare organizations (including advocacy groups), labor organizations (including unions), trade and professional associations, fraternal organizations, employee benefit funds, and veterans' organizations.

Special rules tax all income not related to exempt functions (including investment income) of social clubs, homeowners' associations, and political organizations.

Certain organizations are not generally subject to the unrelated income rules, simply because they are not allowed to engage in any active business endeavors. This is the case, for example, with respect to private foundations and title-holding organizations. As to the former, the operation of an active business (externally or internally) by a private foundation would likely trigger application of the excess business holdings restrictions (see Chapter 11).

Instrumentalities of the United States, like nearly all governmental agencies, are exempt from the unrelated business rules. However, the unrelated income rules are applicable to colleges and universities that are agencies or instrumentalities of a government, as well as to corporations owned by such colleges and universities.

Trade or Business Defined

For the purpose of the federal tax rules, the term *trade or business* includes any activity that is carried on for the production of income from the sale of goods or the performance of services. Accordingly, most activities that would constitute a trade or business under basic tax law principles are considered a trade or business for purposes of the unrelated income rules.

This definition of the term *trade or business* embraces nearly every activity of a tax-exempt organization. Absent a specific statutory exemption (see below), only passive investment activities generally escape this classification. In this sense, every tax-exempt organization should be viewed as a bundle of activities, each of which is a trade or business. (It must be emphasized that this definition has nothing to do with whether a particular activity is related or unrelated; there are related businesses and unrelated businesses.)

Thus, the IRS is empowered to examine each of the activities in the bundle of activities comprising an organization in search of unrelated business. Each activity in the bundle can be examined as though it existed wholly independently of the others; an unrelated activity cannot, as a matter of law, be hidden from scrutiny by tucking it in among a host of related activities. As Congress chose to state the principle, "an activity does not lose identity as a trade or business merely because it is carried on within a larger aggregate of similar activities or within a larger complex of other endeavors which may, or may not, be related to the exempt purposes of the organization." This is known, in the jargon of tax law professionals, as the *fragmentation rule.* For example, the fragmentation rule allows the IRS to treat the income from advertising in an exempt organization's magazine as revenue derived from an unrelated business, even though otherwise the publication of the magazine is a related business.

The federal tax law also states that, "[w]here an activity carried on for profit constitutes an unrelated trade or business, no part of such trade or business shall be excluded from such classification merely because it does not result in profit." In other words, just because an activity results in a loss in a particular year, that is insufficient basis for failing to treat the activity as an unrelated one (including reporting it as such to the IRS). Conversely, simply because an activity generates a profit is not alone supposed to lead to the conclusion that the activity is unrelated (although there are many in the IRS and on court benches who are likely to leap to that conclusion).

Just as *profits* are not built into the formal definition of the term *trade or business,* so too is the element of *unfair competition* missing from that definition. This is somewhat surprising, given that unfair competition is the driving force behind the unrelated income rules. Nonetheless, the IRS and the courts sometimes use the factor of "competition" in assessing whether an activity is related or unrelated to exempt functions.

Another aspect of the tax law definition of *trade or business* is the absence of the element of *commerciality.* That is, there is nothing in the statutory law that generally permits the IRS and judges to conclude that an activity is unrelated solely because it is conducted in a commercial manner, which basically means in a manner similar to the way a comparable activity is carried on by for-profit businesses. But they do it anyway.

Definition of Regularly Carried On

To be considered an unrelated business, an activity of a tax-exempt organization must be *regularly carried on* by it.

Income from an activity is considered taxable only when, assuming the other criteria are satisfied, the activity is regularly carried on, as distinguished from sporadic or infrequent transactions. The factors that determine whether an activity is regularly carried on are the frequency and continuity of the activities, and the manner in which the activities are pursued. (It is in this context that the statutory law comes the closest to using a doctrine of *commerciality.*)

These factors must be evaluated in light of the purpose of the unrelated business income tax, which is to place tax-exempt organizations' business activities upon the same tax basis as their nonexempt business competitors. Thus, specific business activities of a tax-exempt organization will generally be deemed to be regularly carried on if they manifest a frequency and continuity, and are pursued in a manner, generally similar to comparable commercial activities of nonexempt organizations.

Where income-producing activities are performed by commercial organizations on a year-round basis, the performance of those activities for a period of only a few weeks does not constitute the regular carrying on of a trade or business. Similarly, occasional or annual income-producing activities, such as fund-raising events, do not amount to a business that is regularly carried on. However, the conduct of year-round business activities, such as the operation of a parking lot, for one day each week would constitute the regular carrying on of a business. Where commercial entities normally undertake income-producing activities on a seasonal basis, the conduct of the activities by an exempt organization during a significant portion of the season is deemed the regular conduct of that activity.

Thus, a trade or business is regularly carried on by a tax-exempt organization where the attributes of the activity are similar to the commercial activities of nonexempt organizations.

Definition of Unrelated Trade or Business

The term *unrelated trade or business* is defined to mean "any trade or business the conduct of which [by a tax-exempt organization] is not substantially related (aside from the need of such organization for income or funds or the use it makes of the profits derived) to the exercise or performance by such organization of its charitable, educational, or other purpose or function constituting the basis for its exemption." The parenthetical clause means that an activity is not related simply because the organization uses the net revenue from the activity for exempt purposes.

Thus, the revenue from a regularly conducted trade or business is subject to tax, unless the business activity is substantially related to the accomplishment of the organization's exempt purpose. It is clear, then, that the key to taxation or nontaxation in this area is the meaning of the words *substantially related.* Yet the law tells us merely that, to be substantially related, the activity must have a *substantial causal relationship* to the accomplishment of an exempt purpose.

The fact that an asset is essential to the conduct of an organization's exempt activities does not shield the unrelated income from that taxation where that income was produced by that asset. The income-producing activities must still meet the causal relationship test if the income is not to be subject to tax. This issue arises when a tax-exempt organization owns a facility or other assets that are put to a dual use. For example, the operation of an auditorium as a motion picture theater for public entertainment in the evenings is treated as an unrelated activity even though the theater is used exclusively for exempt purposes during the daytime hours. The fragmentation rule allows this type of use of a single asset to be split into two businesses.

A related concept is that activities should not be conducted on a scale larger than is reasonably necessary for the performance of exempt functions. Activities in excess of the needs of exempt functions constitute unrelated businesses.

The law is filled with court cases and IRS rulings providing illustrations of related and unrelated activities. Colleges and universities operate dormitories and bookstores as related activities but can be taxable on travel tours and sports camps. Hospitals may operate gift shops, snack bars, and parking lots as related activities but may be taxable on sales of pharmaceuticals to the general public. Museums may, without taxation, sell items reflective of their collections but be taxable on the sale of souvenirs. Trade associations may find themselves taxable on sales of items and particular services to members, while dues and subscription revenue are nontaxable. Fundraising events may be characterized as unrelated activities, particularly when compensation is paid or when the activity is regularly carried on.

Definition of Unrelated Business Taxable Income

As noted, to be subject to the unrelated income rules, an activity must satisfy (or, depending upon one's point of view, fail) three tests. These tests are built into the definition of the term *unrelated business taxable income.*

That term is defined as "the gross income derived by any [exempt] organization from any unrelated trade or business . . . regularly carried on by it, less the deductions allowed . . . [under federal tax law in general] which are directly connected with the carrying on of such trade or business."

Both this gross income and allowable deductions are computed in conformance with the "modifications" discussed below.

In the case of an organization covered by the unrelated income rules that is a foreign organization, its unrelated business taxable income is "its unrelated business taxable income which is derived from sources within the United States and which is not effectively connected with the conduct of a trade or business within the United States" and "its unrelated business taxable income which is effectively connected with the conduct of a trade or business within the United States."

If a trade or business regularly carried on by a partnership of which a tax-exempt organization is a member (see Chapter 16) is an unrelated trade or business with respect to the organization, the organization, in computing its unrelated business taxable income, must (subject to the modifications) include its share (whether or not distributed) of the gross income of the partnership from the unrelated business and its share of the partnership deductions directly connected with the gross income. However, a tax-exempt organization's share (whether or not distributed) of the gross income of a publicly traded partnership must be treated as gross income derived from an unrelated business, and its share of the partnership deductions is allowed in computing unrelated business taxable income.

Tax-exempt organizations are subject to tax on their unrelated business taxable income at ordinary corporate tax rates or at individual rates if the organization is not incorporated.

Exempted Activities

Despite the foregoing general rules, certain businesses conducted by tax-exempt organizations are expressly exempted from taxation.

Exempted from taxation is a trade or business "in which substantially all the work in carrying on such trade or business is performed for the organization without compensation." Thus, if a tax-exempt organization conducts an unrelated business, with services substantially provided by volunteers, the net revenue from that business is not taxable. For example, this exemption protects from taxation many ongoing charitable fund-raising activities.

Also exempted is a trade or business which is carried on by the organization "primarily for the convenience of its members, students, patients, officers, or employees." However, this exception is only available to organizations that are charitable, educational, and the like, or are governmental colleges and universities.

Further exempted is a trade or business "which is the selling of merchandise, substantially all of which has been received by the organization as gifts or contributions." For example, this exemption shelters the work of exempt thrift stores from taxation.

The term *unrelated trade or business* does not include so-called *qualified public entertainment activities.* A public entertainment activity is any entertainment or recreational activity of a kind traditionally conducted at fairs or expositions promoting agricultural and educational purposes, including, but not limited to, any activity one of the purposes of which is to attract the public to fairs or expositions or to promote the breeding of animals or the development of products or equipment.

To be *qualified,* a public entertainment activity must be conducted in (1) conjunction with an international, national, state, regional, or local fair or exposition, (2) accordance with the provisions of state law which permit the activity to be operated or conducted solely by a qualifying organization or by a governmental agency, or (3) accordance with the provisions of state law which permit a qualifying organization to be granted a license to conduct no more than 20 days of the activity on payment to the state of a lower percentage of the revenue from the licensed activity than the state requires from nonqualifying organizations.

For purposes of the public entertainment activities exception, a *qualifying organization* is a tax-exempt charitable, social welfare, or labor organization that regularly conducts, as one of its substantial exempt purposes, an agricultural and educational fair or exposition.

The term *unrelated trade or business* also does not include so-called qualified convention and trade show activities. A convention and trade show activity is any activity of a kind traditionally conducted at conventions, annual meetings, or trade shows, including, but not limited to, any activity one of the purposes of which is to attract persons in an industry generally (without regard to membership in the sponsoring organization) as well as members of the public to the show for the purpose of displaying industry products or to stimulate interest in, and demand for, industry products or services, or to educate persons engaged in the industry in the development of new products and services or new rules and regulations affecting the industry.

To be *qualified,* a convention and trade show activity must be carried out by a qualifying organization in conjunction with an international, national, state, regional, or local convention, annual meeting, or show conducted by a qualifying organization if one of the purposes of the organization in sponsoring the activity is the promotion and stimulation of interest in, and demand for, the products and services of that industry in general or to educate persons in attendance regarding new developments or products and services related to the exempt activities of the organization, and the show is designed to achieve the requisite purpose through the character of the exhibits and the extent of the industry products displayed.

For purposes of the convention and trade show activity exception, a *qualifying organization* is a charitable, social welfare, or labor organization, or trade association, that regularly conducts as one of its substantial exempt purposes a show which stimulates interest in, and demand for, the products of a particular industry or segment of such industry or which educates persons in attendance regarding new developments or products and services related to the exempt activities of the organization.

For a tax-exempt hospital, the concept of unrelated trade or business does not include the furnishing of one or more of the services allowable to certain cooperative hospital service organizations to one or more other tax-exempt hospitals if (1) the services are furnished solely to hospitals that have facilities to serve no more than 100 inpatients; (2) the services, if performed on its own behalf by the recipient hospital, would constitute exempt activities of that institution; and (3) the services are provided for a fee or cost which does not exceed the actual cost of providing the services, with the cost including straight line depreciation and a reasonable amount for return on capital goods used to provide the services.

The concept of unrelated trade or business also does not include the conduct of bingo games. For this purpose, "a bingo game" is any game of bingo (1) of a type in which usually the wagers are placed, the winners are determined, and the distribution of prizes or other property is made, in the presence of all persons placing wagers in the game, (2) the conduct of which is not an activity ordinarily carried out on a commercial basis, and (3) the conduct of which does not violate any state or local law.

For a charitable, veterans', or other organization, to which contributions are deductible, the term *unrelated trade or business* does not include activities relating to the distribution of low cost articles if the distribution of the articles is incidental to the solicitation of charitable contributions. A *low cost article* is one that has a cost, not in excess of $5.00 (indexed for inflation), to the organization that distributes, or has distributed for it, the item. A *distribution* qualifies under this rule if it is not made at the request of the distributee, it is made without the express consent of the distributee, and the articles that are distributed are accompanied by a request for a charitable contribution by the distributee to the organization and a statement that the distributee may retain the article whether or not a contribution is made.

Also, for a charitable, veterans', or other organization, to which contributions are deductible, the term *trade or business* does not include exchanging with another like organization the names and addresses of donors to or members of the organization, or the renting of these lists to another like organization.

Other exemption rules apply with respect to certain local organizations of employees; the conduct of certain games of chance; and the rental of poles by mutual or cooperative telephone or electric companies.

Exempted Income

Certain types of income are exempt from the unrelated income tax.

Because the unrelated income tax applies with respect to active businesses conducted by tax-exempt organizations, most types of *passive* income are exempt from taxation. This exemption generally covers dividends, interest, securities loans payments, annuities, royalties, rents, capital gains, and gains on the lapse or termination of options written by exempt organizations.

However, there are important exceptions to this exemption for passive income. One is that income in the form of rent, royalties, and the like from an active business undertaking is taxable; that is, merely labeling an income flow as rent, royalties, and so forth does not make it tax-free. Second, the unrelated debt-financed income rules override the general exemption for passive income. Third, interest, annuities, royalties, and rents from a controlled corporation may be taxable.

There are three exemptions pertaining to the conduct of research. Income derived from research for the United States, or any of its agencies or instrumentalities, or any state or political subdivision thereof is exempt from taxation. In the case of a college, university, or hospital, income derived from research performed for any person is exempted. In the case of an organization operated primarily for purposes of carrying on fundamental research, the results of which are freely available to the general public, income derived from research performed for any person is exempted.

There is a specific deduction of $1,000.

Use of Subsidiaries

As discussed more fully in Chapter 15, some tax-exempt organizations elect to spin off their unrelated activities to related taxable subsidiaries, so that the tax on the net income of the unrelated activity will not be borne directly by the exempt organization. This can happen where the managers of the tax-exempt organization are adverse to reporting any unrelated income or where the unrelated activity is too large in relation to related activity.

As to the transfer of funds from a taxable subsidiary to an exempt parent, that income will be taxable as unrelated income to the parent if it is interest, rents, royalties, or capital gains, where the parent has, directly or indirectly, 80 percent or more control of the subsidiary. However, if the subsidiary pays dividends to the tax-exempt parent, the dividends are not taxable to the parent because they are not deductible by the subsidiary.

CONCLUSION

The unrelated income rules represent an attempt by Congress to prevent tax-exempt organizations from unfairly competing with for-profit businesses. These rules generally equalize the tax treatment of unrelated business activities by segregating them, for tax purposes, from the other activities of tax-exempt organizations and taxing them as though they are free-standing business undertakings.

For an activity to be taxable under these rules, it must be a trade or business that is regularly carried on and that is not substantially related to the performance of tax-exempt functions. The use by a tax-exempt organization of the net revenue from an unrelated business to fund related activities is not enough to convert the unrelated activity into a related one.

The law provides a variety of exemptions, whereby certain activities and certain forms of income are excepted from taxation. The most important of these exemptions is for passive income.

In computing taxable unrelated income, a tax-exempt organization may utilize all business expense deductions, to the extent the expenses are directly related to the conduct of the unrelated business.

As tax-exempt organizations endeavor to generate additional income in these days of declining governmental support, proposed adverse tax reform, more sophisticated management, and greater pressure for more services, they are increasingly drawn to fee-for-service activities, some of which may be unrelated to their exempt purposes.

This phenomenon, coupled with the increasing proclivity of the courts to find activities unrelated because they are "commercial" and the unrest over ostensibly unfair competition between tax-exempt organizations and for-profit entities, is clear evidence that this aspect of the law of tax-exempt organizations is constantly evolving and will be reshaped, partly by Congress.

This federal tax law subject is among the most fast-paced of any. All indications are that this trend will continue.

FOCUS ON THE CAMPAIGN TO CLEAN UP AMERICA

The Campaign does not initially intend to conduct any unrelated business activities. Its fee-for-service revenue will be insubstantial and that is expected to come from related businesses (such as seminars and the sale of publications).

However, as the Campaign grows and becomes known, it may find that it can profitably engage in one or more unrelated businesses. For example, it could sell trash bags and like supplies and equipment. It could provide property maintenance services, for individuals or communities. It could consult with government agencies in the development and maintenance of large-scale beautification programs.

Some of these unrelated activities could be conducted within the organization. Others could be undertaken by means of one or more for-profit subsidiaries.

13

The Lobbying
Constraints—and Taxes

Congress has long been concerned with legislative activities—lobbying—
by nonprofit organizations. This concern is particularly manifested in the
federal tax law pertaining to charitable organizations and trade, business,
and professional associations. Moreover, the Treasury Department and
within it the IRS have promulgated extremely stringent regulations and
rules in an attempt to restrict lobbying by nonprofit organizations, most
notably charitable groups. The federal courts have upheld the government
in its efforts to enforce these constraints.

Regulation in this area is very much a current matter. Congress, in 1987,
introduced new rules in an effort to further limit lobbying by charitable organizations and, to some extent, other nonprofit organizations. Likewise, the
Treasury Department and the IRS have recently issued sweeping regulations
in an effort to curb even further lobbying by public charities and related
organizations. (In 1969, Congress adjusted the tax law by flatly prohibiting
lobbying by private foundations.)

In addition to the tax law, other federal law imposes meaningful constraints on lobbying by nonprofit organizations. For example, the Postal
Service will not grant second or third class mail privileges to otherwise qualifying nonprofit groups whose primary purpose is lobbying. Also, under authority of the Federal Regulation of Lobbying Act, lobbying organizations or
individual lobbyists are required to register with the clerks of the House of
Representatives and Senate.

The principal laws regulating lobbying by nonprofit organizations, however, are the federal tax laws. These rules are explored in this chapter.

LOBBYING RESTRICTIONS ON CHARITABLE ORGANIZATIONS

Organizations that are tax-exempt because they are "charitable" in nature (and, as noted, this classification includes educational, religious, scientific, and similar entities) must, to preserve the exemption, adhere to a variety of requirements. One of these is that "no substantial part of the activities" of the organization may constitute "carrying on propaganda, or otherwise attempting, to influence legislation." Due to the considerable and continuing uncertainty as to the meaning and scope of this rule, many a nonprofit organization has experienced much anguish in attempting to fathom the "substantial part" test.

The difficulties of compliance with this legislative activities limitation have been manifold. In reaction to an increasingly intolerable situation, Congress, in 1976, tried to clarify this area but failed, due in no small part to the insistence of the IRS in proposing broad and onerous rules in interpretation of the statutory law. As is so often the case with "tax reform," the law ends up being much more complicated than it was before.

The present state of the law in this area is such that there are three sets of rules. One set of rules is, as noted, applicable to private foundations (no lobbying). The other two sets of rules are available for other types of charitable organizations ("public charities"). (Again, the distinctions between public and private charities is the subject of Chapter 11.) One of these sets of rules, which is available to most public charities, must be elected by them. These are the so-called "elective rules." The third set of rules, the "general rules," are applicable to those public charities that have not or cannot come within the elective rules.

It is by no means clear as to why, as a matter of policy, it is inappropriate for a charitable organization to engage in lobbying in pursuit of its exempt purposes. The law on this subject was originally enacted in 1934, without benefit of hearings, in an effort to stop the activities of a particular organization that had antagonized some members of the U.S. Senate. Case law prior to that date suggests that lobbying may be a legitimate way for a charitable organization to pursue its exempt goals; there is nothing in the common law of charitable trusts (on which the tax law of charities is based) that specifies that lobbying by charitable groups is contrary to their status as charities. One clue as to the rationale for the prohibition was offered by the U.S. Supreme Court in 1983, when it observed that Congress, in enacting the general rules, "was concerned that exempt [charitable] organizations might use tax-deductible contributions to lobby to promote the private interests of their members." Recently, the Treasury Department expressed opposition to any relaxation of the limitation on lobbying by charitable organizations, on the grounds that liberalization of the rules would enable more nonprofit entities to become classified as charitable ones, therefore becoming eligible to attract deductible gifts, in turn helping to aggravate the federal deficit by the resulting increase in the use of the charitable contribution deduction.

Philosophical or policy considerations notwithstanding, the law is the law. Lobbying by public charities is restricted under either set of rules. In either instance, if a charitable organization loses its tax exemption due to lobbying activities, it may not convert to a tax-exempt social welfare organization (see below).

General Rules

The general rules, pertaining to lobbying by public charities, are found in the regulations, IRS rulings, and court opinions that comprise the body of law under the substantial part test. These rules label a charitable organization that has lobbying as a substantial activity an "action" organization—and, needless to say, charitable action organizations are not tax-exempt.

Legislative activities can take many forms. Some amount to "direct" lobbying, which occurs when one or more representatives of an organization make contact with a legislator and/or his or her staff, and/or the staff of legislative committees. Direct lobbying includes office visits, presentation of testimony at hearings, correspondence, publication and dissemination of material, and entertainment.

Lobbying may also be "grass roots" in form. This type of lobbying occurs when the organization urges the public to contact members of a legislative body or their staffs for the purpose of proposing, supporting, or opposing legislation.

Whether in the form of direct or grass roots lobbying, the law, under the general rules, does not differentiate between lobbying that is related to an organization's exempt purposes and lobbying that is not. The function is still lobbying and both types are subject to the proscription. However, a charitable organization that does not initiate any action with respect to pending legislation but merely responds to a request from a legislative committee to testify is not, solely because of that activity, considered an action organization. Also, a charitable organization can engage in nonpartisan analysis, study, and research and publish its results, where some of the plans and policies formulated can only be carried out through legislative enactments, without being an action organization, as long as it does not advocate the adoption of legislation or legislative action to implement its findings. In both of these instances, the organization is advancing education, not engaging in advocacy activities.

As to nonpartisan analysis, study, or research, there can be a fine line between that type of undertaking and lobbying. An organization may evaluate a subject of proposed legislation or a pending item of legislation and present to the public an objective analysis of it, as long as it does not participate in the presentation of suggested bills to a legislature and does not engage in any campaign to secure enactment of the legislation. But, if the organization's primary objective can be attained only by legislative action, it is an "action" organization. In general, then, promoting activism instead of promoting educational activities can deny an organization classification as a charitable entity.

These rules obviously apply to legislative activities—activities undertaken in connection with the championing or opposing of legislation. Therefore, it is necessary to know what does and does not constitute *legislation.* The term *legislation* has several manifestations, principally action by the U.S. Congress, a state legislative body, a local council, or similar governing body, and by the general public in a referendum, initiative, constitutional amendment, or similar procedure. Legislation does not generally include action by the executive branch, such as the promulgation of rules and regulations, nor does it include action by the independent regulatory agencies. Thus, charitable organizations can "lobby" executive branch and independent agencies, with respect to the agencies' rules, without endangering their tax-exempt status for that reason. However, in the view of the IRS, congressional action on cabinet and judicial nominees constitutes *legislating.*

The most important concept under the general rules is the meaning of the word *substantial.* As noted earlier, the law offers no formula for computing *substantial* or *insubstantial* legislative undertakings.

There are at least three ways to measure substantiality in this context. One is to determine what percentage of an organization's annual expenditures are devoted to efforts to influence legislation. Another is to apply a percentage to the legislative activities themselves, in relation to total activities. A third approach is to ascertain (usually with hindsight) if an organization had a substantial impact on the legislative process simply by virtue of its prestige and influence. Case law and IRS practice support the use of all three practices.

Nonetheless, the IRS being the IRS, the matter of substantiality in this setting is usually measured in terms of expenditures. By reason of the use of the term *substantial* in other tax contexts, it is likely that a public charity's annual outlays for lobbying can be up to 15 percent of total expenditures without causing loss of tax-exempt status. (It cannot be emphasized too strongly, however, that this guideline is that of the author's, based upon practical experience, and should not be regarded as a rule of law.)

Whatever the true measure of substantiality, it remains elusive to this date. In reports accompanying tax legislation over the years, the Senate Finance Committee characterized the state of affairs well. Thus, in 1969, the Committee wrote that "the standards as to the permissible level of [legislative] activities under the present law are so vague as to encourage subjective application of the sanction." Later, in 1976, the Finance Committee portrayed the dilemma this way: "Many believe that the standards as to the permissible level of [legislative] activities under present law are too vague and thereby tend to encourage subjective and selective enforcement."

The confusion and frustration with the substantial part test of the general rules led to enactment of the elective rules, discussed next. The chafing under the restrictions also led to litigation, challenging the general rule on constitutional law grounds. Essentially, the courts have upheld the limitation in the face of charges that it violated free speech and equal protection rights. The rationale is that the tax law does not prohibit organizations from engaging in substantial efforts to influence legislation but merely refrains from allowing the federal treasury to subsidize the lobbying efforts. As the U.S. Supreme Court stated in 1983, the constraints pass constitutional muster and "Congress has merely refused to pay for the lobbying out of public moneys."

Lobbying by charitable organizations, or on their behalf by related nonprofit organizations, was the subject of congressional hearings in March of 1987. The result was enactment of even more legislation, designed to give the general rules more strength, as part of the Revenue Act of 1987.

The 1987 legislation introduced a system of excise taxes on excess lobbying outlays for most public charities. Under these rules, if a charitable organization loses its tax exemption because of attempts to influence legislation, a tax in the amount of 5 percent of the *lobbying expenditures* is imposed each year on the organization. (Again, it must be emphasized that this tax does not apply to any organization that is under the elective rules described below or that is ineligible to make that election.) A lobbying expenditure is any amount paid or incurred by a charitable organization in carrying on propaganda or otherwise attempting to influence legislation.

A separate 5 percent tax is applicable to each of the organization's managers (its officers, directors, and key employees) who agreed to the making of the lobbying expenditures (knowing they were likely to result in revocation of its exemption), unless the agreement was not willful and due to reasonable cause. The burden of proof as to whether a manager knowingly participated in the lobbying expenditure is on the IRS. The fact that the excise tax is imposed on an organization does not itself establish that any manager of the organization is subject to the excise tax.

Elective Rules

The elective rules, regarding permissible lobbying by charitable organizations, arose from a desire to clarify the law which has been made unclear by the substantial part test. In other words, the purpose of the elective rules is to offer charitable groups some certainty as to how much lobbying they can undertake without endangering their tax-exempt status. As noted, this purpose has not been fulfilled both because the IRS has made the rules so sweeping and onerous and because so few organizations have elected to use the rules. (One day, Congress may make the elective rules mandatory.)

The elective rules utilize a tax system as well, although none of the taxes fall on individuals involved. The elective rules are not a substitute for the general rules but act as a "safe harbor" guideline, so that a charitable organization that is in compliance with the elective rules is deemed to be in conformance with the general rules.

These rules are named elective because charitable organizations must elect to come under these standards (sometimes termed the *expenditure test,* in contrast to the *substantial part test*). Those organizations that choose to not make the election are governed by the general rules, with all of their uncertainties. Churches, conventions or associations of churches, integrated auxiliaries of churches, certain supporting organizations, and (of course) private foundations may not elect to come under these guidelines.

The elective rules provide a definition of terms such as *legislation, influencing legislation, direct lobbying,* and *grass roots lobbying.* These terms are essentially the same as those used in connection with the general rules. However, in an attempt to define when the legislative process begins (so as to determine when a lobbying process begins), the elective rules offer a definition of legislative *action,* which is the "introduction, amendment, enactment, defeat, or repeal of Acts, bills, resolutions, or similar items."

The elective rules measure permissible and impermissible legislative activities of charitable organizations in terms of sets of declining percentages of total exempt purpose expenditures (which do not include fund-raising expenses). The basic permitted annual level of expenditures for legislative efforts (termed the "lobbying nontaxable amount") is 20 percent of the first $500,000 of an organization's expenditures for an exempt purpose (including legislative activities), plus 15 percent of the next $500,000, 10 percent of the next $500,000, and 5 percent of any remaining expenditures. However, the total amount spent for legislative activities in any one year by an electing charitable organization may not exceed $1 million. A separate limitation—amounting to one-fourth of the foregoing amounts—is imposed on grass roots lobbying expenditures.

Here is where the taxes come in. A charitable organization that has elected these limitations and exceeds either the general lobbying ceiling amount or the grass roots lobbying ceiling amount becomes subject to an excise tax in the amount of 25 percent of the excess lobbying expenditures. With respect to these two limitations, the tax falls on the greater of the two excesses. If an electing organization's lobbying expenditures normally (that is, on an average over a four-year period) exceed 150 percent of either limitation, it will lose its tax-exempt status as a charitable organization.

The elective rules contain exemptions for five categories of activities. The term *influencing legislation* does not include:

1. Making available the results of nonpartisan analysis, study, or research

2. Providing technical advice or assistance in response to a written request by a governmental body

3. Appearances before, or communications to, any legislative body with respect to a possible decision of that body which might affect the existence of the organization, its powers and duties, its tax-exempt status, or the deductibility of contributions to it

4. Communications between the organization and its bona fide members with respect to legislation or proposed legislation of direct interest to them, unless the communications directly encourage the members to influence legislation or directly encourage the members to urge nonmembers to influence legislation

5. Routine communications with government officials or employees

The elective rules contain a method of aggregating the expenditures of related organizations to forestall the creation of numerous organizations for the purpose of avoiding the expenditure test.

Where two or more charitable organizations are members of an "affiliated group" and at least one of the members has elected coverage under these provisions, the calculations of lobbying and exempt purpose expenditures must be made by taking into account the expenditures of the group. If these expenditures exceed the permitted limits, each of the electing member organizations must pay a proportionate share of the penalty excise tax, with the nonelecting members treated under the general rules.

Generally, under these rules, two organizations are "affiliated" where (1) one organization is bound by decisions of the other on legislative issues pursuant to its governing instrument or (2) the governing board of one organization includes enough representatives of the other (that is, there is an interlocking directorate) to cause or prevent action on legislative issues by the first organization. Where a number of organizations are affiliated, even in chain fashion, all of them are treated as one group of affiliated organizations. However, if a group of autonomous organizations controls an organization but no one organization in the controlling group alone can control that organization, the organizations are not considered an affiliated group by reason of the interlocking directorates rule.

There are special reporting requirements imposed upon charitable organizations that are under the elective rules.

LOBBYING RESTRICTIONS ON OTHER NONPROFIT ORGANIZATIONS

The federal law pertaining to tax-exempt status does not impose any lobbying restrictions on nonprofit organizations other than charitable ones. Thus, the only constraint (if it can even be called that) is that the organization pursue its exempt functions (whatever they may be) as its primary purpose and that any lobbying it may do not interfere with that principal requirement. This means that, basically, entities such as social welfare organizations, labor organizations, business and professional associations (business leagues), and veterans' organizations may lobby without restriction.

Indeed, it was this stark contrast in the law between charitable organizations and other types of tax-exempt organizations (even those to which deductible gifts can be made) that gave rise to the above-noted challenges to the general rules on equal protection grounds. But the U.S. Supreme Court ruled that "[l]egislatures have especially broad latitude in creating classifications and distinctions in tax statutes."

It is due to these distinctions, however, that charitable organizations are afforded a major opportunity to sidestep the rigorous rules regulating lobbying by them. That is, a charitable organization can create a related social welfare organization and use it as a lobbying arm. Indeed, some Justices of the U.S. Supreme Court are of the belief that the easy availability of tax-exempt lobbying arms of charitable organizations is the feature of the tax law that prevents the lobbying restrictions on charities from being unconstitutional.

However, there are, in a few instances, other aspects of the federal tax laws that bear on this matter. These are described next.

Associations

Nonprofit membership associations are generally tax-exempt. Most of these are either trade, business, or professional associations (business leagues) or charitable organizations. Others are labor organizations or social welfare organizations. The pertinent common element among them is that all of these associations receive dues revenue and, in most cases, the dues are deductible as business expenses.

There are, in the rules concerning the deductibility of business expenses, limitations on the amount of expenditures in the business context that may be made for lobbying. These rules thus affect the deductibility of dues and in that regard, as a practical matter, have an impact on the way the recipient associations can use the dues revenue.

The business expense deduction rules permit the deduction for two categories of ordinary and necessary business expenses paid or incurred for legislative efforts. The first category permits the deduction for expenses in direct connection with appearances before, submission of statements to, or sending communications to, members or committees of legislative bodies with respect to legislation or proposed legislation of direct interest to the taxpayer. The second category of deduction is for expenses in direct connection with communication of information between the taxpayer and an organization of which the taxpayer is a member with respect to legislation or proposed legislation of direct interest to the taxpayer and the organization.

As noted, these rules apply to the portion of dues paid or incurred by the taxpayer with respect to an organization of which it is a member that is attributable to the expenses of legislative activities.

However, there is no business deduction for amounts paid or incurred in connection with any attempt to influence the general public, or segments of the public, with respect to legislative matters (or elections or referenda). Thus, no deduction is allowed for any expenses incurred in connection with grass roots campaigns or any other attempt to urge or encourage the public to contact members of a legislative body for the purpose of proposing, supporting, or opposing legislation. Communications between an association and its members generally do not constitute the influencing of the general public. But the employees and customers of members of the association do constitute a segment of the general public. Consequently, a communication from a business league that is intended to go beyond its members and is either directly, or through its membership, directed at a segment of the public will constitute grass roots lobbying. Thus, the expenses attributable to that type of lobbying (including the allocable portion of members' dues) are not deductible as business expenses.

Therefore, an association, as a practical matter, will normally avoid engaging in grass roots lobbying, so as not to risk the possibility of causing an audit of its membership, particularly where the members are business corporations and the dues are substantial.

Political Organizations

One type of tax-exempt organization is the "political organization." A political organization, such as a political action committee, is unlikely to engage in lobbying, because legislative activities are not "exempt functions" for a political organization and thus may cause taxation if they are undertaken.

As described in Chapter 4, a political organization must, to qualify for exemption, be organized and operated primarily for the purpose of directly or indirectly accepting contributions and making expenditures for an "exempt function." An exempt function, in this context, is the function of influencing or attempting to influence the selection, nomination, election, or appointment of any individual to any federal, state, or local public office. Lobbying, then, is not an exempt function for a political committee. If lobbying is done in an insubstantial amount by a political committee, the worse outcome from a tax law viewpoint would be the payment of some tax; if done in violation of the primary purpose standard, the outcome would be loss of tax-exempt status.

Other Organizations

As observed earlier, nearly all forms of tax-exempt organizations may engage in lobbying without endangering their tax exemption under federal law.

The exceptions, in varying degrees, are charitable organizations, membership associations, and political organizations.

There are a few instances, nonetheless, where lobbying activities are inconsistent with tax-exempt status. One example of this is the title-holding corporation—either single-parent or multi-parent (see Chapter 4)—which must be operated for the exclusive purpose of holding title to property and paying over the income from the property to its parent. Lobbying by this type of entity would be contrary to the "exclusivity" requirement and would also be inconsistent with the passive nature of the organization. Some governmental units may operate under restrictions that preclude lobbying. However, no type of tax-exempt organization, other than the charitable one, is expressly prohibited from engaging in activities to influence legislation.

Moreover, other federal, state, or local law may operate to prevent or restrict a nonprofit organization from engaging in activities to influence the legislative process.

―――――――――――― FOCUS ON THE CAMPAIGN TO ――――――――――――
CLEAN UP AMERICA

The hypothetical organization being looked at throughout this book—the Campaign to Clean Up America—has exempt purposes that clearly can be furthered by lobbying. However, its primary purposes—volunteer clean-up programs and public education—enable it to qualify as a charitable organization. Still, the Campaign would like to press for federal, state, and local law changes, such as tougher penalties for those who litter and incentive programs for those who collect and dispose of trash found in public places.

The managers of the Campaign have a decision to make: whether to make the election to come under the special lobbying rules for public charities. After consulting with legal counsel, the choice is to not make the election at this time, because the amount of lobbying that is contemplated is less than ten percent of total activities. Also, a substantial portion of the lobbying that is to be done may be grass roots lobbying and the Campaign would like to avoid the narrower range of percentages that the elective rules impose on that type of lobbying. Further, by reason of this decision, the Campaign is not subject to the detailed IRS regulations that will accompany the elective rules and need not annually report its legislative activities to the IRS in the detailed form required of electing organizations.

Indeed, the management of the Campaign has also decided to seriously consider organizing and operating a related social welfare organization for the purpose of conducting lobbying activities, should the level of lobbying increase beyond the 10 to 15 percent range.

14

Political Activities— and More Taxes

Congress and the IRS, as troubled as they are about lobbying activities by various types of nonprofit organizations (see Chapter 13), are even more concerned about political campaign activities by nonprofit organizations. Unlike the vagaries and uncertainties associated with the federal tax law constraints on lobbying activities, however, the federal tax law rules regulating political campaign activities are relatively clear.

Also, unlike the general federal law pertaining to lobbying, there is an extensive federal statute regulating political campaign activity—the Federal Election Campaign Act—and a federal agency that enforces the law in this area—the Federal Election Commission. The election laws and the tax laws are clearly separate sets of requirements, yet there is also interplay between the two. Nonprofit organizations are very much subject to the federal election laws and thus must arrange their activities to be in conformance with those laws as well as the tax laws. Also, state laws operate to regulate intrastate political campaign activity.

POLITICAL ACTIVITIES BY CHARITABLE ORGANIZATIONS

Congress has flatly decreed that charitable organizations may not engage in political campaign activity. The prohibition states that these organizations must "not participate in, or intervene in (including the publishing or distributing of statements), any political campaign on behalf of or in opposition to any candidate for public office." Coincidently, this restriction has the same origin as the lobbying limitations on charitable organizations, in that it originated in the U.S. Senate. There were no hearings on the provision, and its enactment can be traced to one senator's interest in preventing campaign activity (against him) by a particular organization. (As described in Chapter 11, there are separate and more stringent rules against electioneering that are applicable only to private foundations.)

The prohibition on involvement by charitable organizations in political campaigns is said by the IRS to be absolute. Certainly, these rules do not use a substantiality test. Nonetheless, as a practical matter, a minor involvement in a political campaign may not trigger loss of exemption because, as one court put it, "a slight and comparatively unimportant deviation from the narrow furrow of tax approved activity is not fatal."

The concept of an *action organization* (see Chapter 13) is used in the political campaign context also. Thus, an action organization is one that participates or intervenes, directly or indirectly, in any political campaign on behalf of or in opposition to any candidate for public office. And, as noted in Chapter 13, an action organization cannot qualify as a charitable organization. Obviously, therefore, it is contrary to the tax law for a charitable organization to make a contribution to a political candidate's campaign, to endorse or oppose a candidate, or to otherwise support a political candidacy.

Most of the law amplifying the political campaign proscription for charitable groups is in IRS rulings. These rulings, over the years, have been uniformly rigid in their finding that nearly any activity relating to the political process is activity preventing charitable organizations from being tax-exempt. For example, activities such as the evaluation of candidates, the administration of a fair campaign practices code, and assistance to individuals after they have been elected has been found to be prohibited.

However, in recent times, the IRS has relented somewhat, concluding that voter education activities are permissible for charitable organizations. Thus, as an illustration, a charitable organization can prepare and disseminate a compilation of the voting records of legislators on a variety of subjects, as long as there is no editorial comment and no approval or disapproval of the voting records is implied. Likewise, a charitable organization may conduct public forums involving political candidates where there is a fair and impartial treatment of the candidates. In practice, some charitable organizations disseminate information about candidates' voting records and positions on issues in a format that clearly reflects approval and disapproval of positions, and the IRS has not acted to stop the practice. While this practice remains risky, it is less so where the opinionated material is not widely distributed to the general public or not timed to be disseminated on the eve of the election.

Despite the stringent prohibition on political campaign activities by charitable organizations, the law permits these entities to engage in educational undertakings, such as instruction of the public on matters useful to the individual and beneficial to the community. Thus, there is an inherent tension between political campaign activities and educational activities— just as there is with respect to the constraints on legislative activities.

Charitable organizations may thus cautiously enter the political milieu, as part of the process of advancing education. Consequently, charitable organizations have, for example, been permitted to assemble and donate to libraries the campaign speeches, interviews, and other materials of an individual who was a candidate for a historically important elective office, and to conduct public forums at which debates and lectures on social, political, and international questions are considered.

However, in performing this type of educational activity, a charitable organization is expected to present a balanced view of the pertinent facts to permit members of the public to form their own opinion or conclusion independent of that presented by the organization, although the organization may be able to advocate a particular position or viewpoint (but not, as noted, a particular candidate). Thus, while a charitable organization may seek to educate the public on patriotic, political, and civic matters, it may not do so by the use of disparaging terms, insinuations, innuendoes, or suggested implications drawn from incomplete facts. In a sense, this aspect of the prohibition on political activity is not unlike the prohibition on propagandizing that is part of the constraints on lobbying by charitable groups (discussed in Chapter 13).

Until 1988, the only sanction in the law for violation by charitable organizations of the political campaign activities proscription was revocation of tax-exempt status. Congress came to see that sanction as somewhat ineffective, since there was little revenue incentive in the IRS to take such drastic action, and little incentive for an organization involved and those who manage it to strictly adhere to the rules, since they could simply start anew with a successor organization. The enactment of new law in 1987 dramatically changed the rules of the game.

The federal tax law now levies taxes in situations where a charitable organization makes a "political expenditure." Generally, a political expenditure is any amount paid or incurred by a charitable organization in any participation in, or intervention in (including the publication or distribution of statements), any political campaign on behalf of or in opposition to any candidate for public office.

In an effort to discourage the use of ostensibly "educational" organizations operating in tandem with political campaigns, the term "political expenditure" also applies with respect to "an organization which is formed primarily for purposes of promoting the candidacy (or prospective candidacy) of an individual for public office (or which is effectively controlled by a candidate or prospective candidate and which is availed of primarily for such purposes)." In these circumstances, the term "political expenditure" includes any of the following amounts paid or incurred by the organization: (1) amounts paid to or incurred by the individual for speeches or other services, (2) the travel expenses of the individual, (3) the expenses of conducting polls, surveys, or other studies, or the preparation of papers or other materials, for use by the individual, (4) the expenses of advertising, publicity, and fund-raising for the individual, and (5) any other expense "which has the primary effect of promoting public recognition, or otherwise primarily accruing to the benefit of," the individual.

The taxes applicable in the political activities context consist of "initial" taxes and "additional" taxes, like the private foundation taxes (see Chapter 11).

A political expenditure triggers an initial tax, payable by the organization, of 10 percent of the amount of the expenditure. An initial tax of $2\frac{1}{2}$ percent of the expenditure is also imposed on each of the organization's managers (such as directors and officers), where he or she knew it was a political expenditure, unless the agreement to make the expenditure was not willful and was due to reasonable cause. The IRS has the discretionary authority to abate these initial taxes where the organization is able to establish that the violation was due to reasonable cause and not to willful neglect, and timely corrects the violation.

An additional tax is imposed upon a charitable organization, at a rate of 100 percent of the political expenditure. This tax is levied where the initial tax was imposed and the expenditure was not timely corrected. An additional tax is imposed upon the organization's manager, at a rate of 50 percent of the expenditure. This tax is levied where the additional tax was imposed on the organization and where the manager refused to agree to part or all of the correction.

An organization that loses its status as a charitable organization because of political campaign activities is precluded from becoming tax-exempt as a social welfare organization. (This rule is identical to the rule concerning a charity's inability to convert to social welfare status after engaging in substantial lobbying.)

Under certain circumstances, the IRS is empowered to commence an action in federal district court to enjoin a charitable organization from the further making of political expenditures and for other relief to ensure that the assets of the organization are preserved for charitable purposes.

If the IRS finds that a charitable organization has "flagrantly" violated the prohibition against the making of political expenditures, the IRS is required to immediately determine and assess any income and/or excise tax(es) due, by terminating the organization's taxable year.

The foregoing discussion has been deliberately written to refer only to "political campaign activity." This is to be contrasted with "political activity," of which there are essentially two types.

The first of these is what may be termed, for lack of a better term, "activism." This term embraces a wide range of "political" undertakings which may be described as the type of activity that is constitutionally protected as free speech. These activities may be manifested in a variety of forms, such as writings, demonstrations, boycotts, strikes, picketing, and litigation. These activities frequently give the IRS pause in evaluating the status of an organization as a charitable entity but, unless the activities can be fairly characterized as being lobbying or electioneering, there is no basis in the tax law concerning action organizations (as that term is used in its technical sense) for denying tax-exempt status to an organization that engages in those activities or for revoking tax-exempt status in those instances.

Activist activities are usually a permissible method by which a charitable organization can further its tax-exempt purposes. These activities often are not inherently exempt functions but are viewed by the law as being means to further an end result, which is to achieve exempt purposes. As the U.S. Tax Court once wrote, "the purpose towards which an organization's activities are directed, and not the activities themselves, is ultimately dispositive of the organization's right to be classified as a . . . [charitable] organization." However, such activities will jeopardize tax exemption where they are illegal or are otherwise contrary to public policy.

The second type of political activity can, when done, trigger taxes. This tax structure is a byproduct of the rules defining the tax-exempt "political organization" (summarized in Chapter 4 and below).

For purposes of the political organization rules, the law defines the "exempt function" of these entities, which is, essentially, to engage in political activity. These exempt functions are the actions of influencing or attempting to influence the selection, nomination, election, or appointment of any individual to any federal, state, or local public office. The wording of this definition is such that the term "political activity" is broader than the term "political campaign activity." That is, it includes words such as "selection" and "appointment" which can mean processes other than electioneering. For example, if a representative of a charitable organization testifies for or against a presidential appointment to a cabinet position or a judgeship, the organization is not engaging in political campaign activity (because there is no "campaign" and no "election") but is nonetheless engaging in political activity.

In the case of a charitable organization that engages in a political activity that is not a political campaign activity, it will presumably not forfeit its tax-exempt status but will have to pay a tax. The tax is determined by computing an amount equal to the lesser of the organization's net investment income for the year involved or the amount expended for the political activity. This amount is characterized as "political organization taxable income" and taxed at the highest corporate rates.

Unlike the situation with respect to charitable organizations and the lobbying rules, where a charitable entity may operate a related lobbying organization, a charitable organization is not permitted to operate a related political campaign organization (namely, a political action committee). The state of the law on this point is that the activity of the political action committee is attributable to the parent charity, causing the latter to lose its tax exemption. However, it may be possible for individuals who are involved with a charitable organization to establish and utilize an "independent" political action committee. Although the IRS has not addressed the matter, the Federal Election Commission has issued guidelines by which such a committee—technically termed a "nonconnected political committee"—may be created and used. However, a charitable or other tax-exempt organization may operate a political action committee for the purpose of conducting political activities that are not political campaign activities.

POLITICAL ACTIVITIES BY OTHER EXEMPT ORGANIZATIONS

Federal tax law does not impede political campaign activities by tax-exempt organizations other than charitable ones. However, as noted above, federal and state election laws limit the extent to which nonprofit organizations can directly participate in the political campaign process. For example, the Federal Election Campaign Act makes it unlawful for a corporation—including a nonprofit corporation—to make a contribution or expenditure in a federal election.

Because of the campaign law restrictions, most nonprofit organizations do not directly engage in political campaign activities but instead use political action committees. The nonprofit organizations that most commonly use political action committees are trade, business, and professional associations, and labor organizations; a few social welfare organizations maintain political action committees as well.

The parlance of the federal election laws terms these adjunct political committees "separate segregated funds." Thus, that law permits the "establishment, administration, and solicitation of contributions to a separate segregated fund to be utilized for political purposes by a . . . membership organization." The costs of establishing and administering a separate segregated fund (political action committee) are, however, not contributions or expenditures that are prohibited under the federal election law. These costs are termed "soft-dollar expenditures," as contrasted with "hard-dollar expenditures" which are the outlays directly for political purposes (monies given by the membership and expended for the benefit of candidates).

The tax law is particularly confusing on these points, because of the double meaning given the term "exempt function." As described in Chapter 4, the exempt function of a political organization basically is the funding of campaigns (put another way, the making of hard-dollar expenditures). That exempt function is also recognized by the federal election laws. A nonprofit organization that has (without endangering its exemption) a political action committee may make soft-dollar political expenditures but may not, because of the federal election laws, make hard-dollar political expenditures. Yet, under the tax laws, if a nonprofit organization (other than a political organization) engages in an "exempt function" (as that term is defined in the political law context), it is subject to tax, even though it may be engaging in an "exempt function" (as that term is defined in the law pertaining to its tax-exempt status).

The dichotomy between political campaign activities and political activities is also present with respect to nonprofit organizations other than charitable ones. Even though the federal campaign laws prohibit a social welfare, labor, trade, business, or professional organization from making a political campaign contribution (hard-dollar expenditure), that type of organization may nonetheless make a "political" expenditure under the tax laws. As noted above, in this setting, a political activity includes the function of influencing or attempting to influence the selection, nomination, election, or appointment of an individual to any federal, state, or local public office (an "exempt function"). Thus, these types of membership organizations may, for example, support or oppose a presidential nominee for a cabinet position or judgeship. Again, that is a political activity and not a political campaign activity. Therefore, the federal election laws are not a factor but the tax law may force the payment of a tax (but not loss of tax exemption) as the result of participation in that type of activity. For example, the IRS has ruled that an organization that is primarily engaged in social welfare functions may also carry on activities (such as in-kind services) involving participation and intervention in political campaigns on behalf of or in opposition to candidates for public office without loss of tax-exempt status, although the organization may have to pay the political activities tax as a result.

FOCUS ON THE CAMPAIGN TO CLEAN UP AMERICA

The Campaign to Clean Up America has no plans to engage in political campaign activities. As is the case with lobbying activities, the exempt purposes of the Campaign can clearly be furthered by involvement in political campaigns. Certainly, its purposes will be advanced by those in government who agree with its principles and programs, so the Campaign is rightfully concerned about those who are elected and appointed to public office.

Yet, at this stage in its formation, the Campaign cannot afford to jeopardize its eligibility for deductible charitable gifts. Thus, as noted, it will not participate in any campaigns for those who are candidates for public office.

Still, the management of the Campaign is well aware of the relationship between the success of its programs and those who hold public office. Thus, it is seriously considering undertaking political activities, that are not political campaign activities, that are in advancement of its program objectives. At some point, it may prove feasible to establish a political action committee for this purpose.

Also, the management of the Campaign is considering the establishment of an independent political action committee, for the purpose of electing those whose vision of the future includes a litter-free America.

Part IV

Helpful Hints and Successful Techniques

15

Uses of For-Profit Subsidiaries

It is becoming more commonplace, if not frequently essential, for a tax-exempt organization to utilize a for-profit, taxable subsidiary.

The reasons for this phenomenon are many, including situations where (1) the activity to be housed in the subsidiary is an unrelated one (see Chapter 12), and the activity is too extensive to be conducted within the tax-exempt organization, (2) the management of an exempt organization does not want to report the receipt of any unrelated income and so shifts it to a separate subsidiary, and/or (3) the management of an exempt organization is enamored with the idea of use of a for-profit subsidiary.

In most instances, the first of these three reasons is the prevalent if not the sole one. An unrelated business may be operated as an activity within an exempt organization, as long as the primary purpose of the organization is to carry out one or more exempt functions (see Chapter 4). Thus, while there is no fixed percentage of unrelated activity that may be engaged in by a tax-exempt organization, it is clear that at least 51 percent of its activities must be in furtherance of exempt purposes.

Therefore, if a tax-exempt organization engages in one or more unrelated activities where the activities are *substantial* in relation to exempt activities (for example, constituting more than one-half of total activities), the use of a for-profit subsidiary is unavoidable.

STRUCTURAL CONSIDERATIONS

There are several matters of structure to be taken into account when contemplating the use of a for-profit subsidiary by a tax-exempt organization. These include choice of form and the control mechanism.

Establishing a For-Profit Subsidiary

The factors to be considered in determining whether a particular activity should be housed in a tax-exempt organization or a for-profit organization are the same as those that should be weighed when one is contemplating the commencement of a business that potentially may be conducted in either a tax-exempt or for-profit form. These factors are (1) the value of or need for tax exemption, (2) the true motives of those involved in the enterprise (for example, profit), (3) the desirability of creating an asset (such as stock that is appreciating in value) for equity owners of the enterprise (shareholders), and (4) the compensatory arrangements contemplated for the employees.

The law is clear that a tax-exempt organization can have one or more tax-exempt (or at least nonprofit) subsidiaries and/or one or more for-profit subsidiaries. In the latter instance, the tax-exempt parent organization can own some or all of the equity (usually, stock) of the for-profit subsidiary (unless the parent is a private foundation, in which case special rules apply, as described in Chapter 11).

If an activity of a tax-exempt organization is unrelated to its exempt purpose or functions but is not a principal activity, it may be conducted within the exempt organization, without impairment of its tax-exempt status (although taxes would have to be paid on the net income generated by the activity).

Choice of Form

Just as in forming a nonprofit organization, consideration must be given to choice of organizational form when establishing a for-profit subsidiary (see Chapter 2). Most will be corporations—the most common business form and one that enables the exempt parent to own the subsidiary by holding all or at least a majority of its stock.

Some taxable businesses are sole proprietorships; however, this approach is of no avail in the exempt organization context since the business activity conducted as a sole proprietorship is an undertaking conducted directly by the exempt organization and thus does not lead to the desired goal of having the unrelated activity in a separate entity.

Some taxable businesses are partnerships; however, the participation by an exempt organization in a partnership may involve additional legal difficulties (see Chapter 16).

Some states allow businesses to be conducted by means of business trusts, so this approach may be available to a nonprofit organization. However, before this approach (or any other approach involving a vehicle other than a corporation) is used, it is imperative that those involved are certain that the corporate form is not the most beneficial. One important consideration must be that of stock ownership, as stock in and of itself is an asset that can appreciate in value and can be sold in whole or in part.

A potential compromise is the use of a taxable nonprofit organization in which to house the business activity. This approach is a product of the distinction between a nonprofit organization and a tax-exempt organization. The former is a state law concept; the latter is essentially a federal tax law concept. Assuming state law permits (for an activity may be a "nonprofit" one yet still be "unrelated" to the parent's exempt functions), a business activity may be placed in a nonprofit, yet taxable, organization.

In the general business context, those forming a corporation have the additional decision as to whether or not to qualify the entity as an S corporation, which is a corporation that is treated for federal tax purposes the same as a partnership. An S corporation is not taxed, and its net income and losses (to the extent of the stockholders' basis in the corporation) are passed through to the shareholders for tax purposes.

However, this decision need not detain the managers of a tax-exempt organization, because exempt organizations are not permitted to hold stock in an S corporation.

Control

Presumably, a tax-exempt organization will, when forming a taxable subsidiary, intend to maintain control over the subsidiary. Certainly, after capitalizing the enterprise, nurturing its growth and success, and desiring to enjoy some profits from the business, the exempt organization parent would not want to place the activity in a vehicle over which it cannot exercise control.

Where the taxable subsidiary is structured as a business corporation, the tax-exempt organization parent can own the entity and ultimately control it simply by owning the stock (received in exchange for the capital contributed). The exempt organization parent as the stockholder can thereafter select the board of directors of the corporation and, if desired, its officers.

If the taxable subsidiary is structured as a nonprofit corporation, two choices are available. The entity can be structured as a conventional nonprofit organization, in which case the exempt organization parent would control the subsidiary by means of interlocking directorates. Alternatively, the entity can be structured as a nonprofit organization that can issue stock, in which case the exempt organization parent would control the subsidiary by holding its stock. If the latter course is chosen and if the nonprofit subsidiary is to be headquartered in a state where stock-based nonprofits are not authorized, the subsidiary can be incorporated in a state that allows nonprofits to issue stock and thereafter qualified to do business in the home state.

Attribution Considerations

For federal income tax purposes, a parent corporation and its subsidiary are treated as separate entities as long as the purpose for which the subsidiary is formed are reflected in true business activities. That is, where an organization is established with the bona fide intention that it will have some real and substantial business function, its existence will generally not be disregarded for tax purposes. By contrast, where the parent organization so controls the affairs of the subsidiary that it is merely an extension of the parent, the subsidiary may not be regarded as a separate entity. In an extreme situation, the establishment of an ostensibly separate subsidiary may be regarded as a sham.

The IRS generally will respect the separate identities of closely related entities, including situations where the tax-exempt parent wholly owns the for-profit subsidiary.

FINANCIAL CONSIDERATIONS

The principal financial considerations that a nonprofit organization should keep in mind when contemplating the establishment of a for-profit subsidiary are capitalization, compensation, and liquidation.

Capitalization

Assets that are currently being used in an unrelated activity (if any) may be spun off into a related, for-profit organization. However, the extent to which a for-profit corporation can be capitalized using exempt assets involves far more strenuous limitations.

A tax-exempt organization can invest a portion of its assets and engage in a certain amount of unrelated activities. At the same time, the governing board of a tax-exempt organization must act in conformance with basic fiduciary responsibilities and the organization cannot operate for the benefit of private interests (see Chapter 5).

Recent IRS private letter rulings suggest that perhaps only a very small percentage of an organization's resources ought to be transferred to controlled subsidiaries. However, these percentages approved by the IRS are usually unduly low and probably pertain only to cash. In some cases, a specific asset may—indeed, perhaps must—be best utilized in an unrelated activity, even though its value represents a meaningful portion of the organization's total resources.

The best guiding standard in these regards is that of the prudent investor. In capitalizing a subsidiary, a tax-exempt organization should only part with an amount of resources that is reasonable under the circumstances and that can be rationalized in relation to amounts devoted to programs and invested in other fashions. Relevant to all of this is the projected return on the investment, in terms of both income and capital appreciation. If a contribution to a subsidiary's capital seems unwise, the parent-to-be should consider a loan (albeit one bearing a fair rate of interest and accompanied by adequate security).

Compensation

The structure of a tax-exempt parent and a taxable subsidiary may generate questions and issues as to compensation of employees.

The compensation of the employees of the taxable subsidiary is subject to an overall requirement, by reason of the rule that all business expenses must be "ordinary and necessary" to be deductible, that the amounts paid may not exceed a reasonable salary or wage. The compensation of the employees of the parent exempt organization is subject to a like limitation, by reason of the private inurement doctrine (see Chapter 5).

The employees of the tax-exempt parent could participate in deferred compensation plans or perhaps tax-sheltered annuity programs. Deferred salary plans may also be used by the subsidiary, as may qualified pension plans, including so-called "401(k) plans." (See Chapter 10.)

Use of a taxable subsidiary may facilitate the offering of stock options to employees, to enable them to share in the growth of the corporation. The subsidiary similarly may offer an employee stock ownership plan—a plan that invests in the stock of the sponsoring company. The subsidiary may issue unqualified options to buy stock or qualified incentive stock options.

Liquidations

The federal tax law causes recognition of gain or loss by a corporation on a liquidating distribution of its assets (as if the corporation had sold the assets to the distributee at fair market value) and on liquidating sales. There is an exception for liquidating transfers within an affiliated group (which is regarded as a single economic unit), so that the basis in the property in the distributee is carried over.

This nonrecognition exception is modified for eligible liquidations in which an 80 percent corporate shareholder receives property with a carryover basis, to provide for nonrecognition of gain or loss with respect to any property actually distributed to that shareholder. Nonetheless, this nonrecognition rule under the exception for 80 percent corporate shareholders is generally not available where the shareholder is a tax-exempt organization. However, this nonrecognition treatment is available in the tax-exempt organizations context where the property distributed is used by the tax-exempt organization in an unrelated business immediately after the distribution. If the property later ceases to be used in an unrelated business, the tax-exempt organization will be taxed on the gain at that time.

TREATMENT OF REVENUE FROM SUBSIDIARY

While not always the case, most tax-exempt organizations develop an unrelated activity in the anticipation that it will serve as a source of revenue. Thus, the development in or shifting of the unrelated business to a taxable subsidiary should be done in such a way as to not preclude or inhibit the flow of income from the subsidiary to the parent.

Before discussing the appropriate character of the income flow, it is necessary to note that the staff and other resources of an affiliated business are usually those of the exempt organization parent. Thus, the headquarters of the taxable subsidiary are likely to be the same as its parent. This means that the taxable subsidiary will have to reimburse the exempt organization parent for the subsidiary's occupancy costs, share of employees' time, and use of the parent's equipment and supplies. Therefore, one way for dollars to flow from the subsidiary to the parent is as this form of reimbursement, which would include an element of rent.

Another type of relationship between an exempt organization parent and a taxable subsidiary is that of lender and borrower. That is, in addition to funding its subsidiary by means of a capital contribution (resulting in a holding of equity by the parent), the parent may find it appropriate to lend money to its subsidiary. Inasmuch as a no-interest loan to a for-profit subsidiary by an exempt organization parent may endanger the tax-exempt status of the parent and trigger problems under the imputed interest rules, it would be appropriate for a loan to bear a fair market rate of interest. Therefore, another way for dollars to flow from the subsidiary to the parent is in the form of interest.

The business activities of a for-profit subsidiary may be to market and sell a product or service. When done in conformance with its tax-exempt status, the parent can license the use of its name, logo, acronym, or some other feature that would enhance the sale of the product or service provided by the subsidiary. For this license, the subsidiary would pay to the parent a royalty—another way of transferring dollars from subsidiary to parent.

A conventional way of transferring money from a corporation to its stockholders is for the corporation to distribute its earnings and profits to them. These distributions, or dividends, represent still another way in which a taxable subsidiary can transfer dollars to its tax-exempt parent.

As mentioned earlier, certain types of income are exempted from taxation as unrelated income—principally the various forms of passive income.

Were it not for a special rule of federal tax law, a tax-exempt organization could have it both ways: avoid taxation on unrelated income by housing the activity in a subsidiary and thereafter receive passive, nontaxable income from the subsidiary.

Congress, however, was mindful of this potential double benefit and so legislated an exception to the general rule that exempts passive income from taxation: Otherwise passive nontaxable income that is derived from a controlled taxable subsidiary is taxed as unrelated income. Thus, when an exempt organization parent receives rents, interest, or most other forms of passive income from a controlled taxable subsidiary, those revenues will generally be taxable. In this instance, *control* means a direct or indirect 80 percent ownership.

There is an exception to the exception. This rule is predicated upon the fact that the payment of rents, interest, or royalties gives rise to a tax deduction for them for the payor corporation. So, for example, when a for-profit subsidiary pays interest to its exempt organization parent in connection with a loan, the interest payments are deductible by the subsidiary.

However, there is no tax deduction for the payment of dividends. So, when a for-profit subsidiary pays a dividend to its exempt organization parent, the dividend payments are not deductible by the subsidiary. Therefore, Congress determined that it would not be appropriate to tax revenue to an exempt organization parent where it is not deductible by the taxable subsidiary.

Thus, this principle has developed (facilitating tax planning as to which entity if any is to be taxed): If the income paid to an exempt organization parent is deductible by the subsidiary, it is unrelated income to the parent. By contrast, if the income paid is not deductible by the subsidiary, it is not taxable to the parent. The exception to the exception, then, is for dividend income, that is not taxable to an exempt organization parent even when derived from a controlled taxable subsidiary.

SUBSIDIARIES IN PARTNERSHIPS

There is a dimension to the use of a taxable subsidiary by a tax-exempt organization parent that is alluded to in the discussion of exempt organizations in partnerships. This is the attempt by a charitable organization to avoid endangering its tax-exempt status because of involvement in a partnership as a general partner by causing a taxable subsidiary to be the general partner instead.

This can be an effective strategy as long as all of the law's bona fides are satisfied, including the requirement that the subsidiary be an authentic business entity. However, as discussed, if the exempt organization parent is too intimately involved in the day-to-day management of the subsidiary, the IRS may impute the activities of the subsidiary to the parent, thereby endangering the tax-exempt status of the parent by treating it as if it were directly involved as the general partner of the partnership.

The federal tax law concerning the depreciation deduction contains rules reducing the deduction in situations where otherwise depreciable property is being used for the benefit of tax-exempt organizations. These rules are the *tax-exempt entity leasing rules.* The essence of the tax-exempt entity leasing rules is to force investors to compute their depreciation deduction over a longer recovery period where the property is *tax-exempt use property.* The tax-exempt entity leasing rules can cause property to be tax-exempt use property where the property is owned by a partnership in which the tax-exempt organization is a partner or where the property is owned by a partnership in which a for-profit subsidiary owned by a tax-exempt organization is a partner.

Thus, if any property, that would not otherwise be tax-exempt use property, is owned by a partnership that has both a tax-exempt organization and a nonexempt entity as partners, an amount equal to the tax-exempt organization's proportionate share of the property is treated as tax-exempt use property, unless there is a *qualified allocation* of the partnership items (such as gains and losses). In an attempt to prevent property from becoming tax-exempt use property, some exempt organizations did not enter into partnership arrangements directly but instead used for-profit subsidiaries as the partners. Congress, in turn, acted to thwart this technique by causing a taxable subsidiary to be considered a tax-exempt organization for purposes of the tax-exempt entity leasing rules, terming such subsidiaries "tax-exempt controlled entities."

TITLE-HOLDING CORPORATIONS

This discussion of the use of a subsidiary by a tax-exempt organization has been confined to the use of for-profit subsidiaries. Thus, although some of the analysis is relevant to the point, the discussion is not directly focused on situations where the subsidiary also is a tax-exempt organization, such as a membership organization utilizing a related foundation or a charitable organization utilizing a related advocacy organization.

There is, however, a type of subsidiary related to an exempt organization parent that warrants mention, being somewhat of a hybrid entity. This is the *title-holding corporation.* This entity is a hybrid whose activities are generally in the business context yet it is tax-exempt by reason of a relationship with a tax-exempt parent.

Essentially, the function of a title-holding corporation is a passive one: to hold title to property, to pay expenses associated with maintenance of the property, and to at least annually remit any net revenue to the parent organization. A title-holding corporation cannot be engaged in an active business undertaking. This type of subsidiary can be useful in the administration of property and as a device for limiting liability.

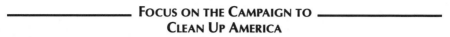

FOCUS ON THE CAMPAIGN TO CLEAN UP AMERICA

At the present, the Campaign to Clean Up America does not have any plans to utilize a for-profit subsidiary. As discussed in the unrelated income context (see Chapter 12), there are potential unrelated businesses for the Campaign. Some of these may ultimately be housed in a subsidiary.

As the Campaign grows, and if federal tax laws allow, the organization may find it productive to utilize one or more for-profit subsidiaries in advancement of businesses selling supplies, equipment, and/or consulting services.

16

Tax-Exempt Organizations and Partnerships

One of the most important phenomena involving tax-exempt organizations is the use of related organizations. There is nothing particularly revolutionary about this technique, as reflected in the discussion in Chapter 15 about the use of subsidiaries by tax-exempt organizations. What is different is the willingness of tax-exempt organizations to simultaneously use so many different forms of related entities, be they for-profit or nonprofit, trust or corporation, taxable or nontaxable.

Some ascribe this development to the economic pressures on tax-exempt organizations resulting from the decline in government funding. Others trace troubles to tax reform. While there is ample basis for finding cause in both of these sources, it is not the entire answer. These two reasons do not explain the trade association surrounded by a charitable foundation, a political action committee, and two for-profit business subsidiaries, one of which is a general partner in a real estate limited partnership. This development is attributable to a factor other than the mother-of-invention theory and that other factor is: Sophistication. Tax-exempt organizations are better managed and better advised than ever before.

The resulting use of partnerships by exempt organizations is largely due to the discovery by them of the availability of partnerships to facilitate what they would like to do in any event. That us, a partnership is essentially a financing technique.

REAL ESTATE ACQUISITIONS

Economic conditions being what they are, managers of tax-exempt organizations are more frequently concluding that the organizations would be financially advantaged if they owned real estate, usually for purposes of housing their offices. An organization is likely to be in a preferable position, economically, if its occupancy costs are fixed rather than subject to the vagaries of the rental market. In addition, it is almost always advantageous to have real property among the assets of an organization. Further, the ownership of real property sometimes offers the opportunity for an organization to conduct program activities at its own location and/or utilize the property to generate additional revenue for the organization. Moreover, in many instances, there is prestige associated with ownership by an organization of its headquarters in relationship to its membership, contributors, or perhaps the general public.

For some nonprofit organizations, ownership of real property has been commonplace. This is certainly the case with institutions such as churches, universities, colleges, schools, hospitals, country clubs, and some major charities and associations. However, real estate ownership—particularly for office headquarters purposes—is becoming more commonplace for a wide variety of charitable, educational, religious, scientific, trade, business, professional, veterans, and other categories of nonprofit organizations.

There are several aspects of real estate ownership by nonprofit organizations. As a general proposition, it is clear that a nonprofit organization will not jeopardize its tax exemption because of acquisition, ownership, and maintenance of real property. In some instances, real property owned by a nonprofit organization will be exempt from a state's property tax. Also, as a general rule, there is no likelihood of tax exemption being impaired where a nonprofit organization leases space in property it owns, whether to other nonprofit entities or to the general public.

There are, nonetheless, a variety of potential unrelated income tax considerations associated with the acquisition, ownership, and maintenance of real property by nonprofit organizations.

In the simplest of circumstances, where a nonprofit organization acquires real property with no financing and uses the property wholly for its tax-exempt purposes, there would be no adverse consequences in terms of tax-exempt status or unrelated income taxation. Federal tax considerations come into play where the property is acquired with the assistance of others (such as by means of a partnership or other joint venture), there is rental or other income involved, financing is utilized, and/or the property is put to an unrelated use.

It is in the property acquisition phase that tax considerations can be prominent and the issue is likely to be whether tax-exempt status would be jeopardized rather than unrelated income taxation.

A common way for an organization (nonprofit or not) to acquire real property, where the organization is unable or unwilling to do so wholly out of its own resources, is to utilize a partnership. The partnership may well be comprised of the organization, the person(s) providing the financing, and the construction company. In many instances, the partnership will be a limited partnership, with the tax-exempt organization being the general partner or one of the general partners. The partnership is the entity that acquires the property, develops it (if necessary), and sometimes continues to operate and maintain the property. Subsequently the nonprofit organization involved may acquire the property from the partnership, such as by purchase or (if the organization is a charitable one) by being the recipient of gifts of the partnership interests.

Certainly, not all partnerships utilized by tax-exempt organizations involve the acquisition and maintenance of real estate. Many partnerships involving tax-exempt organizations are used to acquire and operate capital equipment. Nonetheless, most of these partnerships are employed in the real estate context and this use serves as an appropriate basis for examining the underlying rationale for this technique.

Suppose, for example, that a charitable organization decided that it no longer wished to pay rent for its office space but instead wants to own a building for its use. Its options for deriving the funds necessary to acquire the building are (1) use money it has saved and held for investment, (2) borrow the money, (3) embark on a capital campaign and raise the money from gifts and grants, (4) utilize tax-exempt bonds, (5) acquire the property by means of a real estate limited partnership, or (6) some combination of two or more of the foregoing approaches.

The disadvantages of most of these choices are that the tax-exempt organization usually does not have nor cannot get the money, and/or lacks the time or other resources to attract the funding. The advantages of the partnership approach include the ability of the organization to acquire the building using the funds of others. As observed earlier, a partnership is a financing mechanism—a means to an end.

SOME BASICS ABOUT PARTNERSHIPS

A partnership is a business form, recognized by law as an entity just as is a corporation or trust. It is evidenced by a document that is a partnership agreement. The agreement is between persons who are the partners; the persons may be individuals, corporations, and/or other partnerships. Each partner owns one or more interests, called units, in the partnership.

Partners are of two types: general and limited. Every partnership must have at least one general partner. Sometimes where there is more than one general partner, one of them is designated the managing general partner.

Many partnerships have only general partners, who contribute cash, property, and/or services. The interests of the general partners may or may not be equal. In this type of partnership, that is essentially a joint venture, generally all of the partners are equally liable for satisfaction of the obligations of the partnership and can be called upon to make additional capital contributions to the partnership.

Some partnerships, however, need or want to attract capital from sources other than the general partners. This capital can come from investors, called *limited partners.* Their interest in the partnership is limited in the sense that their liability is limited. The liability of a limited partner is confined to the amount of the capital contribution—the investment. General liability for the acts of the partnership rests with the general partner or partners. A partnership with both general and limited partners is a *limited partnership.*

As observed, the partnership is the entity that acquires the property, develops it (if necessary), and sometimes continues to operate and maintain the property. Where a tax-exempt organization is the general partner, it is not the owner of the property (the partnership is) but nonetheless it can have many of the incidents of ownership, such as participation in the cash flow generated by the property, a preferential leasing arrangement, and/or the general perception by the outside world that the property is owned by the tax-exempt organization (often furthered by naming the building with the organization's name). The tax-exempt organization leases space in the property owned by the partnership. Often, the tax-exempt organization will have the option to purchase the property from the partnership after the passage of a few years.

Partnerships do not pay taxes. They are merely conduits of net revenue to the partners, who bear the responsibility for paying tax on the net income. Partnerships are also conduits of the tax advantages of the ownership of property, and thus pass through preference items such as depreciation and interest deductions.

If an entity fails to qualify under the federal tax laws as a partnership, it will be treated as an *association,* which means taxed as a corporation. When that happens, the entity will usually have to pay taxes and the ability to pass through tax advantages to the equity owners is lost.

As a general rule, a partnership is a very useful and beneficial way for one or more individuals or organizations to acquire, own, and operate a property. However, there can be problems with this approach in the tax-exempt organizations context.

THE TAX EXEMPTION ISSUE

The IRS is not enamored with the thought of nonprofit organizations in partnerships, other than as limited partners in a prudent investment vehicle. To date, all of the controversy has focused on charitable organizations in partnerships, although some or all of the principles of law being developed may become applicable to other types of tax-exempt organizations, such as social welfare organizations and membership associations.

It is the view of the IRS that substantial benefits can be provided to the for-profit participants in a partnership (usually the limited partners) with a tax-exempt organization where the exempt organization is a general partner. This concern has its origins in arrangements involving hospitals and physicians, such as a partnership formed to build and manage a medical office building, with a hospital as the general partner and investing physicians as limited partners. Where these substantial benefits are present, the IRS will—upon discovering them—not be hesitant to assert private inurement and private benefit (see Chapter 5).

It is the current position of the IRS that a charitable organization will lose its federal income tax exemption if it is a general partner in a partnership, unless the principal purpose of the partnership itself is to further charitable purposes. Even where the partnership can so qualify, the exemption is revoked if the charitable organization/general partner is not adequately insulated from the day-to-day management responsibilities of the partnership and/or if the limited partners are receiving an unwarranted return.

The IRS position on tax-exempt organizations in partnerships is questionable, being somewhat unfair and in conflict with basic legal principles. Nonetheless, the present position of the IRS on the subject is far more enlightened than its original position. Indeed, it is apparent that the views of the IRS in this regard are changing, with the IRS now conceding that a charitable organization can (as required) be operated exclusively for exempt purposes and simultaneously be a general partner and satisfy its fiduciary responsibilities with respect to the other partners.

Originally, the IRS was of the view that involvement by a charitable organization in a partnership as a general partner was the basis for automatic revocation of tax exemption, irrespective of the purpose of the partnership. This view was predicated upon the private inurement doctrine. That is, the IRS staked out the position that participation by a charitable organization in a partnership, where the organization is the general partner and private investors are limited partners, is contrary to the organization's tax-exempt status, in that private economic benefit resulted to the limited partners.

However, the courts failed to uphold these views, forcing the agency to relax its stance in these regards. The IRS' lawyers ultimately opined that it is possible for a charitable organization to participate as a general partner in a limited partnership without jeopardizing its tax exemption. The lawyers advised that two aspects of the matter should be particularly reviewed: whether (1) the participation may be in conflict with the goals and purposes of the charitable organization, and (2) the terms of the partnership agreement contain provisions that "insulate" the charitable organization from certain of the obligations imposed on a general partner.

This position of the IRS' legal counsel has opened the way for many favorable private letter rulings concerning charitable organizations in partnerships. Each of these partnerships, however, have been held to be in furtherance of charitable objectives, such as the construction and operation of a medical office building on the grounds of a hospital, the purchase and operation of medical equipment at a hospital, and low-income housing projects. Indeed, to date, the IRS has yet to issue a private letter ruling denying a charitable organization tax-exempt status because of its involvement as a general partner in a limited partnership.

In summary, the current position of the IRS as to whether a charitable organization will have its tax-exempt status revoked (or recognition denied) if it functions as a general partner in a limited partnership is the subject of a *two-part test*. Under this test—which really is a three-part test—the IRS first looks to determine whether the charitable organization/general partner is serving a charitable purpose by means of the partnership. If the partnership is serving a charitable purpose, the IRS applies the second portion of the test. Should the partnership fail to adhere to the charitability standard, however, the charitable organization/general partner will be deprived of its tax-exempt status.

The second part of the two-part test is designed to ascertain whether the charity's role as general partner inhibits its charitable purposes. Here, the IRS looks to means by which the organization may, under particular facts and circumstances, be insulated from the day-to-day responsibilities as general partner and (the true third part of the test) whether or not the limited partners are receiving an "undue" economic benefit from the partnership. It is the view of the IRS that there is an inherent tension between the ability of a charitable organization to function exclusively in furtherance of its exempt functions and the obligation of a general partner to operate the partnership for the benefit of the limited partners. This tension is the same perceived phenomenon that the IRS, at the outset, chose to characterize as a conflict of interest.

SOME ALTERNATIVES TO PARTNERSHIPS

Until or unless the IRS revises its rules in this area, charitable organizations must avoid participation in partnerships where the purpose of the partnership is not itself charitable (or else be prepared to test the government's position in court).

One way for a charitable organization to avoid the dilemma is to establish a wholly owned organization, usually a for-profit corporation, that would serve as the general partner in the partnership. This approach has been upheld by the IRS in private letter rulings. However, as discussed, the tax-exempt entity leasing rules have been revised to make this approach somewhat less attractive.

Some charitable organizations are using a pooled income fund (see Chapter 17). Donors transfer cash and/or property to a pooled income fund, and receive a charitable contribution deduction. The assets of the fund are used to purchase and maintain real property, with the depreciation deduction flowing through the fund and to the income beneficiaries for their use in computing income tax liability. Under some circumstances, the tax-exempt entity leasing rules will be applicable in determining the depreciation deduction.

Another approach is to avoid partnerships or other "pass-through" entities altogether and utilize a leasing arrangement. This works best where a tax-exempt organization acquires unimproved land and subsequently desires to have it improved, such as for its offices. The organization can acquire land and enter into a long-term ground lease with a developer or development group. The developer would construct the building, perhaps giving it the organization's name and otherwise providing all external appearances of the structure being the organization's own building. This leaves the developer or development group in the position of fully utilizing all of the tax benefits. The nonprofit organization leases space in the building, perhaps pursuant to a "sweetheart" lease, and may be accorded an option to purchase the building after the passage of years.

FOCUS ON THE CAMPAIGN TO CLEAN UP AMERICA

As is the case involving the use of a for-profit subsidiary, the Campaign to Clean Up America is not ready, at this stage in its development, for participation in a joint venture or other type of partnership.

There will be opportunities in the future for advancement of the programs of the Campaign by means of one or more joint ventures with other nonprofit organizations. Perhaps, too, a general partnership with a for-profit entity will prove advantageous or maybe a limited partnership as a financing vehicle. Part of this depends upon the success of the Campaign itself; part is dependent upon forthcoming developments in the law of tax-exempt organizations.

17

The World of
Planned Giving

One of the great mysteries in the world of charity is why so few nonprofit organizations take advantage of the most remunerative fund-raising technique there is—planned giving. Those that do venture into the realm of planned giving are inevitably successful if they have given the attempt even half a chance. Since the managers of nonprofit organizations do talk to one another, what is the reason for the failure of planned giving to be commonplace throughout the charitable community?

The reason for this failure is probably twofold. One is that planned giving has, over the years, been seen as mysterious and very complicated, so that the management of many organizations have grown fearful of it. The other is a consequence of that phenomenon that manifests itself all too frequently, which is the "nonprofit mentality" or the tendency of the management of nonprofit organizations to think small and short-sightedly. These two reasons are actually tightly interwoven, as most organizations think about planned giving from time to time but put off implementing a planned giving program to another day—a tomorrow that never comes. Perhaps this is why the old term—deferred giving—is more accurate!

APPRECIATED PROPERTY GIFTS—A REPRISE

The importance of the appreciated property gift is addressed in Chapter 8. In essence, this aspect of charitable giving is based on the fact that one of

193

the chief principles undergirding the advantages of charitable contributions of securities, real estate, and other property is that the deductible amount is generally equal to the full fair market value of the property at the time of the gift. This means that the amount of appreciation in the property (the amount exceeding the donor's basis), which would be taxed if sold, escapes income taxation. (As noted in Chapter 8, there may be some alternative minimum tax complications.) For this favorable result to occur, the property must constitute long-term capital gain property.

Consequently, the key to wise charitable giving is to give property that is long-term capital gain property and that has substantially appreciated in value. The greater the appreciation, the greater the charitable deduction and other income tax savings. The appreciated property gift is, therefore, a core concept of planned giving.

PLANNED GIFTS—AN INTRODUCTION

There are two basic types of planned gifts. One is to utilize a will, whereby the gift comes out of a decedent's estate (as a bequest or devise). The other is a gift made during the donor's lifetime, using a trust or other agreement.

On many occasions, these gifts are called *deferred gifts,* because the actual receipt of the contribution by the charity is deferred until the happening of some event (usually the donor's death). But the term *deferred giving* has fallen out of favor, as some donors gain (to the chagrin of the gift-seeking charity) the impression that it is their tax benefits that are being deferred.

A planned gift usually is a contribution of a donor's interest in money or an item of property, rather than an outright gift of the entirety of the money or property. (The word *usually* is used because gifts using insurance do not neatly fit this definition and because some treat an outright gift of property in some circumstances as a planned gift.) Technically, this type of gift is a gift of a partial interest in property. Thus, planned giving is (usually) partial interest giving.

An item of property has within it two interests. One is an *income interest* and the other is a *remainder interest.*

The income interest within an item of property is a function of the income generated by the property. A person may be entitled to all of the income from a property or some portion of the income, such as, for example, income equal to 6 percent of the fair market value of the property, even though the property is producing income at the rate of 9 percent. This person is said to have the (or an) income interest in the property. Two or more persons (such as husband and wife) may have income interests in the same property and these interests may be held concurrently or consecutively.

The remainder interest within an item of property is the projected value of the property, or the property produced by reinvestments, at some future date. That is, the remainder interest in property is an amount equal to the present value of the property (or its offspring) when it is to be received at a subsequent point in time.

These interests are measured by the value of the property, the age of the donor(s), and the period of time that the income interests will exist. The actual computation is usually made by means of actuarial tables usually promulgated by the Department of the Treasury.

An income interest or a remainder interest in property may, then, be contributed to charity. However, it is infrequent that a deduction is available for a charitable gift of an income interest in property. By contrast, the charitable contribution of a remainder interest in an item of property will—assuming all of the technical requirements are met—give rise to a (frequently sizable) charitable deduction.

When a gift of a remainder interest in property to a charity is made, the charity will not acquire that interest until the income interests have expired. Nonetheless, the donor receives the charitable deduction for the tax year in which the remainder interest in the property for the recipient charity is established. When a gift of an income interest in property to a charity is made, the charity acquires that interest immediately and retains it until such time (sometimes measured by a term of years) as the remainder interest commences. Again, any resulting charitable deduction is available for the tax year in which the income interest in the property for the charity is established.

Basically, the federal tax law requires that a planned gift be made by means of a trust if a charitable deduction is to be available. The trust used to facilitate a planned gift is known as a *split-interest trust* because the trust is the mechanism for satisfying the requirements with respect to the income and remainder interests. That is, the trust is the medium for splitting the property into its two component interests. Split-interest trusts are charitable remainder trusts, pooled income funds, and charitable lead trusts (explained below).

There are some exceptions to the general requirement as to use of a split-interest trust in planned giving. The principal one is the charitable gift annuity that uses a contract rather than a trust. Individuals may give a remainder interest in their personal residence or farm to charity and receive a charitable deduction without utilizing a trust. Also, a trust is not required for a deductible gift of a remainder interest in real property which is granted to a public charity or certain operating foundations exclusively for conservation purposes. Similarly, one may contribute a lease on, option to purchase, or easement with respect to real property granted in perpetuity to a public charity or certain foundations exclusively for conservation purposes and receive a charitable contribution deduction without a trust. Further, a contribution of an undivided portion of one's entire interest in property is not regarded as a contribution of a partial interest in property.

A donor, although desirous of supporting a particular charity, may be unwilling or unable to fully part with property, either because of a present or perceived need for the income that the property provides and/or because of the capital gains taxes that would be experienced if the property was sold. The planned gift is likely to be the answer in this situation, because the donor may satisfy his or her charitable desires and yet continue to receive income from the property. Moreover, the donor receives a charitable deduction for the gift of the remainder interest which will reduce or eliminate the tax on the income from the gift property. Also, there is no regular income tax on the capital gain inherent in the property (although, as noted, there may be some alternative minimum tax consequences). Further, if the gift property is not throwing off sufficient income, the trustee of the split-interest trust may dispose of the property and reinvest the proceeds in more productive property, which will enable the donor to receive more income from the property than was the case prior to the making of the gift.

The various planned giving vehicles are explored next.

CHARITABLE REMAINDER TRUSTS

The most widespread form of planned giving involves a split-interest trust known as the *charitable remainder trust.* The term is nearly self-explanatory: the entity is a trust, which has created a remainder interest that is destined for charity. Each charitable remainder trust arrangement is specifically designed for the particular circumstances of the donor(s), with the remainder interest in the gift property designated for one or more charities.

A qualified charitable remainder trust must provide for a specified distribution of income, at least annually, to or for the use of one or more beneficiaries (at least one of which is not a charity). The flow of income must be for life or for a term of no more than twenty years, with an irrevocable remainder interest to be held for the benefit of, or paid over to, the charity. These beneficiaries are the holders of the income interests and the charity has the remainder interest.

The manner in which the income interests in a charitable remainder trust are ascertained is dependent upon whether the trust is a *charitable remainder annuity trust* or a *charitable remainder unitrust.* In the case of the former, the income payments are in the form of a fixed amount (hence the word *annuity*). In the case of the latter, the income payments are in the form of an amount equal to a percentage of the fair market value of the assets in the trust.

All categories of charitable organizations—both public charities and private foundations (see Chapter 11)—are eligible to be remainder beneficiaries of as many charitable remainder trusts as they can muster. However, the allowability of the charitable deduction will vary as respects the type of charitable organization that is the donee, due to the percentage limitations (see Chapter 8).

Usually, a bank or similar financial institution serves as the trustee of a charitable remainder trust. These institutions should have the capacity to administer the trust, make appropriate investments, and timely adhere to all income distribution and reporting requirements. It is common, however, for the charitable organization that is the remainder beneficiary to act as trustee. If the donor or a related person is named the trustee, the *grantor trust* rules may apply, with the gain from the sale by the trust of appreciated property taxed to the donor.

Conventionally, once the income interest expires, the assets in a charitable remainder trust are distributed to the charitable organization that is the remainder beneficiary. However, the assets (or a portion of them) may be retained in the trust. If a retention occurs, the trust will be classified as a private foundation, unless it can sidestep those rules.

POOLED INCOME FUNDS

A popular planned giving technique is the gift to a *pooled income fund.* Like a charitable remainder trust, a pooled income fund is a form of split-interest trust.

A donor to a qualified pooled income fund receives a charitable deduction for the gift to charity of the remainder interest in the donated property. By the transaction, income interests in one or more noncharitable beneficiaries are created, with the remainder interest in the gift property designated for the charity that maintains the fund.

The pooled income fund basic instrument (trust agreement or declaration of trust) is written to faciliate gifts from an unlimited number of donors and thus the essential terms of the transaction are established in advance for all participants. That is, there is no tailoring of the terms of the transfer to fit any one donor's particular circumstances (as is the case, for example, with the charitable remainder trust). The pooled income fund is, literally, a pooling of gifts.

Contributions to a pooled income fund may be of a considerably lesser amount than those to a charitable remainder trust. Gifts to pooled income funds are generally confined to cash and readily marketable securities (other than tax-exempt bonds).

A pooled income fund receives gifts from a number of donors, with each donor contributing an irrevocable remainder interest in the gift property to or for the use of an eligible charity. Each donor creates an income interest for the life of one or more beneficiaries, who must be living at the time of the transfer. The properties transferred by the donors must be commingled in the fund (to create the necessary pool).

Each income interest beneficiary must receive income at least once each year, determined by the rate of return earned by the fund for the year. Beneficiaries receive their proportionate share of the fund's income. The income share is based upon the number of unit's owned by the beneficiary in the fund and each unit must be based upon the fair market value of the assets when transferred.

Thus, a pooled income fund is essentially an investment vehicle, the funding of which is motivated by charitable intents.

A pooled income fund must be maintained by one or more charitable organizations. This maintenance requirement means that the charity must exercise control over the fund; the organization does not have to be the trustee of the fund (although it can be) but must have the power to remove and replace the trustee. An income beneficiary of or donor to the fund may not be a trustee. However, a donor may be a trustee or officer of the charitable organization that maintains the fund where he or she does not have general responsibilities as respects the fund which are ordinarily exercised by a trustee.

Unlike the case with respect to other forms of planned giving, only certain categories of charitable organizations may maintain a pooled income fund. Most types of public charities can maintain a pooled income fund, while private foundations and some nonprivate foundations cannot. (The distinctions between public and private charities are summarized in Chapter 11.)

The same general tax advantages available as the result of gifts to charitable remainder trusts are available for gifts to pooled income funds. This is particularly true when the gift is made using fully marketable and appreciated securities. The pooled income fund transfer may accommodate a smaller amount (value) of securities than a transfer to a remainder trust. However, if fixed income is an important consideration, the charitable remainder annuity trust (see above) or the charitable gift annuity (see below) will be preferable to a gift to a charitable remainder unitrust or pooled income fund.

CHARITABLE GIFT ANNUITIES

Another form of planned giving is the *charitable gift annuity.* Unlike these other two planned giving methodologies, the charitable gift annuity is not based upon use of a split-interest trust. Rather, the annuity is reflected in an agreement between donor and donee, where the donor agrees to make a gift and the donee agrees to, in return, provide the donor (and/or someone else) with an annuity.

The donor, in fact, is engaging in two transactions, albeit with one payment—the purchase of an annuity and the making of a charitable gift. It is the latter that gives rise to the charitable deduction. One sum is transferred; the amount in excess of that necessary to purchase the annuity is the charitable gift portion. It is because of the dual nature of the transaction that the charitable gift annuity transfer constitutes a bargain sale.

As with the annuity paid out of a charitable remainder annuity trust (see above), the annuity resulting from the creation of a charitable gift annuity arrangement is a fixed amount paid at regular intervals. The amount paid is dependent upon the age of the beneficiary, determined at the time the contribution is made.

A portion of the annuity paid is tax-free, being a return of capital. Where appreciated securities are given, there will be capital gain on the appreciation that is attributable to the value of the annuity. If the donor is the annuitant, the capital gain can be reported ratably over the individual's life expectancy. However, the tax savings occasioned by the charitable contribution deduction may shelter the capital gain, resulting from the creation of a charitable gift annuity, from taxation.

Because the arrangement is by contract between donor and donee, all of the assets of the charitable organization are on the line for ongoing payment of the annuities. (By contrast, with most planned giving techniques, the resources for payment of income are confined to those in a split-interest trust.) That is why a few states impose a requirement that charities establish a reserve for the payment of gift annuities and why many charitable organizations are reluctant to embark upon a gift annuity program. This is unfortunate, because millions of dollars are lost annually by charitable organizations that fail to use charitable gift annuities—and even those who are reluctant to commit to the ongoing payment of annuities can eliminate the risk by reinsuring them.

CHARITABLE LEAD TRUSTS

The foregoing forms of planned giving have this common element: The donor transfers to a charitable organization the remainder interest in the property, with one or more noncharitable beneficiaries retaining the income interest. However, the reverse may occur—and that is the essence of the *charitable lead trust.*

A charitable lead trust is a vehicle by which property transferred to it is apportioned into an income interest and a remainder interest. Like the charitable remainder trust and the pooled income fund, it is a split-interest trust. Pursuant to a charitable lead trust, an income interest in property is contributed to a charitable organization, either for a term of years or for the life of one individual or the lives of more than one individual. The remainder interest in the property is reserved to return, at the expiration of the income interest (the "lead period"), to the donor or some other noncharitable beneficiary or beneficiaries; often the property passes from one generation (the donor's) to another.

The charitable lead trust can be used to accelerate a series of charitable contributions, that would otherwise be made annually, into one year, with a corresponding single-year deduction for the "bunched" amount of charitable gifts.

In some sets of circumstances, a charitable deduction is available for the transfer of an income interest in property to a charitable organization. There are stringent limitations, however, on the deductible amount of charitable contributions of these income interests.

STARTING A PROGRAM

Knowing something about the various planned giving techniques is a start but only that. A planned giving program must be implemented and that takes more than knowing about income and remainder interests.

Some tips on how to launch a planned giving program are found in Chapter 18.

18
Putting Ideas into Action

It is one thing to have an idea; it is another thing to put the idea into actual practice. The chapters in this portion of the book are offered to stimulate ideas. Starting and operating a nonprofit organization is a relatively common undertaking. However, using techniques such as planned giving, subsidiaries, joint ventures, and partnerships is not so common. Not all of these techniques are suitable for all nonprofit organizations at all times. The point is not to overlook a technique that can prove useful for your particular organization.

As always, when approaching something of this sort, professional guidance is a must. Fees for lawyers, accountants, and/or management or fundraising consultants may seem unaffordable at first but in the long run it is usually money well spent.

JOINT VENTURES

A *joint venture* is an undertaking involving two (or more) organizations. In this context, it may be two nonprofit organizations or a nonprofit and a for-profit organization.

In most instances, a joint venture is the product of thinking that two heads are better than one. It is a pooling of resources. Sometimes the resources are financial, although that is most often the case with partnerships. Most often, a joint venture is an aggregation of programs. That is, a typical joint venture in this setting occurs when one organization has a program resource and the other organization has another program resource, and the purpose of the joint venture can only be accomplished or can better be accomplished through a blending of the two.

From the standpoint of a nonprofit organization, two general outcomes are possible. One is that the organization will be approached by another, with the latter seeking access to a resource of the former. The other is that the nonprofit organization will go out seeking a resource of another organization, to carry out a desired program of the first organization.

The management of a nonprofit organization should always have an ongoing business plan that includes an inventory of what it is that the organization is doing or wishes to do. From such an inventory, management may discover that the organization lacks the resources to undertake a particular project. Some nonprofit managers might give up at this point. Others may expend the effort needed to purchase the personnel, equipment, or other resources necessary to tackle the project.

A third option is possible: use of the existing resources of another. This may require some effort and ingenuity, yet can be a preferable alternative to the other options. When one nonprofit organization joins with another organization to advance a particular undertaking, a joint venture results.

A joint venture, thus, can be a medium for furthering program objectives. It can also be a way to further management objectives, although if another nonprofit organization is merely providing management services to another, the provision of services may be an unrelated business of the provider (see Chapter 12).

A joint venture can also be used to advance fund-raising objectives. This is often done with another nonprofit organization. It can also be done with a for-profit organization.

A case in point with respect to the latter is the *commercial co-venture.* This is an unfortunate term, because of the connotation (usually inaccurate) that the nonprofit organization involved is engaged in some activity that is commercial. Moreover, it often is not really a venture—although it can be (and increasingly is).

A commercial co-venture is an arrangement between a business and a charitable organization, whereby the business entity agrees to make a contribution to the charity. The gift is a function of the volume of sales of the company's service or product during a particular period of time. That is, the company agrees to donate to the charity an amount equal to a percentage of sales during the time of the promotion; the fact of the prospective gift is advertised to the consuming public. The charity benefits because of the gift, and the business benefits because of the positive marketing and (hopefully) an increase in the sales volume. The relationship can turn into a true joint venture as the charity itself becomes involved in the promotional aspects of the sales campaign. A word of caution: As the charity becomes more involved in this type of joint venture, the likelihood increases that the business' payments to the charity will be treated as a taxable payment for services rendered and less a charitable contribution.

PARTNERSHIPS

The concept of the partnership is described in Chapter 16. There, the point is made that the partnership can be a general or limited one.

As a practical matter, there is little difference between a general partnership and a joint venture. Both involve a pooling of resources, often programmatic ones. Astute managers of nonprofit organizations will always be alert to opportunities to achieve something using the resources of others. This is not a selfish or unilateral approach since the other party to the venture will also, by definition, be entering into the arrangement for the purpose of achieving some desired end.

Thus, again, nonprofit management should review programs and objectives, to determine if something can be better accomplished (or just plain accomplished) working in tandem with another or others.

Sometimes, the nature of the relationship is that one or more of the partners is bringing to the arrangement something other than programmatic resources. Sometimes, the resource brought is money. It is in this context that a partnership is used as a financing device. This is almost always the case when a limited partnership is utilized. As noted in Chapter 16, the limited partners are investors and the resource they bring to the arrangement is money. Having stated that limited partners are sources of financing, there is one unique aspect of the matter that requires mention in the nonprofit organization context: The limited partners will most likely be those who are supporters of the organization, those who are particularly interested in its programs and objectives. They, then, are acting in a dual capacity: They desire to make an investment and receive an economic return, and they wish to assist the organization. These limited partners tend to be directors, trustees, and/or officers of, and/or substantial contributors to, the organization. Certainly, nonprofit organizations have unique opportunities in this regard.

Therefore, the management of a nonprofit organization should approach the possibility of a partnership, particularly a limited partnership, as a search for funding. This type of financing can be blended with a fund-raising program. Certainly, limited partners and donors can be drawn from the organization's same constituency. For example, an individual can become a limited partner in a partnership where a charitable organization is a general partner, and then subsequently donate his or her limited partnership interest to the organization.

The management of a nonprofit organization, then, should do the following:

- Review all program, administrative, and fund-raising objectives, with a view to the funding of them.

- Develop a program for the financing of each of these functions. In this process, some may be clearly fundable with contributions (in the case of charitable organizations), some may be funded with fee-for-service revenue, some may be funded with membership fees (assuming a membership), and some may be funded with investment income (those funded out of an endowment).

- This process may well yield one or more programs or functions that cannot be fully funded using one or more of these approaches or cannot be funded at all this way. This introduces the possibility of a limited partnership.

Does the organization need or want its own building? How about a new computer system? Or other major equipment or capital asset? What about a facility to further programs, such as a research center or conference facility? These are situations where the limited partnership can be used as a financing mechanism to accomplish these ends.

The process, then, of deciding whether to utilize a partnership or joint venture is really one of matching means to ends. It requires the management of a nonprofit organization to take the most expansive view of objectives and opportunities. It requires abandonment of the nonprofit organization's management to think small and to instead seek to the fullest the exploitation of the organization's potential.

As an illustration, some nonprofit organizations' management only dream of having their own building for their offices. They fear a conventional fund-raising program to that end, believing (in some instances, correctly) that they lack the donor base to accumulate the necessary funds by gifts and grants. Others take a broader view: They assemble board members and other supporters, and cause them to become limited partners in a partnership. Using the capital thus acquired and/or borrowing by the partnership, the partnership acquires the property, creates the offices, leases them (presumably on some favorable basis) to the organization, and passes along to the limited partners all or some of the cash flow of the property and the tax advantages of owning property. In the meantime, the organization can (particularly if a charitable one) raise funds to ultimately purchase the property from the partnership. When the process is completed, the organization has done a remarkable thing: It has acquired its own headquarters, which it can now occupy rent-free, solely using the funds of others.

Some programs of nonprofit organizations can be enhanced by administering them by means of a general partnership. Some functions of nonprofit organizations can be best financed using a limited partnership. As to the latter, the use of a limited partnership needs to be weighed against and integrated with other financing techniques. Without intending to put the matter too crassly, a limited partnership is a way of utilizing the money of others to achieve ends. That ability can be doubly enhanced when coupled with the charitable deduction.

PLANNED GIVING

As observed in Chapter 17, charitable organizations are underutilizing planned giving. Part of the reason for this phenomenon, which is rather remarkable considering the extent of gifts that can be developed by means of the planned giving techniques, lies in the mystery that surrounds planned giving. For many, planned giving is perceived as far too complex. Since planned giving seems so complicated and is believed to not generate badly needed current dollars, the implementation of a planned giving program is usually deferred to another day—that never seems to come.

Still another reason for this less than full utilization of planned giving is found in the erroneous belief that planned giving is only for the larger charities, those that have been in existence for some time and that have an existing constituency. Finally, the lack of planned giving programs can be traced to the thought that the initial process of establishing a planned giving program is too expensive.

None of these reasons for delaying a planned giving are truly valid. Nearly every charitable organization, no matter how small or how new, should have a planned giving program.

The very term *planned giving* usually causes some uncertainty. The two words obviously do not mean that all other gifts are unplanned. As noted in Chapter 17, a far better term would be *integrated giving*. The concept of planned giving means a gift that is of sufficient magnitude that the making of it is integrated with the donor's personal financial plan or estate plan. A planned gift, then, is not an impulse gift; it is planned in the sense that the consequences of the gift (other than to the charity) as they relate, for example, to the donor's family or business, are taken into account before the gift is made and in determining the type of gift that it will be.

Probably the simplest of planned gifts is a bequest in a will. The larger the gift or the more complicated the terms, such as the inclusion of one or more trusts, affect the extent of the planning, but a planned gift it is. Writing a will means formulating a plan. So does the writing of a trust.

Usually an outright gift of cash or property is not regarded as a planned gift, although sometimes an outright contribution of property can be, such as a gift of a business or a partnership interest. A mere gift of an insurance policy may not be regarded by some as a planned gift but the process of deliberately selecting a particular policy for donation to charity and the giving of it can easily entail some serious planning.

Most planned gifts are those that are based on the fundamental principle that property consists of two interests: an income interest and a remainder interest. Planned gifts usually involve the donation to charity of either an income interest or a remainder interest.

A gift of an income interest is made by means of a charitable lead trust. Most remainder interest gifts are made using a charitable remainder trust, a pooled income fund, or a charitable gift annuity.

The fund-raiser can do more in the planned giving field than ask for gifts and collect them. He or she can simultaneously render valuable services to the donor. The donor may end up with more income as the result of the gift. The donor's earnings may be shifted from taxable income to nontaxable income. The donor has been enabled to dispose of property without paying taxes. In many cases, this is property he or she did not really need. The donor may become able to pass property to other family members without incurring estate taxes. Planned giving can yield professional money and property management without cost to the income beneficiaries. It can be the foundation for retirement plans, tuition payments, and memorial gifts. The list goes on and on.

So, if planned giving is so great, why is every charity not using it? The principal reasons have already been stated. However, another reason may be that the organization simply does not quite know how to begin. Here, then, are the ten easy steps to implementation of a successful planned giving program.

Step 1: The members of the organization's board of directors *must* be involved. At this point, *being involved* does not mean as donors—that comes later. It means involved in the launching of the program.

The best way to start this process is by causing the board to pass a planned giving launch resolution. This is a resolution that states that there is to be such a program, who on the staff and among the officers is principally responsible for it, and most importantly, what planned giving methods are going to be used. As to this last point, the resolution should expressly identify the vehicles: wills, charitable remainder trusts, insurance, pooled income fund, or whatever.

Step 2: Most of the board members will not have heard of these things and that opens the way to step 2. At a board meeting, set some time aside for a brief presentation on the basics of planned giving. The presentation should be made by an outsider—a lawyer, professional development counsel, or bank trust officer, for example. The board members should be given some written material to peruse at their leisure afterwards.

Step 3: Once the board has received its initial training and has adopted the launch resolution, step 3 is to develop some prototype instruments. These are documents, with the organization's name in the appropriate places, that can be shown to interested parties. These documents may be will clauses, charitable remainder trust models (both annuity trust and unitrust, and one life and two lives), stock powers, pooled income fund transfer agreements, and/or charitable gift annuity contracts.

Donors will rarely be interested in these prototype documents. Some of the board members may be. Certainly those who are going to be asking for planned gifts should have some basic familiarity with them. However, the greatest use of these instruments will be to provide them to the potential donor's professional counsel, be it lawyer, accountant, financial planner, insurance agent, or securities broker. These persons may be unfamiliar with planned giving and will find actual documents very helpful.

Step 4: Government regulation of planned giving programs is unavoidable, so step 4 is to adhere to the requirements of the law. Asking for a planned gift is still asking for a gift, so it is important to register in each of the states that have charitable solicitation acts if the charity has not already done so (see Chapter 9). If a pooled income fund is to be in the arsenal of planned giving methods, management should be certain to secure a favorable ruling from the Internal Revenue Service as to qualification of the fund before gifts are made. If charitable gift annuities are to be used, state insurance law requirements must be complied with. Likewise, where gifts of insurance policies are involved, it is necessary to be able to establish that the charity has an insurable interest in the lives of the donors.

Step 5: The beginning of the marketing phase. This step may involve a myriad of alternatives but the first must be acquisition of some easy-to-understand brochures on the concept and methods of planned giving that will be distributed to prospective donors. It is far preferable to have separate brochures on each of the techniques, than to have one large booklet. The organization can either write and print its own brochures or purchase them commercially.

Back to the board of directors. They are provided copies of the literature. Now starts the process of getting some (preferably all) of the directors to commit to some form of planned gift. It is not easy causing others to give when the organization's own leadership has not (or worse, will not).

Step 6: The organization should start the process of building a network or cadre of volunteers who will be planned giving advocates to the outside world. This group should be comprised in part of members of the organization's board of directors; other possibilities include individuals from the organization's prior leadership, active members, community leaders, and volunteer professionals (such as lawyers and accountants). These individuals will assist in procuring planned gifts, by making them themselves, by asking others, and/or by influencing others who will do the asking.

This cadre of volunteers will need some training before they are sent out looking for planned gifts. Special sessions with someone knowledgable about planned giving is essential, as is the provision of written materials. The intent is not to make these persons instant planned giving experts or even expect them to procure the gift. Their job is to become sufficiently familiar with the concept and techniques of planned giving so that they know the basics about each method and something about how to correlate these basics with the facts and circumstances of each prospect's situation. The actual "ask" will probably be by a staff person or a professional planned giving consultant.

Step 7: Identify prospective planned gift donors. Of course, this step is, in actuality, an ongoing process. If the organization has a membership, that obviously is the base of individuals with which to begin. The giving history of donors (frequency and amount of gifts) should be reviewed to determine planned giving prospects. Others who are interested in the organization's programs are prospects as well. Even new organizations have those who are supporters and thus potential planned givers.

Step 8: Once the prospective donors are identified, they must be contacted. This is the essence of the marketing phase and how it is done will vary from group to group. One tried-and-true approach is to send letters to the prospects explaining the planned giving program and inviting them to request additional information; those who respond are sent the appropriate brochures. Another approach is to concentrate on one vehicle, such as the pooled income fund or insurance, and market just that method by sending the brochure with the introductory letter. Some organizations, for example, like to lead with a wills program; others have had success opening with a pooled income fund program.

There are many marketing techniques. Some organizations have had success with financial planning seminars, where planned giving is stressed. Others hold seminars, not for donors but for those in the community that advise donors—again, the lawyers, financial planners, accountants, and so on. If the organization has a magazine or newsletter, it should regularly publish items on planned giving. If the organization has an annual meeting or convention, a presentation on planned giving should be on the agenda. One favorite technique is the annual membership meeting where a planned giving booth is among the other displays in the exhibit hall as part of the "trade show."

The marketing aspects of planned giving must be ongoing ones. Some organizations can use all of these techniques. For launching a planned giving program, a combination of a special mailing, a seminar, and coverage in the organization's regular publications can be powerful.

Step 9: The process of actually obtaining the gift once a bona fide prospect has signaled some interest. On this point, it is hard to generalize. For organizations with an emerging planned giving program, the best way to proceed is to have a staff person or a volunteer meet with the prospective donor and work out a general plan, then have a subsequent session with a planned giving professional who can advise the parties as to the specific method that is best for all concerned. Thereafter, a lawyer can prepare the specific instrument. As the organization matures, it can build planned giving expertise into its in-house operations.

Here is an example of a typical planned gift: An individual has been contacted about a charitable organization's planned giving program. Having coincidentally received a large amount of money as the result of a sale of property, he or she is looking for some tax relief. The prospective donor has an interest in the programs of the organization, so he or she and a staff person meets and works out these general guidelines: he or she needs a charitable deduction of X amount and annual income of Y amount. The parties subsequently meet with a lawyer, the numbers are run on a computer, the deduction and income amounts for each planned giving method are reviewed, and a specific arrangement (in this case, perhaps a charitable remainder annuity trust) is developed.

One thing is clear: The organization's staff and volunteers will only learn by doing. As the gifts come in and the various processes that lead to the gifts are experienced, the parties involved will gain greater confidence and will need to rely on the outside professional less. Nonetheless, it is advisable to have a planned giving professional on call at the outset, and thereafter use him or her as circumstances warrant.

Step 10: Indeed, this is step 10, which may have occurred much earlier in the process: the selection of legal counsel or other professional who can work with the organization in the launching and ongoing administration of the program.

As noted, one of the excuses frequently given for postponing the inauguration of a planned giving program (or altogether ignoring the idea of such a program) is that it is not suitable for a new organization. There is no question that a university with decades of graduations has a larger and more solid donor base than a community service group incorporated last week. But that university's relative advantage is not an authentic reason for doing nothing. Every organization has a support base or it would not exist. It may be that, on day 1, there is only one planned gift prospect, yet that is no reason not to ask that one propsect. The largest planned giving program started with one gift.

The other excuse for not implementing a planned giving program is that the organization must channel all of its fund-raising energies into the generation of current dollars. Of all the excuses for not beginning, this is the most plausible. Nonetheless, this is still an excuse, not a reason.

There are two aspects of planned giving that are misunderstood when it comes to the need for current support. One is that there are some forms of planned giving that produce current dollars. Planned giving is not simply waiting 30 years for someone to die. Three planned giving methods that yield current dollars are (1) the charitable lead trust, where the charity is provided immediate income out of the trust, rather than a deferred remainder interest, (2) the charitable remainder trust, where the donor (in addition to giving the remainder interest) gives the portion of the income interest to charity, and (3) gifts of life insurance (or gifts based on life insurance), where the policy can be surrendered if necessary for its cash value or the charity can borrow money using the policy's cash value as collateral.

The other misunderstanding is that planned gifts generate usable support much more quickly than is usually realized. Without becoming too morbid or grasping about it, individuals can die sooner than expected. Or, to state the matter more charitably, not everyone reaches their life expectancy. The odds being what they are, the larger the stable of planned gifts, the greater the likelihood of a speedy return.

Also, the planned gift is ideal for the organization that is amassing a general endowment, scholarship, memorial, research, building, or similar fund. While everyone likes current gift dollars, once a base of investment assets (principal) is established, the investment income can nicely complement the gift support and the organization has the security of knowing that the assets remain in place.

The more it is understood that planned giving means service to the donors and large gifts, the more appreciated it will be. Some money will have to be expended at the outset but it will be minimal in relation to the gifts received. It is simply a matter of getting started—of taking the "deferral" out of this form of giving. Once the program is launched, the mystery will fall away and planned giving will become the most enjoyable and remunerative component of the fund-raising and development program.

BLENDING IT ALL

Innovative and energetic management of nonprofit organizations may well utilize all of these ideas . . . and more. A contemporary nonprofit organization may have subsidiaries, be involved in a partnership, and have a successful planned giving program.

Once again, it cannot be stressed enough that all of these techniques are means to ends. They are ways to cause an organization to acquire what it wants and needs. Usually, this means money—and in many ways all of these suggestions are fund-raising techniques.

The place to begin is the organization's "wish list." What does it want? A building? A computer? An endowment? Thereafter, it is a matter of matching the technique with the wish. Basically, the sky is the limit.

Moreover, these techniques can be blended. A partnership may be the best way to acquire the organization's offices, with an ongoing fund-raising program (including planned giving) used to buy out partnership interests, so as to ultimately directly own the property. A conventional fund-raising program may be used to acquire a computer system but an endowment fund (fueled in part by planned giving) may secure future upgrades and replacements of equipment. A subsidiary or other separate organization may be appropriate to house a particular activity but, as the organization grows, it may be able to absorb the activity within its basic operations, and an ongoing fund-raising program can provide the wherewithal to buy out shareholders or otherwise acquire the assets supporting the activity.

This concept does not have to be expressed in terms of fund-raising programs. Perhaps a joint venture or subsidiary is preferable to any fund-raising.

Generalizations are difficult here. There are many opportunities and many techniques. All an organization has to do is match its wants and needs to these techniques, and the rest is relatively simple.

Part V

Nonprofits: Whither the Future?

19

Whither Nonprofits?
A Short-Range Look

Nonprofit organizations are an expanding component of modern American society. These entities affect the lives of all. They are, as stressed in Chapter 1, a most distinguishing characteristic of our society, differentiating the United States from all other countries in the nation's willingness, when grappling with problems, to rely upon institutions other than governmental ones. They are a treasured national resource . . . or are they?

Many individuals truly treasure nonprofit organizations—and demonstrate this feeling by giving of their money, expertise, and time—for they comprehend the value of pluralism and voluntarism. Most Americans generally have a positive attitude toward nonprofit entities, be it their church, synagogue, hospital, or the old alma mater. Yet there is a minority—a growing one—that is not particularly sympathetic toward nonprofits, and that is, in some instances, hostile toward them. Some in this latter category serve in legislatures, are employees of legislators, preside in courtrooms, or are federal, state, or local regulators. There are some in the U.S. Congress, for example, who see nonprofit organizations as the most unregulated of sectors in our society—and they are working to remedy that perceived "deficiency."

Nonprofit organizations are not on the brink of extinction. They undoubtedly have decades of service yet to come, but there are some troubling signs that suggest that the climate for nonprofit organizations may soon be dramatically different as the result of a shift in the philosophy underlying the law that regulates them—as well as the substance of that law. This chapter will explore three of these signs: the matter of competition with for-profit organizations (and resulting tax policy), fund-raising regulation, and self-regulation. These developments are leading to a fundamental problem: the nonprofits' identity crisis. This phenomenon is explored in Chapter 20.

THE COMPETITION ISSUE

Without doubt, the greatest single issue facing nonprofit organizations today is the charge that they are unfairly competing with for-profit businesses (frequently portrayed as small business). The law issues associated with this allegation are manifold, and range across federal, state, and local law topics, as well as involving constitutional, statutory, and administrative law considerations.

These issues stretch across law areas such as the reach of the IRS for revenue by classifying activities as unrelated ones, the right of charitable organizations to engage in fund-raising as acts of free speech, the determination by governments as to what entities are to be entitled to be recipients of grants and contracts, the ability to mail using preferential postal rates, and the question as to what, if any, changes in the federal tax law are warranted in light of the current fee-for-service activities of nonprofit organizations. Yet, despite this range of topics, the matter is essentially one of federal tax policy. It concerns the ongoing ability of nonprofit organizations to remain exempt from federal, state, and local income, sales, use, and property taxes.

This is a subject that has attracted little research. Despite many months of allegations and comprehensive congressional hearings in 1987, the substantive inquiry into the matter of competition by nonprofit organizations has yet to be done. There have been some studies and general articles but there has been little true research on this point. Instead, the subject is flavored with misconceptions, predispositions, a great amount of emotion, and—the element that will determine much of the nature of the evolving law on the subject—politics.

Recently, there has been great pressure from the small business community for review of this matter, at both the federal and state levels. The federal government itself is participating in the effort through the U.S. Small Business Administration. In November, 1983, the SBA's Office of Advocacy issued a report that has been subsequently updated concluding that many types of tax-exempt organizations are engaging in commercial activities in competition with the nation's small businesses and that this phenomenon is increasing. Institutions cited in the report for engaging in unfair competition include educational institutions, healthcare providers, and nursing homes; competitive activities were found to include audio-visual services, analytical testing, research, computer services, and the sale of hearing aids. The report singled out technological services provided by colleges and universities in the name of research, sales of health products by clinics, sales of excess computer capacity, operation of tours, and a variety of studies and services generally denominated consulting.

Following the issuance of this report, the small business community began organizing its campaign. A Business Coalition for Fair Competition was formed that is spearheading efforts to revise the laws in this regard at both the federal and state levels. This issue was also a prominent one at the 1986 White House Conference on Small Business. The subject is of growing interest in both the popular media and specialized publications.

In part because of the pressure from the small business community, Congress is in the process of reviewing the current application of the unrelated business income rules. However, the examination is ranging beyond that subject and into the realms of commercial and entrepreneurial activities, undertakings that ostensibly are competitive with for-profit businesses. Aspects of this review are expected to focus on the underlying rationale for tax-exempt status for many nonprofit entities.

All too many believe that this set of issues is essentially a matter of the federal tax treatment of unrelated business income. This is understandable, inasmuch as the unrelated trade or business rules presently in the law were written as the result of charges of unfair competition (see Chapter 12). However, today's allegations of unfair competition are complaints about activities that, under existing law, are related to the tax-exempt organizations' functions. As a consequence, much of the debate is shifting the discussion to the matter of overall qualification for tax-exempt status. Congress seems ready to revise the law if necessary to accommodate these concerns.

The core of the legal issues involving competition between nonprofit and for-profit organizations is found here. Will emerging law provide more specific definitions of the term *unrelated business?* Will there be overarching rules, such as an equation of competitive activities with unrelated ones, or will new rules focus on particular activities, such as publishing, consulting, research, and/or product sales? Will activities now denominated fundraising, cause-related marketing, or commercial co-venturing be considered taxable or disqualifying activities? Will specific limitations be placed upon the ability of tax-exempt organizations to incur unrelated income? To what extent will the law prohibit or require the use of for-profit subsidiaries or joint ventures? The immediate future probably holds the answers to these questions.

These and subsequent inquiries are forcing law writers and the nonprofit community to reassess the criteria underlying the concepts labeled nonprofit and tax-exempt—concepts explored in Chapters 4 and 5.

Concurrently, the courts have been more disposed to finding activities nonexempt or unrelated functions of tax-exempt organizations—not through the application of the conventional unrelated income rules but rather because of the conclusion that the activities are commercial or competitive with tax-paying organizations. Recent developments reflect this trend, whether it involves the marketing of insurance programs to members of associations, the selling of advertising, or the publishing activities of allegedly educational or religious organizations. Thus it is that, just about the same time that the doctrines of commerciality and competitiveness in the tax-exempt organizations law context are taking hold in the court opinions, Congress may be embarking upon the process of engrafting these concepts onto the statutory law.

Congress is studying the various types of income-producing activities being conducted by nonprofit organizations, the resulting revenue, the extent of competition between nonprofit and for-profit organizations, the use of joint ventures and partnerships, and any correlation between the expansion of income-producing activities and federal budget cuts. As part of this inquiry into the contemporary efficacy of the unrelated income rules, there is exploration of the relationship between business activities and tax-exempt status, the rationale for tax exemption for various types of income (including that from endowment funds), the current criteria for determining unrelated income (including the suitability of various existing exemptions for certain categories of activities), and any fostering of unfair competition with taxable businesses. Also under examination is whether the IRS has an adequate and balanced enforcement program in this area, the portion of unrelated income that is actually being reported to the government, and whether the existing information and tax returns are adequate to identify the relatedness of business activities and satisfy other compliance needs.

It is educated guesswork at this point as to what all of this activity will yield in the way of new law. A vast amount and variety of proposals are under examination. The SBA analysis, for example, urges these possibilities (some inconsistent with others): an outright prohibition in the federal tax laws on unrelated business activities, a higher income tax on unrelated business activities, a more specific federal tax law definition of the term "unrelated trade or business," a percentage limitation on allowable unrelated business activities, repeal of some of the statutory exceptions to the unrelated income rules, and use of tax differentiation factors between nonprofit and for-profit organizations in the cost comparison process followed under the federal procurement law. The SBA concluded that federal policymakers "must undertake a thorough evaluation of the changing role of the nonprofit [organization] in our society and economy." The report found that "[a]ppropriate revisions in federal statutes and regulations governing nonprofits are necessary to reflect the existence of the commercial nonprofit sector, and to remedy the unfair competition now imposed on for-profit small business."

Irrespective of whether the nonprofit community agrees with those propositions, that is the way the issue is being framed for debate. There is a potential that all of this will lead to nothing—or to an in-depth inquiry into the federal and state law distinctions between for-profit and nonprofit organizations, the rationale for the tax exemption of certain types of nonprofit organizations, and the matter of whether some existing tax exemptions are outmoded and whether some new forms of tax exemption are required. It is probable that the result of this legislative process will be the introduction of many new aspects of the law of tax-exempt organizations, including perhaps some rewriting of the criteria for achieving and maintaining tax-exempt status.

A major battle is shaping up—on the line is the future of the terms in law of nonprofit and tax-exempt organizations. Along with these impending law changes is the potential for a substantial alteration in the entire economic and regulatory climate for nonprofit organizations.

FUND-RAISING REGULATION

Fund-raising regulation, at the federal and state levels, is experiencing another great surge (see Chapter 9). As to the latter, more and more states are getting into charitable solicitation regulation, imposing registration, reporting, and a myriad of other requirements upon charities and those who assist them in the fund-raising process. States that have formerly foregone the desire for a fund-raising law have suddenly decided that their citizens now need one. States with fund-raising regulation laws are making them tougher. Those who administer these laws—the state regulators—are applying them with new vigor.

These state laws require compliance by charitable organizations that engage in fund-raising. They apply to these charities, by the law of the state in which the organization is located and by the law of each of the other states in which the organization solicits contributions. Further, these laws directly impact charities by reason of the regulation of those who help them raise funds, namely, professional fund-raisers, paid solicitors, and commercial co-venturers.

Without doubt, these charitable solicitation acts are generally well-intentioned. Most state legislators vote for them, thinking they are performing a public service. There are fund-raising abuses taking place, and the public needs and deserves a place to lodge complaints and be assured that the frauds are prosecuted and punished. The law is clear that each state, in the exercise of its police power, has the authority to enact and enforce this type of law. Indeed, the states' attorneys general have considerable inherent authority to regulate in this field even without the statutory backup.

Sometimes, however, the cure is worse than the disease. Fund-raising regulation, under today's version, is one of those instances. The typical contemporary state charitable solicitation act is a monster. These laws are unnecessarily complex, onerous, stringent, and burdensome. They are usually written by a legislator or regulator with a motive to get someone or are otherwise ill-conceived. These laws are frequently authored by individuals with a dim view of what they are doing and administered by bureaucrats with a negative view toward philanthropy. In too many cases, the zeal to control fund-raising is leading to the creation of little regulatory empires, staffed at taxpayers' expense by lawyers and investigators whose skills are sorely needed in far more important government service. The paperwork and the costs imposed upon charities and their professional consultants exceeds any value these overreaching laws may provide.

The ridiculousness of the situation can be readily seen when one stops to think about what is being regulated. We are not talking about public health and safety here. This is not drug trafficking or nuclear waste disposal. This is charitable giving! Some public education and disclosure by soliciting charities is all that is needed. If an individual is uncertain about a particular charity and cannot obtain some wanted information, there is a very simple solution: Don't give.

The shame of it all is that the legislators and regulators have lost perspective on what it is they are regulating. Philanthropy is the lifeblood of the American pluralistic system. Billions of dollars are annually provided for services and other benefits that government cannot and will not supply. Giving to charity is, obviously, what fuels this machine. But fund-raising regulation is damaging the legitimate gift solicitation process. (Do not forget that charitable fund-raising is a constitutionally protected act of free speech.) In short, charitable fund-raising is overregulated—unnecessarily, harmfully, and counterproductively.

Two examples of this point should suffice. Both of them are referenced in Chapter 9: the improper use of percentages in regulating by means of limitations on fund-raising costs and the nonsensical interpretations of the definitions of the terms professional fund-raiser and professional solicitor.

The use of percentages in this setting has been repeatedly criticized and found unconstitutional by federal and state courts all the way up to the U.S. Supreme Court. Yet the legislators and regulators persist in using these restrictions anyway. The regulators are absolutely rabid about fund-raising expenses, even though it has been repeatedly shown (and common sense dictates) that the relative size of an organization's fund-raising costs bears no correlation as to the quality of its program.

The foolishness in the applicability of the definitions can be seen, for example, in the impact of the state charitable solicitation acts on telemarketers who assist charitable organizations in fund-raising. Most of the fund-raising regulation zealotry is being directed at the quickie promoters, those who roll into town for a weekend with a circus or some like attraction and who roll out of town with most of the money. Yet the statute-writers cannot seem to find the ability to develop law regulating these types. It is a virtual scandal that all of fund-raising, be it capital, annual giving, direct mail, or planned giving programs, is heavily regulated so that purveyors of tickets to vaudeville acts can be monitored.

Chapter 9 contains a reference to the meaning of the terms *professional fund-raiser* and *solicitor.* When it is remembered that the term *solicit* includes the seeking of gifts over the telephone, in the eyes of most of the regulators, a telemarketer becomes a solicitor. (To their credit, a few regulators refuse to apply their laws in this extreme fashion.) Generically, a telemarketer is not a solicitor. In saying that, the assumption is that the telemarketer does not receive the funds from the solicitation. That is an important distinguishing characteristic. A true *professional solicitor* is one who requests a contribution on behalf of a charity, receives all of the gift proceeds, retains the fee and the amount to cover expenses, and remits the balance to the charity. Frequently, another characteristic of a solicitor is that compensation is determined on the basis of a percentage of funds received. Further, the transactions usually are such that the donor realizes that the solicitor is not an employee or volunteer of the donee charity but is functioning in an independent capacity.

Under normal circumstances, when a gift is made to a charity as the result of a telemarketing effort, the gift is—literally—made to the charity. Compensation is on a set fee basis, rather than on the contributions received. And those called believe (harmlessly) that the caller is a direct representative of the charity, not some independent taker of most of the gift amounts. In fact, the usual telemarketer is such a representative, functioning as an agent of the soliciting charity.

Except for the disparaging connotation usually associated in the fund-raising context with the term *solicitor,* there would be no harm in classifying telemarketers as solicitors if it were merely a matter of definitions. However, the matter is far more than that, simply because, in their craze to drive out the circus promoters, the statute writers have made life miserable for those who are categorized as solicitors, by imposing on them a battery of tough requirements that are not imposed on others.

What is to be done? First, charities and those who support them must come to more fully appreciate this dilemma, just as there needs to be greater recognition of the law warp the telemarketers are in. The states are overreacting and overregulating—and the public (and federal legislators) are concluding with greater frequency that increasing regulation reflects a need for increasing regulation, not realizing that the regulation is feeding upon itself. In other words, there is no problem of great magnitude here but the expanding scope of regulation is conveying the impression that there is—an instance of the law developing backwards.

Second, there must be some organized effort to change these laws. One charity or telemarketing firm cannot do it alone. Third, any remedial efforts must not make the same mistake that many legislatures are currently making. That is, sweeping definitions will not do. The corrective legislation must be narrow and precise, so as to rectify the particular problems but not at the same time ignore the abuse situations. It can be done but it will take much work.

Couple all of this with the emerging reach of federal regulation of fund-raising (see Chapter 9) and it is clear that whether or not the fund-raising regulation system is altered will have a great bearing on the process of raising funds for charitable purposes and on the success of nonprofit organizations in general. No one—not donors, donees, consultants to charities, regulators, or the public—is served by this present of affairs. It cries out for correction and the status of nonprofit entities in the future will be shaped by the outcome.

SELF-REGULATION

There are those who hold the view that the nonprofit community escaped some forms of regulation by government because of the extent to which it regulated itself. Holders of this view tend to believe that self-regulation of the nonprofit sector is no longer adequate to do the job—that now government must regulate the sector even more than it presently does.

Irrespective of the validity of this view, the fact is that self-regulation in the nonprofit sector is on the rise—dramatically so. But the word on this does not seem to be getting out, so that the sector will ironically likely be facing the prospect of more governmental regulation at a time when nongovernmental regulation is increasing.

Nongovernmental regulation of nonprofit entities comes in three basic forms. One is regulation by the so-called watchdog groups. These are self-appointed bodies that call themselves voluntary agencies and serve as a source of information about nonprofit organizations for the media, researchers, and the general public. They promulgate standards, prepare and disseminate reports on nonprofit organizations, and distribute lists identifying the entities that do and do not meet the standards. The public, including donors and grantors, tend to give these ratings and reports considerable credibility and act (give or do not give) accordingly, thereby giving the voluntary agencies a degree of real-life clout and leverage that they would not otherwise have.

The two most well-known watchdogs are the Philanthropic Advisory Service of the Council of Better Business Bureaus and the National Charities Information Bureau. These agencies endeavor to monitor most of the charities that solicit contributions from the general public. There are other such agencies, established to provide standards for smaller groupings of nonprofit organizations, such as the Evangelical Council on Financial Accountability and the National Religious Broadcasters Ethics and Financial Integrity Commission.

The problem has been that sometimes these watchdog groups have been unfair in their practices. They set standards that lack common sense or are inconsistent with points of law. Organizations that operate in a perfectly lawful manner and have meaningful programs find themselves on a widely distributed list of organizations that "fail to meet standards"—and the general public believes the organizations are poorly run and direct their support elsewhere. The reports are sometimes unfairly written, with heavy emphasis on negative points, some of which are immaterial. On occasion, the agencies are poorly staffed, using the services of individuals who lack adequate training on the subject and/or who have an anti-philanthropic mindset.

For better or worse, the reach of these watchdog groups, and the number of them, is on the increase. Thus, so is this form of self-regulation.

The second form of self-regulation is through codes of ethics. These are statements of principles established by membership organizations (associations) and therefore apply only to those individuals who are members of the entity. The point of these codes is to hold the members to at least minimal standards of ethical conduct, all for the ultimate protection of the public. One problem, quite obviously, is the determination of what is ethical behavior for a particular group of individuals representing one profession, business, trade, discipline, field of interest, or whatever. Because so many considerations must be accommodated, the typical code of ethics tends to be a very general and vague statement of broad principles—making it a document very difficult to interpret and apply in relation to a particular set of facts.

Even where a nonprofit organization devises a detailed code of ethics, another problem arises: What to do with it? There are two basic choices: Ignore it (rendering the process of writing it rather pointless) or enforce it. If a code of ethics is properly enforced, the organization must have an ethics committee that reviews cases (including the holding of hearings), a detailed statement of the procedures for processing a case, an appeals procedure, and a series of meaningful sanctions (reprimand, censure, suspension, expulsion). Here, a phenomenon sets in: If an ethics enforcement mechanism is in place, people will use it, and that leads to more people using it, which leads to the nonprofit organization having to expend a meaningful portion of its time acting as a court system. Proper enforcement of a code of ethics is a substantial commitment.

Enforcement of a code of ethics does not occur in a legal vacuum. There are serious antitrust and defamation considerations. An individual who has been found "guilty" of violating a code of ethics is likely to be unhappy about being embarrassed in front of his or her peers, losing a job, failing to be promoted, or whatever, because of (or allegedly because of) the ethics violation. This individual is a potential plaintiff, with all of the implications for organizational and personal liability.

Despite the legal considerations, however, the development and enforcement of codes of ethics is on the rise, as organizations strive to make their constituency more professional. Again, the nonprofit sector is actively engaged in self-regulation.

The third form of self-regulation in the nonprofit world is certification. This one comes in other names, including credentialing and accreditation, but essentially means the conferring of a designation on an individual who has met particular criteria. The certification process is akin to licensure and, again, is a manifestation of the desire to enhance the professionalism of a particular group. The designation is intended to benefit the public, by identifying those in a particular field who are accomplished and thus suitable for selection when their services are needed. For example, there are certified financial planners, certified association executives, and certified fund-raising executives.

Unlike codes of ethics, to which all members of an association are expected to adhere, a certification program is a voluntary one, in that a member of a group can but need not pursue certification. Still, when a certification program is in place, there is a natural pressure to become certified or else risk the perception of "second class" status. Here again, then, is a form of self-regulation of the nonprofit sector.

The ramifications in law for nonprofit organizations in the administration of a certification program are not unlike the administration of a code of ethics. There is always the prospect of lawsuits by unhappy individuals who fail to achieve, or lose, accreditation. Here again, there is the prospect of defamation, antitrust violations, and charges of due process transgressions. Some organizations compound this risk by making compliance with a code of ethics a requirement for ongoing certification.

One thing is clear: In the years to come, nonprofit organizations will be laboring under the burden of more regulation. Much of it will come from government, but a lot of it will flow from the nonprofit community itself, with nonprofits being the regulators and their constituencies the regulated.

WHERE ARE NONPROFITS HEADED?

From a lawyer's vantage point, the question is easy to answer: They are headed for more regulation. Again, more regulation does not (necessarily) mean extinction. But, additional regulation is a threat, for it raises suspicions in the minds of some, tempts more than a few legislators into seeking even more, and generally is a drag on the system (most notably, when it comes to charitable giving).

There are two things the nonprofit community can do to improve matters in these regards. The betting is here that neither will be done, in part because they are somewhat inconsistent but largely because of human nature (adherence to the status quo, inertia, fear of the unknown). One entails self-restraint, the other more involvement in the political process.

Addressing the latter point first, the nonprofit community has come a long way in recent years in participation in the legislative process at the federal level. It is more adept than ever in influencing the legislative process as practiced by the U.S. Congress. And this is not easy. If the matter is not handled with some sensitivity and skill, the nonprofit world's emissaries to the legislatures become perceived as merely another pack of lobbyists—often a counterproductive development—instead of the well-intentioned group pursuing the public weal that they are. Also, as Chapters 13 and 14 point out, it is action in the face of considerable sanctions when nonprofit organizations venture into the realm of legislative and political campaign activities.

Still, there is much to be done in this department. Here are four suggestions.

1. Much more involvement in the grass roots. Looking at this one from a federal standpoint, legislators (particularly those in the House of Representatives) pay attention to their constituency. Representatives of nonprofit organizations must befriend their members of Congress, and visit them often, in Washington and in the districts. These legislators can become informed as to the organizations' programs and other activities, including fund-raising plans and problems. (Legislators can identify with this, for they are fund-raisers too.) Nonprofits must learn to lobby when adverse legislation is not imminent; keeping up the relationships month to month, year in and year out, makes the real lobbying easier and more effective—and, in the long run, less necessary. Some of this type of activity is not involvement in the legislative process in any event, so the sanctions are not always a problem. Further, nonprofit organizations, including charitable ones, can usually lobby much more than they believe.

2. Nonprofit organizations need to do much more to affect public opinion about them. Ideally, there would be ongoing media coverage of their good works. Articles, press releases, studies, op-ed columns, and the like should routinely flow. Nonprofit organizations can engage in research activities and other projects that yield substantive results to community and business leaders, and legislators and their staffs. Greater public relations would enhance the image of nonprofits, educate and remind the public of their heritage and role in contemporary society, and—in the process—probably pave the way for more successful fund-raising. When the public is favorable toward a particular subject, the politicians tend to be as well and even the opponents find the opposing harder going.

3. The nonprofit community must do more in the field of self-education. Somehow, those who manage and advise nonprofit organizations must learn more about the basics of the law affecting nonprofit organizations. (This book is written in that spirit.) Much difficulty could be avoided, whether it be an IRS audit or a matter of personal liability of a director, if just the fundamentals were mastered. Conferences and seminars abound but, for some reason, those that need the word are not getting it. There are massive gaps in understanding of, for example, fund-raising regulation (and techniques), the requirements for keeping

tax-exempt status, the unrelated income rules, and the annual reporting obligations. A very current illustration of this is the growing tendency of charitable organizations to regard every payment to them as
a deductible charitable gift, when that is clearly not the case. Some
members of Congress have challenged the nonprofit sector to rid itself
of this problem, through dissemination of corrective information—
before Congress takes on the cause through more stringent legislation.
This and comparable efforts must be launched, and soon.

4. The nonprofit community needs to make better use of political action
   committees for its own purposes. Members of Congress and other legislators, like nonprofit organizations, need financial support—and
   they tend to be responsive to those who provide it to them. The world
   needs some PACs for the nonprofits' causes. Even those in the charitable community could experiment with the use of independent political
   action committees.

As to the matter of self-restraint, one aspect of this has already been discussed: the hope for a cooling of the regulatory zeal associated with self-
regulation. There is another dimension to this, which is directly associated
with the "pig theory." This principle has it that a good idea can evolve into a
massive mistake, that adversely affects everyone, when the idea is pushed to
its outer limits. That is, the idea as implemented in the early stages is a good
one but as others begin to use it the idea becomes transformed into something different and certainly something more extensive, and the practice ex-
pands until it attracts the attention of a legislature, which either taxes the
income involved or outlaws the practice altogether, by means of very restric-
tive legislation that not only wipes out the entire undertaking (including the
original good idea) but leaves the community more restricted and regulated
than was the case before the good idea was initially implemented. A manifestation of the pig theory can be seen in the evolving doctrine of commerciality. This doctrine cuts across tax exemption and unrelated income issues,
and applies to nearly all forms of nonprofit organizations.

Many nonprofit organizations have become obligated, to sustain themselves and their beneficiaries, to pursue funding from new sources, now that
some of the conventional ones are proving insufficient. (This is, by the way,
no secret in Washington, DC; the General Accounting Office recently observed that "[a]s a result of growing federal deficits and reduced government
spending for social services, tax-exempt organizations are being asked to assume a greater share in the funding of these services" and "[t]herefore, it is
likely that in seeking sources of funds, tax-exempt organizations will continue to increase their UBI activity.") As they turn to the fee-for-service approach, they (as noted above) embark upon fund-raising ventures that, while
innocent enough at the outset, expand economically and in visibility until
the business community is antagonized and until some legislative body is

activated. Two cases in point are the enactment by Congress in 1984 of the tax-exempt entity leasing rules and in 1986 of the tax rule causing the offering of "commercial-type insurance" to be either a basis for loss of tax exemption or an unrelated business. Other cases in point that are shaping up are income-producing affinity card programs and multi-charity commercial co-venturing. Before the doctrine of commerciality matures, it is likely to challenge many existing notions of what is required to qualify as a tax-exempt organization, rewrite portions of the law of unrelated income taxation, and pit some nonprofit organizations against others.

The overall future for nonprofit organizations is bright, although along the way they are going to have to achieve a better public understanding of their role in society and, to some extent, learn to live with a redefinition of that role. There is much that nonprofit organizations can do to affect these developments, including the four proactive techniques suggested above, blended with the self-restraint. It is, admittedly, a tall order.

20

Whither Nonprofits?
A Long-Range Look

Despite the problems and challenges for nonprofit organizations chronicled in Chapter 19, it is expected that most nonprofit entities will, overall, fare quite well over the coming decades. What separates the nonprofit organization of today from the successful nonprofit organization of tomorrow is resolution of the nonprofits' identity crisis. The seeds of that process were sown in 1987.

This was an extraordinary year in the development of the law of tax-exempt organizations. Unfortunately, from the standpoint of nonprofit organizations, much of the development was in negative contexts. Indeed, 1987 may be characterized as the year of charity-bashing.

1987: IDENTITY CRISIS SURFACES

Not since 1969 has there been such a spate of general antipathy towards tax-exempt organizations. Even in that year, however, the bashing was more focused, being levied upon private foundations (see Chapter 11). In 1987, the hostility against charitable organizations was widespread and generally indiscriminate.

Why this negativism? The answer is far from clear, although several theories present themselves. Probably all are legitimate factors and there are undoubtedly additional ones. Also, the relative importance to be assigned to the elements that can be identified is difficult.

There was nothing inherent in 1987 that caused this phenomenon, but it is curious that so much happened within this year.

The official manifestations of the intense review of the law of tax-exempt organizations in 1987 principally were the three sets of hearings held before the House Subcommittee on Oversight of the House Ways and Means Committee. These hearings examined these practices by charities: legislative activities, political campaign involvements, fund-raising, private inurement, and commercial and competitive activities. Already, the first set of hearings has resulted in the adoption of legislation concerning lobbying and political activities (see Chapters 13 and 14). The hearing on television evangelism is not expected to lead to any legislative recommendations. The hearings on the unrelated activities rules are leading to a series of recommendations for change in that area of the federal tax law (see Chapter 11).

Other manifestations include proposals contained in the many revenue-raising options being developed by congressional committee staffs and the continuing flow of developments at the state level in the regulation of fund-raising for charity (see Chapter 9).

Of course, a great amount of this activity in 1987 had its origins in developments that commenced months and even years beforehand. Likewise, what happened in 1987 in this area spilled over into 1988 and will continue for months and years thereafter.

Still, an unusual amount of anti-nonprofit organization activity unfolded in 1987 and it is interesting to speculate on the reasons for this confluence of factors.

There are, as noted, several factors. One of them, and superficially perhaps the most important of them, is coincidence. How else to explain, within the same year, the guilty pleas of those who (allegedly) misused the National Endowment for the Preservation of Liberty, and the collapse of Jim and Tammie Bakker's Praise The Lord empire? Likewise, complaints about lobbying and political campaign activities by charitable organizations have been rumbling for some time, as have commercial and competitive practices by charities and other nonprofit organizations, but why congressional hearings on both subjects (plus the hearings on television evangelism) in the same year?

Another aspect of the matter that is somewhat akin to coincidence but is actually a separate factor is the simultaneous convergence, for purposes of policy resolution, of (seemingly) unrelated tax-exempt organization policy issues. These include the need to confront the proper tax treatment of nonprofit hospitals, the distinctions between commercial testing and exempt function research, the sales of certain items in university bookstores and museum gift shops, and the pressures building between commercial fitness centers and traditional charitable institutions such as the YM/WCAs.

Another aspect of this phenomenon is the recent media coverage accorded charitable organizations. The coverage of tax-exempt, particularly charitable, organizations by the print and broadcast media rarely focuses on the good works of these organizations but, instead, all too often portrays them as commercial entities (such as because of their investment practices), or borderline fraudulent entities (such as stories about [allegedly] inappropriate fund-raising practices), or entities that are the objects of scorn and ridicule (such as the television evangelists).

The factor of media coverage, however, is also of great import because of its influence on other developments, discussed next.

Still another factor is the (ostensible) need of the federal government for more revenue. The issue of the need to reduce the federal deficit is growing and tax-exempt organizations are increasingly being looked to as sources of revenue. The proposed law changes emanating out of this development are not being advocated out of substantive policy deliberations; rather, they are being propelled by the sheer need for the revenue that would be derived. The most obvious proposal in this regard is the idea, surfacing all too regularly, of a 5 percent tax on the net investment income of nearly all tax-exempt organizations.

The foregoing four factors are all, to some degree, superficial ones and do not seem to get to the heart of the matter. Nonetheless, they are real and important, and tend to reflect and in some instances facilitate more deep-seated reasons for the focus on tax-exempt organizations in 1987.

There seems to be an alteration in the thinking of the political leadership in this country on the subject of nonprofit organizations. Nonprofits do not appear to be as sacrosanct in their eyes as these organizations once did. The universities, the hospitals, even the churches, seem more open to their challenge today than yesterday, thus, the attacks on the YM/WCAs and the hospitals.

But why have the political leaders become so emboldened? It is not like 20 years ago, when the late Representative Wright Patman took on private foundations—that undertaking was frequently characterized as a populist fighting entrenched and unproductive wealth. That stance was popular (and thus politically easy to assume) throughout most of America. But taking on charities and other tax-exempt organizations across the board is another matter.

There are several reasons underlying the politician's bold attacks on charities and other tax-exempt organizations. Some are necessarily superficial. One is desperation—the above expressed (alleged) need for additional federal revenue. Another is grandstanding—many nonprofit organizations are not part of a voting constituency. Another is frustration—some members of Congress really do not like the idea of charities engaging in lobbying. Another is successful government relations by others—the small business community is well-represented in Congress. Another is resentment—anger with one nonprofit organization (for example, the PTL) spills over onto other nonprofit organizations.

But, as noted, these are relatively superficial considerations. There is probably something more profound taking place to account for this boldness in our politicians. A possibility is a decline in the respect previously accorded nonprofit organizations by the general public. Most members of Congress take stances on political issues only to the extent those stances are encouraged, or at least tolerated, by the voters.

Why would the general public lose some degree of respect for nonprofit organizations? Again, the superficial reasons are the easiest to identify. One possibility is that the general public is beginning to take nonprofit organizations for granted, forgetting what a unique American institution they are and forgetting how crucial they are to the preservation and enhancement of American societal values. Another possibility is tax reform, bringing more pressure for more revenue, thus triggering greater resentment in those who must pay taxes, in turn focusing more attention on those that do not pay taxes (such as, obviously, tax-exempt organizations). Another possibility is the negative media coverage that has tainted all nonprofit organizations in recent months and years.

But these reasons do not explain it all. At a deeper level, the general public may be confused. The precise identity once ascribed to nonprofit organizations is, in many instances, gone. Today, many nonprofit organizations and small or large businesses look the same. Hospitals may be the most stark example. But other illustrations abound. Research, fitness, publishing, conferencing, touring, product sales, counseling—all these and much more are done by nonprofit organizations and for-profit organizations. An identity loss at the organizational level is producing an identity crisis at the individual level of perception.

Yet the analysis cannot stop at this point. What started the public confusion? Partly, apparently, it just happened, as nonprofit organizations evolve in an increasingly complex and competitive society. That is, as America moved from an industrial (manufacturing) economy to a services (information) economy, nonprofits became involved in industries once solely the province of for-profits. More sophisticated management has changed the character of many nonprofit organizations. Tax reform, government funding cutbacks, and demands for more services have played a role.

However, some of this confusion is a product of actions by the nonprofit community. Tax-exempt organizations are not necessarily a band of innocents. Some, with huge endowments, physical plants, massive staffs, government relations programs, high-profile fund-raising and development programs, and aggressive investment activities (including involvements in joint ventures and creative uses of for-profit subsidiaries) have shaken the traditional view within the general public as to what a nonprofit organization is.

This is not to imply that charitable (and other nonprofit) organizations have done anything wrong or otherwise illegal by engaging in these confusion-producing activities. This is to suggest, however, that nonprofit organizations are changing in character and activities (but not purposes) faster than the ability of much of the general public to favorably perceive them.

Some may be thinking that nonprofit organizations are anachronisms. This does not appear to be the case, as evidenced by the frequent reference to them by the futurists.

Another dimension of this may be that some confusion is also being caused by the inability of the statutory law to keep pace with the contemporary and evolving practices of nonprofit organizations. Oddly, the courts are developing different principles and are having little difficulty in keeping up with the innovative activities of nonprofit organizations.

The heart of the matter may be, then, one of a loss of identity for nonprofit organizations. It is quite possible that developments in the federal tax law in the coming years will redefine the role of nonprofit organizations in general, or at least some of them. Will the criteria for tax exemption remain the same? How about the criteria for charitable giving? Will there be an expansion of reporting and other disclosure requirements . . . and penalties? What about a rewriting of the definition of related and unrelated activities? What will be the use of criteria such as commerciality and competition with business?

This convergence of events is forcing the nonprofit community to explain what it means to be *nonprofit* and *tax-exempt,* and why it differs from being *for-profit,* and why the present law of tax exemptions, tax deductions, and the like should remain. Likewise, if there are abuses of tax-exempt status occurring—particularly any that cannot be corrected under existing law—the nonprofit community should be forthright about it. A battle is shaping up and on the line is the future of the legal terms *nonprofit* organizations and *tax-exempt* organizations.

The emerging doctrine of *commerciality* seems to presume that, since for-profit organizations obviously engage in commercial activities, if the activity is to be found in the for-profit sector, it is an impermissible (taxable) activity when and if conducted in the nonprofit sector.

Should this presumption be the rule? If so, presumably some exceptions would have to be made for traditional activities conducted in the nonprofit sector. Two clear instances of this historical conduct is the operation of nonprofit schools and hospitals, even though there are proprietary counterparts. Thus, the existence of one proprietary school or hospital would not preempt the field for nonprofits, so that there could no longer be nonprofit (nontaxable) schools or hospitals. Presumably, the same would be true for other institutions, such as museums and libraries.

But what about program activities such as conferences, publications, and consulting? Since there are counterparts of these activities in the for-profit sector, are they inherently commercial activities and thus automatically unrelated ones? If so, the commerciality concept bears directly on eligibility for tax-exempt status as well as on unrelated income taxation, inasmuch as, in many instances, these activities are primary (if not the only) ones.

What about the new entry of one or more for-profit organizations into a field previously occupied solely by nonprofit organizations? Does that introduce commerciality into the field, making the activity taxable when conducted by nonprofit organizations? And does the field become nontaxable for nonprofits only when and if the for-profit organizations abandon that field?

One of the challenges for the nonprofit sector over the coming years will be whether it can succeed in defining its role in American society, to the satisfaction of the general public, and thus the legislators and the regulators.

This is a capitalist society and perhaps nonprofit organizations are to be secondary to for-profit ones when it comes to similar activities. However, the concern is that, in our zeal to protect small business or otherwise address particular legislators' pet peeves, the nation's nonprofit organizations will be significantly harmed with noncorresponding benefit to society. Even if there was a corresponding benefit, it would be augmentation of the role of government in providing social and other services. While others may champion that outcome (and while that philosophy may underlie some of the recent proposals to revamp the law of unrelated income taxation), it would be shortsighted and would dramatically alter for the worse the manner in which our society is organized and operated.

EXAMPLE: TAX PENALTIES

Sometimes the best defense is a good offense. In recent years, the nonprofit sector has been on the defense, time and time again, in relation to the development of federal tax law, particularly by Congress. Others propose new rules to meet new problems and, for the most part, the nonprofit community opposes them. This leads to the view among legislators that the independent sector is interested only in protectionism, rather than problem-solving, which in turn lowers the sector's credibility and thus effectiveness with the legislatures. Reduced effectiveness frequently stimulates more adverse legislation and the cycle continues—or worsens.

What is it that nonprofit organizations can do to seize the moment and stop this slide in credibility and effectiveness? One idea lies in the nature of the sanctions used to enforce the law of tax-exempt organizations. Traditionally, the regulatory sanction used to enforce the federal tax law in this area has been revocation of tax exemption. Over the years, other, less draconian (usually) sanctions have crept into the law, in the form of taxes (principally excise taxes) and civil penalties.

This process began in 1950, when Congress enacted the income tax on unrelated business activities (see Chapter 12). Again, in 1969, Congress enacted a battery of penalties in the form of excise taxes applicable to private foundations (see Chapter 11). And, legislation in 1987 brought a panoply of taxes and penalties in the exempt organizations context, in subjects ranging from lobbying and political campaign activities to fund-raising disclosure (see Chapters 13 and 14). With these and other penalties (such as those for failure to timely file a complete annual information return or for failure to make those returns or the application for recognition of exemption available for public inspection (see Chapters 6 and 7), the regulatory emphasis has shifted away from the all-or-nothing sanction of loss of exemption to the use of penalties.

Perhaps the nonprofit sector should build on this trend, to show a willingness to cope with real problems and to, not incidentally, curb some abuses before they grow into major issues and massive legislation. Here are some ideas.

The IRS is rightfully concerned about the manner in which annual information returns are being prepared these days. All too often, the returns are late, incomplete, sloppily prepared, and unresponsive to the questions. Part of the fault for this lies with the IRS, because the return is often vague or confusing. There are indications that the IRS will be improving the return, with or without more legislation, and that Congress will be legislating expansions of the return. In conjunction with this revamping of the return, consideration should be given to a strengthening of the penalties, to induce compliance. The penalty of $10 per day (maximum of the lesser of $5,000 or 5 percent of the gross receipts of the organization for the year) may have to be increased, by increasing the per-day penalty (such as to $100) and/or increasing the maximum penalty to be paid with respect to any one return. Hardly anyone outside of government likes to advocate greater penalties on tax-exempt organizations but the noncompliance problem is a serious and worsening one, with a higher penalty likely to be one of the solutions.

Another penalty structure that warrants revisiting is the one levied for failure to comply with the fund-raising disclosure rules (see Chapter 9). Here, the penalty ($1,000 per day, up to $10,000 annually) is too stringent. This is particularly the case now that the IRS is interpreting the rule to apply to solicitations of membership dues and assessments. Thus, nonprofit organizations should advocate a reduction of that penalty, such as to $100 per day. Why should the penalty be higher for failure to make the fund-raising disclosure than for failure to timely file a complete annual return? At the same time, the nonprofit sector should advocate extension of the disclosure rule and the accompanying penalty to charitable organizations, where they solicit payments that are not deductible as charitable gifts (see the discussion in Chapter 8). This, too, is a growing problem and needs to be nipped now, rather than waiting for more restrictive legislation later.

Many of the well-publicized and embarrassing episodes adversely affecting the nonprofit sector involve violations of the private inurement doctrine (see Chapter 5). Perhaps the time has come to develop penalties for public charities along the lines of what Congress did in 1987 with respect to impermissible lobbying and political campaign activities, which is to enact taxes that are potentially imposable on the individuals who willfully cause the exempt organization to engage in the forbidden act(s). Thus, the independent sector could advocate sanctions that are imposed on the individuals who engage in acts of private inurement, instead of more rules on the organizations who are being manipulated by these individuals. One way to do this is to underlie the private inurement rules with a series of penalty taxes somewhat akin to those imposed in connection with the self-dealing rules applicable to private foundations (see Chapter 11). This would not be a popular stance within the nonprofit community but it would show leadership in addressing a pressing problem and again ward off the very real possibility of more repressive legislation later. This same approach could be engrafted upon the revisions upon the unrelated income rules that are being written.

Probably there is little enthusiasm within the top levels of the independent sector for advocating—of all things—more penalties on their memberships. Yet something must be done and the sector must do more toward contributing to solutions.

THE LONGER VIEW

As noted, all too many regard tax-exempt organizations as a quaint anachronism of another era—forms of institutional life no longer suited for the organizations of today and the future. The thought that exempt organizations, or most of them, are destined for extinction may be tested against the thinking of futurists.

For example, Alvin Toffler, writing in *The Third Wave,* envisions great change in the nature of "increased diversity" in "ideas, political convictions, sexual proclivities, educational methods, eating habits, religious views, ethnic attitudes, musical tastes, fashions, and family forms." This development (stimulated by what he terms the "de-massification" of society), he believes, will lead to a splintering and/or reshaping of many of society's institutions—both a decentralizing and a fragmenting process. If nothing else, this result would mean more tax-exempt (or at least, nonprofit) organizations. As an illustration, Toffler sees this de-massification phenomenon occurring in U.S. political life, when he describes the "sudden, bewildering proliferation of high-powered splinter groups." Concerning the future of nonprofit organizations, Toffler clearly expects not only more of them but an expanded role for them.

Toffler predicts a greater diversity in organized religion and the emergence of new religions. He expects that a "host of new religions, new conceptions of science, new images of human nature, new forms of art will arise—in far richer diversity than was possible or necessary during the industrial age." He foresees new educational organizations and new educational methods. Toffler predicts restructuring of curricula, revisions in the concept of grading, increased parental influence on the schools, and a lessening in the number of years of compulsory schooling; in general, he expects new forms of consultancies, massive changes in the modes of educational instruction (because of the advent of word processors, home computers, and telecommunications), and new opportunities in instruction and publishing. He predicts new advances and diversification of organizations in the fields of health and science. Nonprofit organizations should be in the forefront of what Toffler terms "[f]antastic scientific advances," yet ironically also very much involved in the resistance to new technology, being part of the organizational effort of "humanizing the technological thrust." He sees significant changes in healthcare delivery systems, with obvious implications for the nonprofit community.

Concerning the nation's political system, Toffler calls for nothing less than the "design of new, more appropriate political structures." One of the pathways to this objective is "imaginative new arrangements for accommodating and legitimating diversity—new institutions that are sensitive to the rapidly shifting needs of changing and multiplying minorities." Nonprofit organizations will certainly be a part of this process, both as entities that help to design the new political process and as participatory elements of it.

In his wide-ranging analysis of life tomorrow, Toffler speculates on some of the needs in the future and on ways to satisfy them. Many of these ways would require the use of nonprofit organizations.

For example, Toffler discusses some of the problems that cannot be solved by national governments individually (such as inflation, activities of transnational corporations, arms trade, outer space governance, and interlocking currencies). He states that "[w]e desperately need, therefore, to invent imaginative new institutions at the transnational level to which many decisions can be transferred" and calls for "consortia and teams of nongovernmental organizations to attack various global problems."

Likewise, he writes of the need to enable a variety of minorities to regulate more of their own affairs. To this end, he speculates, "[w]e might, for example, help the people in a specific neighborhood, in a well-defined subculture, or in an ethnic group, to set up their own youth courts under the supervision of the state, disciplining their own young people rather than relying on the state to do so." He rationalizes this suggestion in terms embodying some well-recognized tax law doctrines for such groups: "Such institutions would build community and identity, and contribute to law and order, while relieving the overburdened government institutions of unnecessary work."

In still another example of new nonprofit organization life forms, Toffler postulates the use of "semi-cults"—organizations that "lie somewhere between [the application of] structureless freedom and tightly structured regimentation." These groups are envisioned by him as a means to impose a certain degree of structure where and as long as it is required, yet enabling persons to freely return to productive life in society. He also suggests a variant of these entities to provide community services.

The conclusions of another futurist, John Naisbett, parallel those of Toffler. Writing in *Megatrends,* Naisbett also finds the shift from an industrial society to an information society, the "evolution of a highly personal value system to compensate for the impersonal nature of technology," the transformation from national economics to a world economy, the emphasis on long-term concepts rather than short-term thinking, the change from centralization to decentralization, the shift from institutional help to self-help, the evolution from representative democracy to participatory democracy (within both government and large corporations), and the change from hierarchies to networking.

While Naisbett, like Toffler, found no occasion to specifically address the future of nonprofit organizations as such, he foresees growth in the human potential and self-help movements, massive changes in the delivery of education and healthcare, new political initiatives, the development of networking, and the emergence of new religions—all of which will inevitably utilize nonprofit organizations. Neither of these futurists wrote of any need to preserve tax exemption for nonprofit organizations—perhaps they simply assumed that this will continue. Toffler, for one, is not opposed to this type of utilization of the tax system, however, since in his book he calls for the application of tax incentives to help accomplish particular objectives.

The point of the foregoing is not to endorse any particular vein of futurist thinking or the necessary evolution of any particular form of tax-exempt organization but to suggest that unfolding societal needs are likely to heavily entail the active involvement of nonprofit (tax-exempt) organizations. Toffler's prognostications indicate an exciting and meaningful future, replete with a large dosage of the American tendency to create *associations.* The Toffler premise suggests that nonprofit organizations are an integral part of the American societal and political structure, and that the concern for the immediate future is not whether nonprofit groups are a dying breed but whether they are to be seriously endangered by evolving tax and fundraising regulation policy.

It is projected that nonprofit (hopefully, tax-exempt) organizations very much remain in the nation's future. As to the law, the future also holds considerable changes in tax law, fund-raising law, and other law matters such as personal liability and compensation forms that will govern the nation's nonprofit organizations in both the coming years and over the longer perspective.

Glossary

Abatement. In general, a decrease or diminution; in the nonprofit organization tax law context, the relieving of a tax liability, such as the ability of the IRS to abate nearly all of the "excise taxes" imposed upon "private foundations" (IRC § 4962).

Actuary. One who creates actuarial tables, including those used in the "planned giving" context in calculating "income interests" and "remainder interests."

Additional tax. In the "private foundations" context, the "excise taxes" that are assessable, following assessment of the "initial taxes," in enforcement of the rules; also known as "second-tier" taxes.

Adjusted gross income. In the case of an individual, "gross income" less certain deductions (IRC § 62).

Advisory committee. A group of individuals who serve as advisors to the "board of directors" of a "nonprofit organization"; a technique for attracting well-known persons to service for an organization without causing them to become involved in its actual governance.

Agricultural organization. An organization described in IRC § 501(c)(5).

Alternative minimum tax. A federal tax intended to make certain wealthy and/or sophisticated taxpayers pay some taxes, thus the word "minimum"; it is an "alternative" tax in that it is paid, if larger, rather than the "regular income tax"; the tax is determined, in part, by adding the value of a taxpayer's "tax preference items," including the appreciation element in "contributions" of "appreciated property" (IRC §§ 55–59).

Amateur sports organization. An organization organized and operated exclusively to foster national or international amateur sports competition if the organization is also organized and operated primarily to conduct national or international competition in sports or to support and develop amateur athletes for national or international competition in sports (IRC § 501(j)).

Annual information return. The return that is required to be filed by most "tax-exempt organizations" annually with the IRS (Form 990).

Annuity. A regular payment of a set amount of money for life or lives, or for a period of years, such as the annuity payable as the result of creation of a "charitable gift annuity" or a "charitable remainder trust."

Apostolic association. A religious organization that has a common treasury or community treasury, even if it engages in business for the common benefit of its members, where the members of the organization include in their gross income their entire pro rata shares, whether or not distributed, of the taxable income of the organization (IRC § 501(d)).

Application for recognition of exemption. The IRS form by which a "nonprofit organization" seeks recognition of tax-exempt status from the IRS (Form 1023 or 1024).

Appraisal. The determination of the fair market value of a property, as in the valuation of property that is the subject of a "charitable contribution."

Appraiser. An individual who is in the business of making "appraisals," as in an independent appraiser mandated in connection with gifts of property with a value in excess of $5,000.

Appreciated property. Property that has increased in value; property the fair market value of which is greater than its cost basis (IRC §§ 170(b)(1)(C) and 170(e)).

Appreciation element. The component of value of an item of property that is the difference between the property's cost basis and its fair market value.

Articles of incorporation. See "articles of organization."

Articles of organization. The generic term for the document used to create a "nonprofit organization"; "articles of incorporation" in the case of a corporation; a "constitution" in the case of an unincorporated association; a "trust agreement" or "declaration of trust" in the case of a trust.

Association. An organization, usually nonprofit and tax-exempt, that has a membership, of individuals and/or organizations.

Attorney. A word commonly used as a synonym for "lawyer"; anyone acting on behalf of another with the authority to do so (as in power of attorney).

Audit. The process whereby the IRS examines the books and records of an organization, and witnesses, in search of compliance with the internal revenue laws (IRC §§ 7601–7611).

Award. A gift of cash or property in recognition of an achievement, usually taxable to the recipient unless immediately transferred to a "charitable" organization (IRC § 74).

Bargain sale. A transaction whereby a person transfers property to a "charitable" organization for less than its fair market value, thereby making the transaction part sale and part gift (IRC § 1011(b)).

Basis. The cost amount for the acquisition of an item of property, plus certain subsequent expenditures (IRC § 1012).

Benevolent. A term sometimes used as a synonym for "charitable"; it is of broader scope than "charitable" and not formally used in the federal tax law rules, although sometimes used in the state and local law context.

Benevolent life insurance association. An organization described in IRC § 501(c)(12).

Bequest. A gift of personal property made by means of a will.

Black lung benefit trust. An organization described in IRC § 501(c)(21).

Board of directors. Two or more individuals who serve as the governing body of an organization; see "board of trustees."

Board of trade. An organization described in IRC § 501(c)(6).

Board of trustees. The same as a "board of directors," except that the organization involved is usually a "trust" and/or a "charitable" entity.

Business league. An organization described in IRC § 501(c)(6).

Bylaws. The document of an organization that contains its rules of operation; in some jurisdictions, the term "code of regulations" is used.

Capital asset. Property held by a person, whether or not connected with a trade or business, not including inventory, depreciable property used in a business, certain literary or artistic compositions, and certain publications of the United States government (IRC § 1221).

Capital campaign. A "fund-raising program" designed to generate "contributions" for a "charitable" organization's "capital," usually for a building, major item of equipment, or an "endowment" fund.

Cause-related marketing. Fund-raising techniques used to generate non-gift revenues, involving "related" and/or "unrelated" activities; the term usually includes "charitable sales promotions" and other forms of "commercial co-ventures."

Cemetery company. An organization described in IRC § 501(c)(5).

Chairperson of the board. An individual selected, usually by a "board of directors," to be the leader of the board; this is not usually an "officer" position, although it can be when so provided in "articles of organization" and/or "bylaws"; in some instances, an individual denominated "chairman" or "chair" of a board.

Chamber of commerce. An organization described in IRC § 501(c)(6).

Charitable. The description of a purpose, activity, or organization that the applicable law, such as the federal tax law (principally, IRC § 501(c)(3)), regards as meeting at least one of the "charitable" objectives referenced in Chapter 4.

Charitable contribution. A "contribution" made to a "charitable" organization; sometimes, a contribution made to a noncharitable organization for a "charitable" purpose.

Charitable contribution deduction. A "deduction" available, under certain federal, state, and local laws, for an amount of money or property transferred to a "charitable" organization (e.g., IRC § 170).

Charitable gift annuity. An arrangement whereby property is transferred to a "charitable" organization in exchange for an "annuity," with the donated value of the property in excess of the value of the annuity a "charitable contribution."

Charitable lead trust. A trust used to facilitate the contribution of a "lead interest" or "income interest" to a "charitable" organization (IRC § 514(c)(5)).

Charitable organization. An organization that is organized and operated for what the applicable law, such as the federal tax law (principally, IRC § 501(c)(3)), regards as a "charitable" purpose.

Charitable remainder trust. A form of "split-interest" trust used to facilitate the contribution of a "remainder interest" to a "charitable" organization; a trust that is a charitable remainder annuity trust or as a charitable remainder unitrust (IRC § 664).

Charitable sales promotion. An undertaking that essentially is the same as a "commercial co-venture."

Charitable solicitation acts. State laws that regulate the process of soliciting "contributions" for "charitable" purposes.

Civic league. An organization described in IRC § 501(c)(4).

Commercial. A manner of conduct of an activity by a nonprofit organization in a way similar to the way in which for-profit organizations conduct the same activity; the only federal law statutory illustration of this to date are the rules concerning "commercial-type" insurance (IRC § 501(m)).

Commercial co-venture. An arrangement between a for-profit organization and a (or more) "charitable" organization, whereby the for-profit entity agrees to make a "contribution" to the charitable entity, with the amount of the contribution determined by the volume of sales of products or services by the for-profit organization during a particular time period.

Commerciality. The emerging doctrine whereunder an activity that is conducted in a "commercial" manner is deemed, for that reason alone, to be a nonexempt activity.

Community chest. An organization described in IRC § 501(c)(3).

Consideration. The element of value in a bargain; something exchanged to receive something in return, as in both parties to a "contract" receive consideration.

Constitution. See "articles of organization."

Consultant. One who provides services to an organization in a capacity other than as an "employee," such as an accountant, fund-raising counsel, or lawyer; an independent contractor.

Contract. A set of promises between two or more persons that creates, revises, or eliminates a legal relationship; a set of promises underlain by "consideration."

Contribution. A transfer by one person to another of money or property without an expectation of any material return; a transfer of money or property without "consideration."

Contribution base. An amount equal to what is, essentially, an individual's "adjusted gross income," used in computing the extent to which "charitable contributions" are deductible in a year (IRC § 170(b)(1)(F)).

Cooperative hospital service organization. An organization that performs, on a centralized basis, one or more specified services solely for two or more hospitals and that is operated on a cooperative basis (IRC § 501(e)).

Cooperative service organization of educational organizations. An organization that is organized and operated solely to collectively invest in securities for the benefit of public and private schools, colleges, and universities (IRC § 501(f)).

Cooperative telephone company. An organization described in IRC § 501(c)(12).

Credit union. An organization described in IRC § 501(c)(14).

Crop financing organization. An organization described in IRC § 501 (c)(16).

Cruelty prevention organization. An organization described in IRC § 501 (c)(3).

Declaration of trust. A proclamation by a person of the existence of a trust; see "articles of organization"; cf. "trust agreement."

Declaratory judgment. In the law of tax-exempt organizations, a declaration by the U.S. Tax Court, the U.S. Claims Court, or the U.S. District Court for the District of Columbia as to whether an organization is tax-exempt as described in IRC § 501(c)(3), a "charitable" organization (IRC § 170(c)(2)), a "private foundation" or "public charity" (IRC § 509), or a "private operating foundation" (IRC § 4942(j)(3)) (IRC § 7428).

Deduction. An item (usually an expenditure) that is subtracted from adjusted gross income to arrive at taxable income, such as the "charitable contribution deduction."

Deferred compensation plan. A program whereby one or more employees of an organization are compensated for services rendered currently but the receipt of the compensation is deferred until a subsequent point in time (such as retirement).

Determination letter. A letter from the IRS "recognizing" the tax-exempt status of a "nonprofit organization."

Development program. In many ways, a program that is the same as a "fund-raising program," although this type of program usually emphasizes "capital campaigns" and/or "planned giving programs."

Devise. A gift of real property by means of a will.

Direct lobbying. An attempt to influence the development of "legislation" by contact with legislators, their staffs, or staffs of legislative committees, such as by meetings, correspondence, and/or testimony at hearings (cf. "grass roots lobbying").

Donor acquisition. A "fund-raising program" where the emphasis is on the acquisition of new donors to a "charitable" organization (who hopefully will continue to give); also known as "prospecting."

Donor renewal. A "fund-raising program" where the emphasis is on acquiring "contributions" from those who have previously given (the donor base) to a "charitable" organization.

Dues. Amounts of money paid to an organization for membership services; where these services are "consideration" and the organization is a "charitable" one, the dues are not deductible as "charitable contributions."

Electioneering. The process of intervening or otherwise participating in the campaign for or against the election of a candidate for public office.

Elective rule. In the context of "lobbying" activities by "public charities," the rule that enables qualifying "charitable" organizations to elect to come under certain standards for more mechanically determining allowable "lobbying" (IRC § 501(h)).

Employee. One who provides services to an organization where he or she is under the direct supervision and control of the organization (the "employer"); usually, the services are provided on the premises of the employer, using the resources of the employer, and under working hours and conditions set by the employer.

Employees' beneficiary association. An organization described in IRC § 501(c)(9).

Employer liability trust. An organization described in IRC § 501(c)(22).

Endowment. An accumulation of contributions that are not expended for program but that are held for investment, with the earnings thereon devoted to program activities, either generally or in a "restricted" manner.

Estate. A term with many meanings, including the property of an individual owned by him or her at death; federal tax law defines a "taxable estate" (IRC §§ 2051–2057).

Excise tax. In the "tax-exempt organizations" context, the sanctions sometimes used to enforce tax law prohibitions, for example, the "private foundation" rules and the "elective rule" in the "charitable" organizations "lobbying" field.

Exclusion. In the tax context, an item of income that is excluded from the concept of "gross income," such as a scholarship (IRC § 117).

Executive committee. A subgroup of directors of an organization that has particular influence over the affairs of the organization.

Executive director. An employee of an organization who is assigned the principal responsibility for administering the organization; sometimes termed "president" or "executive vice president"; this may be an "officer" position.

Exempt function revenue. Funds derived by a tax-exempt organization from the performance of an exempt function, such as revenue from the sale of publications or fees received for conferences or seminars.

Farmers' cooperative. An organization described in IRC § 521.

Feeder organization. An organization, not tax-exempt, that distributes all of its net income to a tax-exempt organization (IRC § 502).

Fiduciary. One who is bound to look after the affairs of another using the same standards of care and prudence as he or she would use in attending to their own affairs, as in a trustee of a trust.

Foundation. See "private foundation."

Fraternal society. An organization described in IRC § 501(c)(8) or IRC § 501(c)(10).

Fund-raiser. One who is employed (see "employee") or retained (see "consultant") to assist a tax-exempt organization (usually a "charitable" one) in the raising of funds, conventionally in the form of "contributions" and "grants," and more recently in the form of "exempt function revenue" or "unrelated" revenue; also known as "professional fund-raiser" or "professional fund-raising counsel."

General partnership. A partnership where all of the partners are equally liable for satisfaction of the obligations of the partnership.

Grass roots lobbying. An attempt to influence the legislative process by contacting the general public, or a segment of it, for the purpose of encouraging those individuals to contact the appropriate legislators; cf. "direct lobbying."

Gross income. Except as otherwise provided in the IRC, all income from whatever source derived, including compensation for services (IRC § 61(a)); gross income does not include "gifts" (IRC § 102).

Group legal service organization. An organization described in IRC § 501(c)(20).

Homeowners' association. An organization described in IRC § 528.

Horticultural organization. An organization described in IRC § 501(c)(5).

Identification number. A number assigned to organizations by the IRS; also termed an "employer identification number" (used even when the organization does not have any employees) (IRC § 6109).

Income interest. The right to receive all or some portion of the income from property for a stated period of time, either alone or with others.

Independent sector. The segment of U.S. society represented by nonprofit, principally "charitable," organizations; also known as the "voluntary sector," "nonprofit sector," or "private sector."

Initial tax. Principally in the "private foundations" context, the "excise taxes" that are initially assessable in enforcement of the rules; also known as "first-tier" taxes.

Institutions. In the "tax-exempt organizations" context, entities such as churches, universities, colleges, schools, and hospitals; these entities are not "private foundations" (IRC § 509(a)(1)).

Internal Revenue Code. The statutory body of federal tax law developed by Congress and administered by the IRS (referenced throughout as "IRC"; the current version of which is the Internal Revenue Code of 1986, as amended).

Internal Revenue Service. The agency of the federal government with the principal responsibility for regulating the activities of tax-exempt organizations (referenced throughout at the "IRS"); a component of the Department of the Treasury.

Joint venture. An undertaking of two or more organizations and/or individuals for the accomplishment of a particular purpose; an arrangement closely akin to a "general partnership."

Labor organization. An organization described in IRC § 501(c)(5).

Lead interest. The same right to income as an "income interest; so named because, in the "planned giving" context, an income interest precedes (leads) the "remainder interest."

Legislation. General rules of human conduct which are consciously and deliberately made by a legislative body; a declaration of general principles by a legislative body to be applied (usually prospectively) to all persons or general classes of persons.

Limited partnership. A partnership comprised of at least one "general partner" and at least one "limited partner," the latter being one whose liability for acts of the partnership is limited to the amount of investment.

Literary organizations. An organization described in IRC § 501(c)(3).

Lobbying. An activity usually associated with an attempt to influence a legislative process; generically, it means being in the lobby, so it can also mean attempts to influence the outcome of executive branch or regulatory agencies' decisions, or actions of a legislative branch that are not "legislation."

Modifications. Term used in unrelated business tax context to describe the rules used to exclude certain forms of income, such as "passive income," from taxation (IRC § 512(b).

Mutual ditch and irrigation company. An organization described in IRC § 501(c)(12).

Mutual insurance company. An organization described in IRC § 501(c)15).

Mutual telephone company. An organization described in IRC § 501(c)(12).

Net earnings. Gross earnings less operating expenses; in for-profit organizations, net earnings are often passed along to owners (e.g., dividends paid to stockholders).

Nonprofit organization. An entity that is not organized so that its "net earnings" inure to the benefit of individuals in their private capacity.

Not-for-profit activities. Activities for which a business expense deduction is not available (IRC § 183); often confused with "nonprofit" activities.

Officer. An individual who, by reason of an organization's "articles of organization" and/or "bylaws," or by law, is assigned certain duties in the operation of an organization.

Operational test. Rules applied (most frequently in the IRC § 501(c)(3) context) to determine whether an organization's operations are such as to merit tax-exempt status for it.

Organizational test. Rules applied (most frequently in the IRC § 501(c)(3) context) to determine whether an organization's "articles of organization" are such as to merit tax-exempt status for it.

Paid solicitor. See "solicitor."

Partnership. See "general partnership" and "limited partnership."

Passive income. Income that is not generated from the active participation in a business, usually annuities, capital gain, dividends, interest, rents, and royalties.

Person. An entity, either an organization (corporation, unincorporated association, trust, partnership, or estate) or an individual.

Political organization. An organization described in IRC § 527.

Pooled income fund. A form of "split-interest" trust, by which "contributions" of "remainder interests" in money or property to "charitable" organizations are made (IRC § 642(c)(5)).

Professional solicitor. See "solicitor."

Private foundation. A "charitable" organization that is usually funded from one source (an individual, family, or business), that receives its ongoing funding from investment income (rather than contributions), and that makes grants for "charitable" purposes to other persons rather than conduct its own programs (IRC § 509(a)); cf. "private operating foundation."

Private inurement. The doctrine, most prevalent in the IRC § 501(c)(3) context, that causes a "tax-exempt organization" to lose or be denied tax-exempt status where the organization is operated for the private gain of a "person."

Private operating foundation. A "private foundation" that operates one or more "charitable" programs (IRC § 4942(j)(3)).

Public charity. A "charitable" organization that usually is one of the "institutions" and thus not a "private foundation" (IRC § 509(a)(1)).

Publicly supported charity. A "charitable" organization that is not a "private foundation" because it receives the requisite amount of financial support from the public (IRC § 170(b)(A)(vi) and 509(a)(1) or IRC § 509(a)(2)).

Qualified amateur sports organization. See "amateur sports organization."

Real estate board. An organization described in IRC § 501(c)(6).

Recognition of tax exemption. The process engaged in by the IRS in determining that a "nonprofit organization" is a "tax-exempt organization."

Regular income tax. Term used to describe the basic federal income tax, to distinguish it from the "alternative minimum tax."

Related activity. A program activity that is in furtherance of the purposes of a "tax-exempt organization" (IRC § 512).

Remainder interest. The element of an item of property that causes outright title of the property to pass to a person (usually a "charitable" one) after the "income interest" in the property has expired.

Restricted gift. A "contribution," usually to a "charitable" organization, that is accompanied by documentation mandating that it be applied to a particular purpose of the organization, rather than used for its general operations.

Royalty. Payment made for the right to use property, usually as a fixed amount paid each time the item of property is sold or otherwise used.

Self-perpetuating board. A "board of directors" that is elected to office by themselves, rather than by, e.g., a membership.

Shipowners' protection and indemnity association. An organization described in IRC § 526.

Social club. An organization described in IRC § 501(c)(7).

Social welfare organization. An organization described in IRC § 501(c)(4).

Solicitor. A "person" who is paid by a "charitable" organization to engage in the act of requesting "contributions" to the organization; also known as a "paid solicitor" or "professional solicitor."

Split-interest trust. A trust that is established for the purpose of creating an "income interest" and a "remainder interest" in one or more items of property (IRC § 4947).

Supplemental unemployment benefit trust. An organization described in IRC § 501(c)(17).

Supporting organization. A "charitable" organization that is not a "private foundation" because of its supportive relationship to one or more other organizations, with the supported organization or organizations usually the "institutions" or "publicly supported charities" (IRC § 509(a)(3)).

Tax preference item. An item, usually a deduction or credit, that enables a taxpayer to reduce taxable income for regular income tax purposes.

Taxable income. For individuals who elect to itemize deductions, "adjusted gross income" less itemized deductions and the personal exemptions; for individuals who do not itemize their deductions, "adjusted gross income" less the standard deduction and the personal exemptions (IRC § 63).

Tax-exempt organization. A "nonprofit organization" that is exempt from one or more federal, state, and/or local taxes, most frequently the federal income tax (IRC § 501); also known as "tax-exempt entities."

Teachers' retirement fund association. An organization described in IRC § 501(c)(11).

Testamentary trust. A trust created by a will.

Title-holding company. An organization described in IRC § 501(c)(2) or 501(c)(25).

Trade association. A form of "business league" that is attempting to improve conditions in a particular trade, business, or profession.

Trade or business. An activity carried on for the production of income from the sale of goods or the performance of services (IRC § 513(c)).

Trade shows. A function, usually of a "trade association," consisting of the exhibiting of products and services of interest to the association's membership, usually undertaken in conjunction with the association's annual membership convention.

Trust agreement. An agreement between two or more "persons" for the purpose of creating a trust; cf. "declaration of trust."

Union. An organization described in IRC § 501(c)(5).

Unrelated activity. An activity of a "tax-exempt organization" that is not undertaken in furtherance of the organization's tax-exempt purposes, other than most administrative, investment, and "fund-raising" activities (IRC § 512).

Veterans' organization. An organization described in IRC § 501(c)(19) or 501(c)(23).

Voluntary employee beneficiary association. An organization described in IRC § 501(c)(9).

Nonprofit Organization Checklist

Managers of nonprofit organizations will find the following checklist helpful in keeping track of the various legal statuses and responsibilities of their organizations. Advisors to nonprofit organizations may want to photocopy these pages and keep one set in each client's files.

THE BASICS

Form of organization:

_____ Corporation

_____ Unincorporated association

_____ Trust

_____ Other

Type of articles of organization:

_____ Articles of incorporation

_____ Constitution

_____ Declaration of trust

_____ Trust agreement

_____ Other

Date organization formed _____

Place organization formed _____

Date(s) of amendment of articles _____

Date operational rules (e.g., bylaws) adopted _____

Date(s) of amendment of rules _____

Fiscal year _____

Membership ____ Yes ____ No

   If yes, annual meeting date _____

   Notice requirement _____

Chapters ____ Yes ____ No

Affiliated organizations _____

Board of directors (trustees):

   Origin _____

   Number _____

   Quorum _____

   Voting power _____

   Terms of office _____

   Annual meeting date _____

   Notice requirement _____

Officers:

   Origin _____

   Titles:

      ____ President

      ____ Vice President

      ____ Treasurer

      ____ Secretary

      ____ Other

   Terms of office _____

Committees:

   ____ Executive

   ____ Nominating

____ Development

____ Finance

____ Long-range planning

____ Other

States in which qualified to "do business" _____

State annual report due _____

TAX COMPLIANCE

Tax-exempt (federal)? ____ Yes ____ No

Descriptive IRC section (e.g., IRC § 501(c) (3)) _____

If IRC § 501(c3) organization:

____ Public ____ Private

If public IRC § 501(c3) organization:

____ Church

____ University

____ College

____ School

____ Hospital

____ Medical research organization

____ Donative publicly supported charity

____ Fee-based publicly supported charity

____ Supporting organization

____ Other

If private IRC § 501(c3) organization:

____ Standard private foundation

____ Private operating foundation

____ Exempt operating foundation

____ Other

If IRC § 501(c3) organization, has IRC § 501(h) election been made? ____ Yes ____ No

Date of IRS determination letter _____

If publicly supported IRC § 501(c3) organization:

    Date advance ruling period ends(ed) _____

    Date definitive ruling issued _____

Annual information return due _____

Form 990-T required? _____ Yes _____ No

State tax exemptions:

    _____ Income—classification issued _____

    _____ Sales—classification issued _____

    _____ Tangible personal property—classification issued _____

    _____ Intangible personal property—classification issued _____

    _____ Real property—classification issued _____

    _____ Other—classification issued _____

County tax exemption information _____

City tax exemption information _____

Tax returns due:

    State _____

    County _____

    City _____

    Other _____

Payroll taxes filings _____

OTHER MATTERS

Charitable solicitation laws registered under:

    States _____

    Counties _____

    Cities _____

Bond information _____

Lobbying registration _____

Political action committee law compliance _____

Insurance information _____

Leases _____

Other contracts _____

Name and address of:

    Accountant:

    Executive director:

    Fund-raiser:

    Lawyer:

    Insurance executive:

    President:

    Registered agent(s):

Index